A Hand to Guide Me

DENZEL WASHINGTON
WITH DANIEL PAISNER

Meredith® Books
Des Moines, Iowa

Meredith Books
1716 Locust Street
Des Moines, Iowa 50309–3023
meredithbooks.com

Cover Photo by Jeff Katz

First Edition. Printed in the United States of America.
Library of Congress Control Number: 2006921327
ISBN 13: 978-0-696-23049-3
ISBN 10: 0-696-23049-6

" children have never been very good
        at listening to their elders, but they
have never failed to imitate them. "
—JAMES BALDWIN

ACKNOWLEDGMENTS

A book like this is not written in a vacuum. As the title suggests, it's not just my fingertips on this one. I had an enormous amount of help coordinating and compiling the interviews, and for that I offer a special thanks to Kurt Aschermann at the Boys & Girls Clubs of America. It was Kurt who brought this project to me and convinced me to do it, which was typical of his energy and foresight. Over the years, no one has done more to advance the interests of the clubs than Kurt. It has been a great pleasure to work with him, and I wish him well as he moves on to his new venture at Charity Partners.

Kurt had some invaluable help at the clubs in getting this book off the ground, most notably from Frank Sanchez, Evan McElroy, and Roxanne Spillett. Frank in particular carried the ball on this, cajoling dozens of prominent folks from the clubs' alumni rolls, and then dozens more from outside the clubs, to share their stories about role models and mentors and formative influences in their lives. Without his extra efforts, we wouldn't have a book.

Dan Paisner took the handoff from Frank Sanchez, conducted the interviews, and found a way to make each subject's voice distinctly their own, all the while helping to give the book shape and focus. He also helped me to organize my own thoughts and set them down on paper in a manner consistent with the other memories shared here. Without his extra efforts, we wouldn't have a book either.

Stan Pottinger, president of Barnstorm Books, our book producer, along with Melisse Rose came up with the idea for this book. Stan has been our biggest problem solver and sounding board as we've worked our way toward publication. Without him ... well, you see where I'm going here.

Linda Cunningham, Larry Erickson, Mick Schnepf, Erin Burns, and Amy Nichols of Meredith Books and publicist Sandi Mendelson all deserve thanks for believing in this project and lending their considerable talents.

There's also John Silbersack, Alan Nierob, Frank Curtis, and Alan Kaufman, who gave their key professional assists.

Mostly, though, I want to thank the 73 caring, thinking individuals who agreed to share their reflections and help me to make the all-important point that we don't go it alone. —*Denzel Washington*

MY OWN STORY

SO THAT WE MIGHT FOLLOW
DENZEL WASHINGTON ...8

CONTRIBUTORS

CLOSING THOUGHTS

THE PATH TO PURPOSE

Jeff Katz

so that we might follow
DENZEL WASHINGTON
NATIONAL SPOKESPERSON,
BOYS & GIRLS CLUBS OF AMERICA

Let's start with a verse from Proverbs: "Train up a child in the way he should go, and when he is old he will not depart from it."

Powerful words, don't you think? It's a simple sentiment too, and yet I'm amazed how many people lose sight of it these days. Anyway it's a line that's been bouncing around in my head as I put this book together, because I've been reminded on almost every page of the importance of shaping our children and laying a strong foundation from which they might soar. Show me a successful individual and I'll show you someone who didn't want for positive influences in his or her life. I don't care who you are or what you do for a living—if you do it well I'm betting there was someone cheering you on and showing you the way. I'll even lay odds.

There's a line from one of my movies, *The Bone Collector,* that ties in to what we're talking about: "Destiny is what we make it." In the movie I played a quadriplegic homicide detective named Lincoln Rhyme, on the trail of a serial killer. There's a scene with Angelina Jolie's character where my guy gets to talking about the hand he's been dealt and the meaning of fate and fortune and destiny. It's one of the real turning point, epiphany-type scenes of the movie because Lincoln Rhyme was planning his suicide before he met up with Angelina Jolie. Then he got caught up in this case, and soon enough there were sparks between the two lead characters. Suddenly there was every reason to live where just a moment earlier there'd been no reason at all.

We're all destined to leave some kind of mark. I really believe that. We're all meant to walk a certain path at a certain time in a certain direction for a certain purpose. I believe that too. But I also believe we miss our marks from time to time, and without a certain push in the right direction we might never find the path we were meant to follow. This book is about that certain push, that helping hand we've all had to reach for in order to get where we're going. Train up a child in the way he should go, and he might get to where he's meant to be headed all along.

I've had that push in my life, going back as far as I can remember. So have the folks you're about to meet in these pages—actors, athletes, musicians, doctors, lawyers, politicians, business leaders—they've all had the guidance of someone or something, at some time or other. They've all built on that guidance and internalized it and made it their own. After all you don't get to the top of your game or the top of your field or the top of the charts entirely on your own, and I want to celebrate the good people who have helped us get where we're going. Every one of us has a story to share. Every one of us looks back on a parent or a coach or a teacher or a role model who set us straight and steered us right. Doesn't matter if you've gone on to become a ballplayer or a firefighter or the president of the United States. Doesn't matter if you've struggled to keep your family together under one roof or if you've just been named Employee of the Month down at the factory. If you've achieved any kind of real and lasting success, if you've made any kind of difference, it's more than likely there was someone there to help point the way.

For me, the first push outside my own home came at the Boys Club in Mount Vernon, New York. I spent a lot of time there as a kid—first out of necessity, then because there was no place else I'd rather be. I was there most days after school and most weekends until I went away to high school. At some point I started working and I couldn't get to the club as often as I might have liked, but it remained very much a lifeline, a path to purpose. See, my parents didn't have the time to take me to this or that activity the way parents do today. They couldn't always be home when I was done with school. They were too busy working. My mother worked in beauty salons. My father was a preacher. He had a couple churches—one in Virginia, the other in New York. In addition to that, he always had at least two full-time jobs. So he was always working, always on the road, always going out of his way to help some other family in need or crisis. And my mother had her hands full running back and forth to work and trying to keep the household going.

THE CENTER OF EVERYTHING

In my neighborhood the Boys Club was the center of everything. It was my whole world, just about, from the time I was 6 years old. It was where I learned how to play ball, where I learned how to focus and set my mind on a goal, where I learned about consequences, where I learned how to be a man. And at the heart of it all was a powerful force of nature named Billy Thomas. He pretty much ran the place—and let me tell you, he was a local treasure. Billy helped a lot of kids because he took an interest. He cared. And he made each of us feel like we had something to offer, like we were someone special. For my money, though, Billy Thomas was the someone special. I just thought this guy was it, you know? He had it so completely together that just sitting back and watching him go about his business was an education, and that's what I did. I'd catch myself trying to walk like Billy, trying to shoot a foul shot like Billy, trying to carry myself like Billy, trying to treat other people with the same respect and dignity he might offer. Even his handwriting was fascinating to me. He was an artist, and you could see it in the way he signed his name. There was a real flourish to it, and to this day I look at my signature and think back to how I used to copy Billy Thomas. It's in the way I sign my name. It's in the way I write a letter. It's in most everything I do.

Another great push found me at a barbershop called Modernistic, on Third Street in Mount Vernon. That's where I worked starting when I was 11 or 12. The job eventually pulled me from the Boys Club, as making money became more and more important. I still kept my hand in down at the club, but I was itching to work. Soon enough the barbershop became its own kind of lifeline for me, its own path to purpose. The place was run by a man named Jack Coleman, who took me on as a kindness to my mother. At least that's how I always look back on it. She was in the beauty shop business and she set me up as Mr. Coleman's cleanup guy. I thought it was the best job in the world. I had all kinds of hustles back then. You walked in the shop and I could tell right away how much money you had. I'd check out your shoes and I'd just know. I'd have people bringing me their dry cleaning, and I'd take it out and deliver it back to their house. I'd run all kinds of errands. They'd step out of Mr. Coleman's chair and I'd be on them with a whisk broom, brushing off their collar, saying, "Man, how you doin' today?" Or, "Man, you look good." There was money to be made all day long, especially if you were respectful and solicitous. My thinking was, if you had some loose change dangling around in your pocket on the way in the door, I'd do what I could to see that money into my pocket before you left.

What an education! What a bunch of characters! It was a real neighborhood joint, and Mr. Coleman wasn't just the head barber. He was like Modernistic's master of ceremonies. I thought he was it too—another someone special, another someone to look up to. He had his own business. He called his own shots. He presided over this wonderfully eccentric assortment of souls who paraded in and out of his shop all day long—chess masters, college professors, neighborhood businessmen. That's probably where I got my first acting lessons—at the barbershop, sweeping up and listening to all these stories from all these colorful individuals who could spin a tale or two.

There was a sign on the wall that said, "Credit is dead, it was killed by the last man who didn't pay." That gives you an idea of the tone and tenor of the place. Mr. Coleman was another strong individual, like Billy Thomas, and he ran that place like an extension of his own personality. I'll never forget how the shop used to close at 6:30, and someone would invariably walk through that door at 6:35 and say, "Oh, am I late?" And Mr. Coleman would say, "No, you're early. You're first. You're first one up tomorrow morning."

But of course I wasn't planning to stay at the Modernistic forever. It was just a place to hang my cap for the time being, to hustle some loose change on afternoons and weekends, and to collect some life lessons from the regulars. Besides, my mother didn't want me to stand 16 hours a day over somebody's head like she and Mr. Coleman had to do. She wanted something better for me. She worked too hard, she used to say, to see me walk the same path. She expected me to go to college, and I meant to meet her expectations—although, to be honest, I didn't have the first idea what I'd do when I got there.

THINKING BIG

The Boys Club, that's where I looked for hope and purpose and direction. That's where I learned to dream—to think big—and for that I've got to give Billy Thomas his props. He had us thinking that anything was possible and that even the sky didn't present any kind of limit. That type of thinking was essential for a kid like me. Hey, it's key for every kid, but it's especially important for kids who might be too easily tempted to turn down some lesser road. See, a lot of my friends in and around Mount Vernon weren't just headed for trouble—they'd already run face-first into it. There was a long list of kids in town who weren't going to make it out of Mount Vernon alive, and for a time I was on that list. There were gangs; there was violence, drug and alcohol abuse, and all the things that plague our lower-class, urban communities—and for that matter our middle- and upper-class suburban communities as well. You can't avoid these negative influences no matter where you live or how much money you've got in the bank. Sure, I got into my share of trouble in Mount Vernon—which is why the Boys Club was all the more important, and a guy like Billy Thomas was all the more vital.

One of Billy's great innovations was to hang college pennants from the walls of the club's main hall—one for each school his "kids" went on to attend. There weren't a lot of them, but there were enough. The deal was when you graduated high school and went away to college, you had to send Billy one of these banners, and he'd put it up proudly on the wall for the rest of us to see. He didn't say anything about it, didn't make any kind of big deal out of it. He just put them up and let them speak for themselves. I used to look at these names, these places, and think, "Man, anything is possible!"

Boston University. Syracuse. Vanderbilt. Marquette. Schools I'd never even heard of. Places I'd never even heard of. Places I didn't think I'd ever see.

Gus Williams, a great ballplayer from my neighborhood, was a couple years ahead of me in school. He went out to USC on a basketball scholarship, and I can still remember standing out in that hallway, looking up at his USC pennant and thinking, "Hmmm, so those are the school colors. Hmmm, so that's the Trojan, the mascot." I must have looked at that thing for hours. I didn't even know where California was, couldn't imagine what the sun looked like out there, what the air smelled like. I'd never been anywhere outside Mount Vernon, but I just stared at that pennant and thought, "OK, this guy I know, this guy I grew up with, he's out in California right now on a scholarship. He made it." And then I thought, "You know, if Gus can make it then I can make it too." Like I said, Billy knew what he was doing with those banners.

I sent my banner back to Billy, same as everyone else, but first I went off on a partial scholarship to a prep school called Oakland Academy in upstate New York, across the river from Poughkeepsie. There were only about six of us inner-city kids at Oakland—kids who might be labeled "troubled youth" in today's politically correct climate. Truth was we weren't troubled so much as we were caught between school and the streets. Somehow my mother realized that she needed to get me out of Mount Vernon and away from the negative influences that found me outside the Boys Club and the barbershop if she wanted me to survive and thrive. So that's what she did. Thank God for that. And, mercifully, she even found a way for someone else to help foot the bill, because she could not have afforded the tuition on her own. Thank God for that too.

My mother paid what she could the first two years I was at Oakland. I didn't understand how much she was scraping in those days to meet even a relaxed schedule of payments. I've since come to realize it was a point of pride to her to be able to contribute to my private school education. I came to that realization in a public way, because she never really talked about it. I did an interview on *60 Minutes* once, and one of Ed Bradley's producers went out and found the old accounts ledger from Oakland, and I saw that my mother was paying $16 here, $37 there, $109 there. Whatever she had, whenever she could afford it. Odd numbers. You know, $48, $21, whatever she had managed to save that month. And I looked at those figures recorded in that old Oakland ledger and saw my mother breaking her back to lift me up, one small payment at a time.

I had an English teacher at Oakland named Mr. Underwood who would always start the day by having us read the *New York Times*. That was something new for me. He was also my homeroom teacher, and every morning there'd be a fresh copy of the paper laid out on each of our desks, and we'd spend the first 15 minutes or so of each day reading the *Times*. In the beginning I'd just thumb through the sports pages to see how my favorite teams were doing. But over time I started to read some of the other sections as well. It's a habit I try to keep up to this day, staying plugged in to the world by reading the newspaper. That opened up a whole world to me back then. That's where I first learned about Steuben Glass, because they used to run an ad every day on the same page of the paper. But I also started learning and caring about what was going on in the rest of the world. Vietnam was winding down, Watergate was ramping up, and the civil rights movement was bringing about some positive and substantive change—and I was learning to soak it all in through the morning paper.

I played football at Oakland. In my head, they had a big-time program. Well it was as big-time as a six-man football program could be, but that was just fine with me because in my head I was a big-time player. I used to wear number 40, in honor of Gale Sayers. He was my guy. The way he moved, the things he could do on the football field. He was it too. In the Boys Club, sports was a great big deal. It was everything, and Gale Sayers had it going on. He was like Michael Jordan or Tiger Woods or Muhammad Ali to my friends and me. He was the standard, and where I grew up, when I grew up, there weren't a whole lot of African-Americans out there for me to look up to. I suppose if I'd had an interest in drama as a kid, I might have looked to someone like Sidney Poitier, but athletics was what got me going. So as a kid I looked to guys like Gale Sayers and Jim Brown.

All my friends wanted to be Jim Brown, but I wanted to be Gale Sayers. He was my idol on the football field, which is why I was so pumped when Gale Sayers came to see me, when I was doing *Julius Caesar* on Broadway. He came backstage after the show and he gave me a couple T-shirts, which he signed, and I was like a 9-year-old kid all over again.

Not long after Gale Sayers' visit, I was contacted by a guy whose uncle used to run the Oakland Academy. He also came to see me in *Julius Caesar*, and somehow he'd come into possession of some old 8-millimeter footage of our championship game from my senior year in high school. He brought that along to give to me, thinking I'd want to take a look at it. Now, in the watery eye of memory, I'd replayed that game over and over. And in my watery eye of memory, I looked good. It had been 34 years since that game, and the way I remembered it I'd scored every touchdown, shook every tackle, and made every cutback the way the coach drew it up in the locker room. We had gotten killed, but I'd scored every touchdown—that's how it registered.

NOTHING LIKE GALE SAYERS

I'd been telling my kids these stories for years, and by this point I'd gotten old enough and forgetful enough and probably full enough of myself that I could no longer tell which parts of the story I'd embellished and which parts were true. So I checked out this guy's footage, and it was a little grainy. It wasn't all jumpy and fast, the way that old 8-millimeter film can sometimes look; whoever was holding the camera had a steady hand. I'd never seen myself play football on film, and I'd never been more anxious to see myself on film. Didn't matter how many movies I'd made; this was a bigger deal than any premiere. So I sat down with my oldest son, who's also a football player, and we watched it together. It turned out I was pretty good. It turned out I did score all our touchdowns. It turned out I had some moves. I looked nothing like Gale Sayers, mind you, but I had some moves.

I watched it that one time with my son, but he hung onto it and he kept going back to it, and he tells me now that he's watched it over and over. He says, "Dad, your stance was just like mine." And I say, "No, your stance is just like mine." I mean, I was here first, right? It's *my* stance. But the great thing is he watches the tape before he goes to his games. He says it's his inspiration. His mother and I have worked hard to lay a positive foundation for him and for all our children—and here we stumble across this 34-year-old footage of one of my high school football games, and that's what he grabs onto.

I ended up staying close to home when it came time for college, because it was what we could afford. I went to Fordham University in the Bronx, just down the road from Mount Vernon. I wanted to be a football player. Actually I played football and basketball. I was a walk-on, and at that time Fordham had a really strong basketball team. The football team hadn't been much of a powerhouse for some time, but the basketball team was another story. A couple years before I got there, they were the number 3 team in the country. Digger Phelps was the coach before he went on to Notre Dame. But there I was, thinking I could play at this big-time level. I hadn't been recruited. I didn't have a scholarship. But I went out for the team and I made it. I didn't play much, but I made it. The football team too. That was my Boys Club swagger, I guess. That was Billy Thomas telling me I could do anything. I thought I was unbeatable, you know, and when you're young enough and cocky enough you can pull off almost anything, especially if you've got a little bit of ability to back it up.

That was me—I had just enough ability to back it up. And just enough ego to make up for the fact that I never started a single game as a basketball player or a football player. I hardly even got into the games. And there's just enough of that ego left over for me to claim that P. J. Carlesimo, my freshman basketball coach, couldn't see my talent and that's why he sat me on the bench the entire season. We joke about it now, whenever we run into each other, but I still wish he played me a little more.

Even so I took in a great many lessons from him—about hard work, about drive, about perseverance. That was P.J.'s big thing, that perseverance is your best talent. I wasn't a great basketball player, but I worked hard.

My idea was to try everything the school had to offer, from the locker room to the classroom. I studied everything. At first I thought I wanted to be a doctor. I took classes in chemistry, biology, all the basic sciences. Then I thought I'd be a lawyer. After that a journalist. At some point I realized I was working my way toward the arts. I can't say for sure how that happened or when, but it happened. There were some stops and starts in there too, because I left Fordham for a while, midway through my junior year, so I could take some time to figure out what it was I really wanted to do—which is really just a euphemism for saying I was on academic probation.

Before I was asked to leave, though, somebody tipped me to this public speaking class and I signed up, and looking back I might have signed up because there was a pretty girl in the class or because I'd heard it would be an easy B. That was the way I made my decisions in those days. I didn't plan out my life, I lived it. When you're 20 years old, I guess that means you bounce from one path to the next until you hit on the one you're meant to travel.

I wish I could remember the name of the old guy who taught that class. He used to have these elastic bandages hanging out from his pant leg. It was the strangest thing. He wrapped his legs—both legs, I think—and he couldn't do a good enough job of it to keep the bandages from unraveling by the end of the day. It's strange, the things you remember, but a lot of what he taught has stayed with me as well. He had us reading Shakespeare, and his passion for the theater became a part of me—not right away, but he sowed the seeds. This particular professor was involved with the theater club on the Bronx campus, and one day it fell to me to do a scene from *Hamlet*, and I wasn't happy about it. In fact I was completely terrified, and if I could have raced from the classroom when I was through I would have done just that because I thought I was terrible. It was painful. I wanted nothing to do with the theater or school after that, and my grades started to really fall. I had to leave Fordham the following semester because I just wasn't cutting it.

THE CALL TO THE STAGE

That summer following my aborted junior year, I went to work at Camp Sloane, a YMCA camp in Lakeville, Connecticut. The counselors there put on a talent show for the kids. I put together these little poems and rhymes and skits for the kids in my cabin, and we stood up on stage and did our bit. After the show this guy named Miles Joyce came up to me and said, "Man, you ever thought about being an actor?"

I thought back to that public speaking class, and me reading *Hamlet*, and shrugged off the compliment like I had it coming. I'd also directed plays when I was a younger counselor at Camp Rainbow, the Boys Club camp in Fishkill, New York. I was 13 years old, and I directed a takeoff on Batman and Robin that we called Flatman and Ribbon (another fine contribution to the theater). "Well, you know, I took a class," I said to Miles Joyce, playing it casual. "You know, I did do a little *Hamlet*."

That September, 1975, I re-upped at Fordham for my second go-round as a junior—I was a "junior and a half" on the five-year program—and at the last minute I switched to the school's midtown campus in Lincoln Center, which had a real drama program. I'm still not sure what I was thinking, but I guess there was something about it that was attracting me. I had to give up football and basketball, but I didn't mind, because soon enough I had found something I loved to take their place. I never would have thought it, but I became as passionate about drama and acting as I had ever been about football and basketball. And somewhere along the way I had to give up my idea of being a journalist, although I'll let you all in on a little secret: I still think of myself as an investigative reporter. That's what I do as an actor, the way I approach each new role. I learn everything I can about the character, the period, the setting, whatever's going on in the story, so that I can put what I know into the performance. If I do that part of my job well the audience will never see it, because it's part of the hidden work of an actor. So it all ties in.

I was blessed at Fordham to cross paths with Robinson Stone—Bob to his friends and students. He was my English teacher, but he had acted for many years, and he was involved in the theater program as well. He knew his stuff. He was in *Stalag 17*. He was in *Othello* on Broadway with Uta Hagen, Paul Robeson, and Jose Ferrer. He'd accomplished a lot, and he was eager to share what he knew. Very quickly he became a real positive presence in my life when I was trying on this idea of becoming an actor. He was enormously helpful and encouraging.

I wound up appearing in a student production of *Othello*, and after that he ended up writing a recommendation for me when I was auditioning for a couple graduate school programs in drama: Yale, SMU, a few others I no longer remember. I ended up going to the American Conservatory Theater, and Bob Stone wrote the director a letter that basically said, "If you don't have the talent to nurture this young man, then don't accept him." He put it on them, which I thought was an interesting way to go.

It turned out to be an effective approach, because I was accepted. I still have the letter. I keep it with me when I travel, along with a bunch of other personal stuff—the program from my father's funeral, things like that. Touchstones to keep me connected when I'm on the road or on location, because I'm one of those guys who needs a little reminder every now and then, a little push. I guess we all need those little prompts and props and visual aids telling us where we've come from in order to keep focused on where we're going.

That letter of recommendation was a big deal, which is why I still carry it with me. I read it at the time and wondered if Bob Stone was talking about someone else. I read it now and try to find the young man he was going on and on about in the young man I actually was. He wrote, "Do take him if you want some genuine experiences of inspiration, and if you want the excitement of aggrandizing a talent which is finally going to be among the most exciting and fulfilling of our time." I must have reread that letter a hundred times, and each time I think, "Wow." I remember what a charge it was to take in those kinds of positive statements about myself when I was only 22 years old. What a rush! To have someone believe in you that much is a tremendous boost. It left me thinking, "Well something's going on here. I better pay attention to it, and nurture it, and see it through."

Some people might hear those words and think them some kind of burden, but I took them as a blessing. That's another key: I knew I was blessed, and I know now of course that we're all blessed. But Bob Stone's words, back then, they kept me going. It's not like I walked around thinking, "Well he thinks I'm so great, so it must be so." But he gave me something to live up to. He lit a fire in me. He might have been blowing smoke, gushing, saying all those nice things about me to help me get into an acting program. But when times got tough, when I wondered when I'd catch my first break, I kept telling myself, "It'll all work out," reminding myself that something big was coming.

A BLESSING

When I read those words I felt no pressure at all, because I knew my talent was a blessing from God. These gifts, this talent— it wasn't me. Yes, destiny is what we make it, but we're helped along. Yes, I worked hard. Yes, I made some sacrifices until I finally made it. Yes, luck is where opportunity meets preparation. But first and foremost it's a blessing from God, which is the foundation of everything. It's the extra push we need to take us where we're meant to go. It's not just because of what Bob Stone wrote and said. It's not just because it was my destiny. This man believed in me and that was huge. He even had an agent friend of his come to see me in *Othello*, so he did open doors for me. I might not have gone through all those doors, but he held them for me. For *me*. And because he believed in me, I believed in myself.

There's a great saying, "From those to whom much is given, much is expected." You hear that line a lot, but I always think, "Well, what's the definition of much? Is it monetary? Is it how many times you're on television? How many square feet you've built into your house? How many deals you've closed or negotiations you've won? And how much is much?"

We've all been blessed in one way or another. We've all received our share of good fortune, so that's my definition of much. A single blessing is all the bounty in the world, and if you've been blessed at all you're meant to pass some of that on. You're meant to set a positive example. That's our responsibility.

I was watching *Crimson Tide* not too long ago, and I remembered when the movie came out I received a letter from a young black kid who said, "I never thought I could be a captain of a nuclear sub. I never thought about it. I didn't think it was possible."

But it is possible. Anything is possible. And that's what I wrote back to this kid. I wrote, "You never know."

I met another kid one day when I was in the store buying magazines. He came up to me all excited and said, "Oh Mr. Washington, *Man on Fire*, you helped me to get sober." He started quoting all these lines and scenes from the movie, telling me he'd been sober nine months. And I said to him, "You never know who you touch." And he said, "Thank you, brother. God bless you, brother."

So you never know who you touch. You never know how or when you'll have an impact, or how important your example can be to someone else. Even when you're acting in a movie that's meant merely to entertain, you strike a chord in someone and you end up enlightening.

My family members were pretty supportive when I told them I wanted to be an actor. They could see I was passionate about it. They could see I had a talent for it. They could see it meant something. What they couldn't see was how I might make a living from it, but at that early stage they didn't place too much emphasis on that. I mean, I was still in college. I was meant to explore all these new things, and if I could grab on to something and make it my own—if I could really own it—then I'd be in a better position to meet the next challenge or opportunity that came my way.

As a parent I try to take the same view with my children. It's not always easy, but I try. I'll give you an example. My son John David, the football player, is a much better athlete than his old man ever was. He's paid a price for it too. He broke his clavicle. He had knee surgery. He has bad ankles. His ribs are constantly banged up. But he loves it—and like I said, he's good at it. He played in a high school all-star game with all these big-time players: Vince Young, who went on to play for Texas; Marcus Vick, who went on to play for Virginia Tech; Lorenzo Booker, from Florida State. These were great, great players from all around the country, and down there on that same field was my son.

The scouts were out, naturally, and there were a bunch of schools interested in him. But what impressed me most about that whole recruiting process was an exchange I had with the athletic director at Morehouse, who called me one day and told me he wanted to give John David a scholarship. I was thrilled at their interest, as I knew John David would be, but we didn't need the money.

"Well that's great," I said, "but why don't you set aside that scholarship and give the money to someone who really needs it?"

I didn't mean to sound full of myself or anything, but I'd had some success as an actor, and I'd put away a couple dollars, and I really thought the money should go to some kid whose parents couldn't afford to send him to college. I said, "Why don't you just accept him to your program, and we'll pay our way?"

The athletic director's answer really surprised me and sent a powerful message. He said, "We're not giving you a scholarship, Denzel. We're giving John David a scholarship."

I said, "I'm listening." And underneath it I thought, "OK, I like the way this man thinks."

He said, "He earned it."

He was dead on, because he recognized how important it is to own our successes, to grab on to them like they mean something—because they most certainly do. It wasn't about whether we could afford to send our son to Morehouse; it was about letting our son know that he earned his way in on the back of the game he loves. It was about validation. And it was the kind of validation I could never give him as a father—because, hey, I'm his father. I'm supposed to pump him up with praise and love and support. It's in my job description. But this athletic director, he was coming at it from a different place, and that's what I liked about it. He wasn't doing me any favors; he was doing a solid for John David, because John David earned it.

And do you know what? We've never really talked about it in just this way, but I'm guessing this scholarship offer represents for John David a lot of what I've taken from that letter of recommendation I still carry with me. It's like a giant pat on the back, and in his case John David had to worry if

Morehouse wanted him because of who his father was, or because of who he was on the football field—and I'm proud to say his performance on the field during his four years at Morehouse erased any doubt in his mind that he got in on my name.

All of which takes me to the book you now hold in your hands, which is also a kind of validation. Years ago, 1975 to be exact, I met a woman named Ruth Green at my mother's beauty shop. It was the spring of what should have been my junior year at Fordham. (When I was a junior-and-a-half, for those of you keeping score.) I was sitting in my mother's shop deciding what I wanted to do with my life, and I could see this woman in the mirror, sitting under the hair dryer. Every time I looked up, I caught her looking at me. She was looking at me and looking at me, and I didn't know what was going on.

Then all of a sudden she said, "Somebody get me a pen."

She had a prophecy, and she wanted to put it down on paper. She told me I would speak to millions of people. (OK, so she got that right.) She told me I would travel the world. (Got that right too.) She told me I would make a positive difference. (I'm guessing the jury is still out on that one, but I'm hoping it comes back in my favor.) At one time I wanted to be a preacher, like my father, and I thought maybe this woman was picking up on that, but now that I look back on it I'm guessing she was talking about something else. And now that I've had some success as an actor, and traveled the world, and made a couple movies that have contributed at least in small part to the way we all look out on that world, I'm reminded of this woman's prophecy and I take it very much to heart. I do. And I carry her words with me, along with the program from my father's funeral, and the letter of recommendation from Bob Stone, and all those other touchstones of a lifetime, because taken together they're what made me who I am.

I think we all have a responsibility to give something back, to leave this world a better place for our having been here. For me that means giving something back to the good people who helped to shape me and give my life purpose and direction. And that's the Boys & Girls Clubs of America— at the national level, and at my home club in Mount Vernon. So that's what I do. For the past several years, I've been a proud spokesperson for the organization. It's a role I've taken on gladly because I can't think of a more noble or fulfilling mission than to guide our young children and to lift them up and set them down on the right path. That's the mission of the clubs all across this great land—in our inner cities and our outlying communities, in rich neighborhoods and poor and every place in between.

If you ask me, being successful means helping others. I look around at people who have accomplished all kinds of great and worthwhile things, and I think, "OK, so what have you done with what you have?" We all know about the awards you've won and riches you've received, but at the end of the day it's not about what you have or even what you've accomplished. It's about what you've done with those accomplishments. It's about who you've lifted up, who you've made better. It's about what you've given back. It's like that saying "You'll never see a trailer behind a hearse." You know, you can't take it with you. The Egyptians tried that, and it didn't work.

A PUSH FROM SOMEONE ELSE

And so I mean to shine a light on the Boys & Girls Clubs' mission by asking a wide assortment of successful people to share their memories about role models and mentors and positive influences in their lives, because these things are universal and these things matter. My hope is that in this chorus of voices, readers might find an empowering message and a stirring reminder that we all get where we're going with a push from someone else.

Some of the folks you're about to hear from are household names, and some are known to just a few people outside their households. Many are alumni of Boys & Girls Clubs in their hometowns, and others have taken on a leadership role with the clubs as adults. Others are friends and colleagues of mine who've shared their stories with me over the years and who have agreed to share them again here. Still others are people I've reached out to because I've admired the way they've lived their lives and thought they might have something to offer in this context.

If there's a bottom line to this group it's that all of them have achieved a significant level of success in their chosen field and that all of them have overcome a hardship or two. Julia Roberts, a friend and colleague, once said in reference to her work that she was an ordinary person with an extraordinary job. Well that's kind of what we've got here with this collection of good people: ordinary folks, from ordinary beginnings, accomplishing extraordinary things. Whatever it is they set out to do, and however unlikely it might have seemed, they made it happen—with a little bit of help along the way. And with God's blessings.

There's John Singleton, the acclaimed motion picture director, who looked to his single-parent father as the inspiration not only for his breakthrough film, *Boyz 'N The Hood*, but also as a model for how to live his life with strength and compassion, even on the hard streets of South Central Los Angeles....

There's Chick Big Crow, executive director of the Boys & Girls Club in Pine Ridge, South Dakota, who draws courage and inspiration from the tragic death of her daughter SuAnne, a standout high school athlete who was killed in a car accident. Chick Big Crow now runs the first club on Indian land to honor SuAnne's memory....

There's John Antioco, CEO of Blockbuster Inc., who learned the basic principles of good business and personal service while riding his father's milk truck as a young boy and helping with deliveries....

There's my good friend Daryl "Chill" Mitchell, an accomplished actor, who was paralyzed in a motorcycle accident and who inevitably looked to the late Christopher Reeve to help him discover what it meant to roll through life in a wheelchair, beneath the helpless gaze of friends and family....

There's Toni Morrison, the Pulitzer Prize-winning novelist, who found in a tossed-off comment from her father the template for a life well and meaningfully lived....

There's former President Jimmy Carter, who took such a shine to a woman who worked as a caretaker on his family farm that he now singles her out as an abiding and formative influence. This woman could pick more cotton and shake more peanuts than any other person in Georgia, President Carter recalls, and she could catch more perch, but she also set such a dignified example that she affected his thinking on racial equality....

There's Bob Woodward, the noted investigative reporter, who sought the guidance of his boss, *Washington Post* publisher Katharine Graham, while he was about to break the biggest news story of his generation, and who recalls her steadfast refusal to accept his initial contention that he and his partner Carl Bernstein would never get to the bottom of the Watergate story....

There's Wesley Clark, the former NATO commander, who sparked to the discipline of his childhood swim coach and credits his time in this young man's tutelage as his first test of character....

There's Antwone Fisher, the Hollywood screenwriter whose self-titled script became my directorial debut, who managed to lift himself up from such hardscrabble beginnings (his unwed mother was in prison when she gave birth to him) by convincing himself that the heralded accomplishments of people in his Cleveland community were his for the taking....

There's Alex Rodriguez, the future Hall of Famer, who went out to take grounders at third base under the guidance of his boyhood baseball coach the night he learned he'd been traded from the Texas Rangers to the New York Yankees and would have to master a new position, reminding us of the never-ending importance of hard work and dedication....

There's the beautiful and beautifully talented Debbie Allen, another great friend, who was about to hang up her dance shoes and try on another career when she met Alvin Ailey and his groundbreaking dance troupe and came away with a new sense of self and who she was meant to be....

Yes, destiny is what we make it after all. Same goes for legacy and opportunity and principle and all those good things. Humility too. Every individual you're about to meet in these pages has remained humble, and that's been my mantra for as long as I can remember—probably not when I was a kid, but in my young adult life, most definitely, and it's something I've tried to model for my children as well. Receive your gifts with open arms, but don't wear them on your sleeve.

But if there's one lesson to be learned from the voices you're about to hear, it is that it's not only on us. It's on the folks around us as well. And mostly, it's on our ability to keep open to their example. That's the underlying message in these pages, that you can draw a line from every great success back to some rock-solid foundation. A parent. A teacher. A coach. A role model. It all starts somewhere. And for me, that somewhere is with God. I'm not here to tell other folks what to believe, but I'll tell you what I believe, and this is what works for me. It's why I'm setting these thoughts to paper right now. It's why I'm here—by the grace of God.

Ordinary people accomplishing extraordinary things? Perhaps. But I'll go one better and suggest that we're all extraordinary in our own way, and that it's what we do with our extraordinariness that sets us apart and makes all the difference.

Read on and see if you don't agree.

what we called second base

HANK AARON
RETIRED PROFESSIONAL
BASEBALL PLAYER

I was raised by my mother, my father, my aunt, my uncles. In our part of Mobile, Alabama, everybody knew everybody else. Everybody was friends. Everybody knew everybody's kids, and if you did something wrong you got two or three whuppings before you got home to the main one.

Uncle Bubba taught me what it would take to make it as a ballplayer. He played in the old Negro Leagues, but he got homesick and came home. Happened to a lot of players in those days, only making a hundred dollars or so a month, almost starving, just to play baseball. They'd play for a while and then come home. Uncle Bubba came back and worked at the Alabama Dry Dock and Ship Building Company in Mobile, fixing ships that were coming into the dock. Same work my daddy did. One week on, two weeks off. Not exactly steady work, but steady as it came.

Growing up in Mobile, like in most southern cities, you could either play baseball or become a schoolteacher. Those were the options for most black kids. You couldn't be anything else. It was like Yogi Berra used to say: "I left school and it was closed, and I went back and it was closed." That's what Yogi said, and that was the truth. I didn't play any organized ball until high school, but I played. It wasn't sandlot ball; it was in the cow pasture. We made fields out of what we could, wherever we could. Slid into what we called second base. We had one ball to play with, and it was precious. It was raggedy and taped-up and everything else, and if it got lost everybody would look for it, not just you. We all needed that one ball.

I was one of eight kids. There are only three of us now, but we all held our heads high. That was our parents' doing. There's not a single one of us who ever spent a day in jail, which in that part of the country, that time in our history, that's saying a lot. Black kids, especially little boys, we were always out there running around. I could have stolen a pencil or looked at someone the wrong way and been sent to prison for 20 years. It would have been so easy to get into some kind of trouble, even a small trouble.

But I was blessed to live in a part of Mobile where everybody looked out for you. It wasn't much. Dirt streets, four houses on the road, no electric lights, but it was tough to stray, because everybody was looking out. A couple blocks over, same city, it could have been entirely different, so I always tell people I was blessed to live in that one little area. Go a little bit farther and chances are I probably wouldn't have made it. Go a little bit farther and there'd have been a whole other set of eyes on me, or maybe there'd have been nobody watching at all.

" my parents, my aunts and uncles, our friends and neighbors—they all set it up so that I could succeed. "

It wasn't luck that we ended up living in that particular neighborhood. My parents created that environment for me and my brothers and sisters. They were drawn to folks who believed the same things they believed. They surrounded themselves and their children with good examples, and they expected us to learn from them.

My mother, I don't ever remember her being out of the house after nine o'clock at night. She was always there for us. My father was out trying to make a living, but even when he wasn't there, he was there, if you know what I mean. My mother, she called me "Man," because I was such a big baby, and whenever she called me it was for a reason. She was not to be played with. When she called your name, best that you listen or be prepared to wait until the weekend until your daddy got ahold of you and he would give you a whupping for Monday, Tuesday, Wednesday, Thursday, Friday—all of 'em.

Whatever I was doing, I always felt I was doing it because that's the way I was taught. In baseball, they teach you how to do things a certain way. I used to hold the bat cross-handed, and I had some success hitting, but no way would I be able to hit in the big leagues hitting cross-handed. It's the same in life. Your parents teach you how to do certain things and then you carry them out—the fundamentals. To this day I think about the lessons my mother taught me and the way she carried herself. My daddy too. Everything I've done, it comes from them and those lessons they taught us when we were kids.

All of us, no matter who—if you're successful you can look back and think, "Hey, I didn't get here by myself." You can be black, white, green, purple, whatever. If you're successful, you can always look back to somebody else. Some teacher might have pushed you, some coach, somebody else. Somebody who came before you who set it up so you wouldn't have it so hard. For me it was also Jackie Robinson, Larry Doby, Don Newcombe. Those guys—what they stood for, how they carried themselves—they lit a path so I might follow. My parents, my aunts and uncles, our friends and neighbors—they all set it up so that I could succeed.

I don't know what I did. Some people say, "You did your part." Well, I don't know. If I did do something, I'd like to do it three more times, because I'm sure I didn't do it as well as I could have.

Hank Aaron

fighting for
something greater
MUHAMMAD ALI
BOXER

Many of the great influences in my life have come to me as an adult, and if
I had to choose just one I would say Nelson Mandela. After I retired from
professional boxing in 1981, I decided to dedicate my life to helping others. I
would no longer be facing challengers in the ring, but there were (and are) far
bigger and more vicious opponents like poverty and hunger and intolerance
in the world arena.

As I became more involved with different organizations, and more aware
of what was happening in various places around the world, Nelson Mandela's
story stayed with me. Madiba, as he is known in South Africa, became for me
a symbol of what it means to sacrifice one's life for a cause as great as freedom.

He was the world's most famous prisoner, but to me he was one of the world's greatest heroes.

Madiba was released in 1990, and I traveled to South Africa to meet him in 1993. By then, he was President Mandela. I found a man not resentful or cynical, but a person who radiated love and warmth. This was amazing! Seeing Madiba like this strengthened my belief in standing up for what is right. His personal characteristics became relevant to the goals and aspirations of facing the tough opponents.

" a man not resentful or cynical, but a person who radiated love and warmth. "

Nelson Mandela is a man of great honor, strength, and integrity, but he was always fighting for something greater than himself, and that was the freedom of an entire nation. More than anyone else in the world, he embodies the hopes and dreams of a true, lasting justice and equality, not just for South Africans but for all people. It is Madiba—through his unselfish and constant presence on the international stage raising awareness about AIDS, peace, debt relief, environments—who most inspires us to think responsibly of the people who surround us.

Muhammad Ali

revelations
DEBBIE ALLEN
DANCER/CHOREOGRAPHER

If I had to narrow it down to one person who really influenced me and put me on a path, it would have to be Alvin Ailey. I met him when I was a freshman in college. Prior to that time, I had trained seriously at the Houston Ballet Foundation where I was the only black student. Following that I auditioned for a major dance school and was rejected. I felt it was my blackness that kept me out. It wasn't what they appreciated. Oh, it was articulated, all right. I was told to go into something else, that dance was not what I needed to do. And so I stopped dancing. I went to Howard and pledged sororities and was set to study Greek and be a scholar, and blah, blah, blah, blah, blah.

But my mother had saved money for me to go to a dance festival that summer. It was the summer of 1968, and I went off to the American Dance Festival in New London, Connecticut. I suppose I wasn't ready to give up dancing just yet. It was a six-week program, and that's where I met Alvin Ailey and his amazing company.

It was a wonderful festival. Martha Graham and a lot of great people were there. But when I saw Alvin Ailey's American Dance Theater and started working with them and learning their repertory, I was transformed. Judith Jamison was there. Dudley Williams. George Faison. Sylvia Waters. All these wonderful dancers. And I had never seen a company like that, until I met all these people.

> " his company, his choreography, his spirit, his elevation of our culture into the highest of highs in concert dance gave me a new sense of who I was and who I could be. "

When I saw "Revelations" and "Blues Suite," I saw a reflection of myself and a path for myself. And I threw my toe shoes away. I wanted to dance barefoot, and dance in some heels and a tight blue dress and a swirling white skirt with a Sunday hat and an umbrella.

Alvin Ailey's choreography spoke to something in me. We were both from Texas and he was the quintessential American choreographer. He was a phenomenon, and I was there in his presence. It was exciting and magical and wonderful. The other dancers wanted me to join the company. I was in class with them, they were teaching us every day, and I was dancing my little ass off. Dudley, the leading male dancer in the company, was training me, and so were Judy and Sylvia and George. You have to understand, this was a truly amazing experience. At the end of those six weeks I had morphed into another Debbie Allen. Alvin Ailey gave me some corrections and delighted in my dance numbers. I remember him smiling and laughing, because I was outdancing everybody. I spent more *time* with Judy and Dudley and the rest of the company, but it was *his* presence that did it. His company, his choreography, his spirit, his elevation of our culture into the highest of highs in concert dance gave me a new sense of who I was and who I could be.

At the end of the summer, I went back to Howard and danced. I joined Mike Malone's dance company and that was the beginning. Then I met Louis Johnson, who was a famous choreographer, and I continued to dance.

We've all remained friends, so they know what they mean to me—Dudley, Sylvia, Judy, all of them.

I did a documentary once, and I was interviewing Dudley, and he started talking about me and telling me how wonderful it was to see me that young and dancing so beautifully. Judith Jamison is the artistic director of Alvin Ailey's company now, and my daughter has been training under her for the past several years, so we're all still connected.

What would I have become if I hadn't gone to that festival that summer? Well, I probably would be an anthropologist and a scholar. But when you're a dancer in your soul, it's hard to walk around that. That's like a river. You can't just jump across that river. You have to swim through it and start dancing again on the other side.

Debbie Allen

"You can do this"

WALTER ANDERSON
EDITOR IN CHIEF, *PARADE* MAGAZINE

I grew up in Mount Vernon, New York. I belonged to the same Boys Club that Denzel Washington ultimately belonged to, except I'm a bit older. I was raised in a tenement on the south side of Mount Vernon, along the edge of the Bronx. I lived on 11th Avenue and Third Street, and the Boys Club at the time was on 10th Avenue.

My father was a violent alcoholic, and if you knew Mount Vernon, you knew that 11th Avenue was a very violent place at the time. Yet I was often safer on the street corner than I was in my own bed. My brother was a fighter and my sister was a street gang leader, so you get some sense of what it was like in my household and in my neighborhood.

I was also a violent child, which was not unusual for that neighborhood. But there were two islands in my childhood where I could go. One was the Mount Vernon library, where I could go and read, and the other was the

Boys Club, where I could be comfortable and not be afraid. I didn't fight because I was a bully, I fought because I was afraid, and I fought a lot. But in the club I never fought, and at the library I never fought, because in those places I was never afraid. Those were my islands.

I'll get back to those islands in a moment, but first I want to mention the most influential person in my childhood, a woman named Ilza Williams. She was probably the only educated person in our neighborhood. She had three sons—Otis, Keith, and Barry. Barry was the youngest, and he was my best friend, and there were many things we did not have in common. My house was loud; his house was peaceful. I lived in a tenement; he lived in a real house. He was tall and thin; I was much shorter and heavier. He was black and I was white. But what we really had in common was his mother, who encouraged us both. She was very interested in our friendship. No child could come within two blocks of Mrs. Williams without having to discuss homework. She was a teacher in the New York City school system, in the Bronx. She was always slipping me something to read: Dickens' *Great Expectations,* for one. She'd begin by telling us a story. She'd tell us about this boy going to a graveyard, and all of a sudden he hears a voice, and we were at the edge of our seats. And then she would say, "Well, if you want to find out the end of the story, go get the book and read it."

She raised our expectations, and I didn't always live up to them. Despite Mrs. Williams' influence, I got into my share of trouble. And yet no matter what I did, she wouldn't give up on me. She persuaded my parents to take me out of public school and put me into parochial school, and I became the first and only child expelled from that parochial school. When I got thrown out of parochial school, she had me tested for a school called Winward, where Barry went to school, and they took me in and gave me a scholarship. I took two grades in one year.

After that Mrs. Williams persuaded my parents to have me tested for Westminster and Cherry Lawn, two prep schools, and I was accepted into both but I declined to go. I said, "Mrs. Williams, you can trust me now, but I want to go back to public school and be with my friends." I took one look at the kids at those prep schools—how they looked, how they dressed—and it was clear I was not one of them. I looked different. I talked different. I was very uncomfortable and extremely self-conscious. She was not happy, Mrs. Williams, but in the end she respected my decision.

A year and a half later, failing nearly all subjects, I quit high school at age 16 and joined the Marines. I didn't think Mrs. Williams would be too happy about that either, so I tried to avoid her, but I kept hearing her voice in my head.

> " no matter what I did,
> she wouldn't give up on me. "

One night I couldn't sleep. I was just walking around the barracks, and it suddenly struck me that in just a few years I'd be getting out of the Marine Corps, and I'd be 21 and an adult and it was terrifying. Five o'clock that morning reveille came, and I went to see the first sergeant and I said, "I want to go to school." I could just picture Mrs. Williams looking on and offering her approval and thinking, "It's about time."

The first sergeant and some other officers and NCOs encouraged me to study for my GED exam, which I did. Apparently I did very well because then they had me study for the one-year college GED, which I also passed. Then they sent me to electronics school in San Diego. When I met my fellow Marines who were going to take these courses with me, I found every one of them was a legitimate high school graduate who had also either attended or graduated from college.

Once again I was terrified. It was a terrible, depressing day. I didn't have any background in the sciences. I didn't think I could do this. And then I remembered how Mrs. Williams used to tell me, "You can do this, Walter. You can do this."

Because that educated person had encouraged me, I believed in her for that one day. And that helped me get by that one day. And then I got by another day, and I kept hearing her voice saying, "You can do this, Walter."

At the end of the year, I graduated seventh in our class of 24. Normally they promoted the first three graduates to lance corporal, but because I had come from so far behind they promoted me as well, and in time they promoted me to corporal and then to sergeant. I ended up serving closer to five years than four, and when I got out of the Marine Corps I became a newspaper reporter, a newspaper editor, a general manager, and editor of the largest magazine in the world. I wrote five books and appeared on television. I spoke on stage in front of all kinds of audiences all around the

world. I had friends who were Nobel laureates and Pulitzer Prize winners. But everything I've accomplished in my adult life all put together is not as large as the day that those anonymous officers promoted me to lance corporal, because that was the first time in my life that somebody said, "I believe in you." And I would not have been in that position were it not for Mrs. Williams.

Now, if we take a step back, I can return to the two islands I mentioned earlier, the Boys Club and the Mount Vernon library, the two places where I felt safe. If I had not had those two islands on which to plant my feet, I don't know that Mrs. Williams would have had such a positive impact. Every child needs a place where he can feel comfortable, where he can explore, where he can be himself, where people take an interest in him. And to have those islands, those places of peace, on the south side of Mount Vernon—well, it was everything.

personal service
JOHN ANTIOCO
CHAIRMAN AND CEO, BLOCKBUSTER INC.

My dad was a milkman. From the time I was very young I worked with him on the milk truck, doing the various things you do as a milkman. You load the truck. You deliver the milk. You collect the bills. You canvass new accounts. And then the next day, you do the same things all over again. I watched him work, and I didn't realize it at the time but I guess I was taking notes.

He was kind of an opportunistic guy. Not only did he establish a route in the lower middle-class, Irish-Italian neighborhood of Brooklyn, but he went into the Hispanic community and the African-American community too. He was a bit of a pioneer, going into these neighborhoods that were maybe a little more challenging, a little more than some of his competitors were willing to take on. He had some single-family homes on his route, but it was mostly apartment buildings and projects. This was the 1950s and the early 1960s, and as I looked on I began to pay attention to how he approached his

life and his work. I learned how to relate to people, because his big focus was always on personal service. I learned how to appreciate the value of a dollar. And I also learned that there were some things I didn't want to do with my life, like deliver milk, because it was exhausting work.

His daily routine? He'd wake up somewhere around three o'clock in the morning, head out to the dairy, unload the empties from the day before, reload the truck, and get back on the road and start making deliveries by four. Ideally he'd try to be done with his deliveries by seven or eight o'clock in the morning. Then he'd take a short break before going out on his collection route or canvassing new accounts. It was a long day. On Saturdays when I rode with him, we usually wouldn't get home until four or five o'clock in the afternoon.

And that's how it was for him, all day, every day, year in, year out, in all kinds of weather. In the summer you got the added joy of putting the milk in the little cold boxes and laying a chunk of ice on top to make sure the milk lasted until the people got to it when they woke up in the morning. He went seven days a week for a while, and then as I got older he switched to a Monday-Wednesday-Friday, Tuesday-Thursday-Saturday kind of alternating schedule. He kept at it even after we moved out to Long Island. I would go with him on Saturdays even then, until I established my own independent life as a newspaper carrier.

His big thing was keeping his customers happy. His thinking was that anybody could deliver a couple quarts of homogenized white milk, so he tried to add products that people liked—things like orange juice, eggs, sour cream, cottage cheese. Adding those products made his deliveries more complicated, but it set him apart from his competitors. It gave him a little bit of an edge. He was always looking for the best price, the best deal from his suppliers. He was a real penny-pincher in terms of cost control, but he was also a good businessman. He grew up in the Depression, so he never was a risktaker, in terms of overexpanding or branching out to buy a dairy of his own or establishing multiple routes. No, he stayed with his one route until he went into semiretirement.

The penny-pinching and saving was a constant theme of my father's life. I spent countless afternoons watching him do repairs on his truck, because he wasn't about to pay anybody to do that and always thought he could do it better and cheaper himself. I would rather have been out playing stickball.

I have memories of listening to the sounds of a ball game in the background while I helped my father repair his truck. He thought it was important that I learn that stuff, so I wouldn't have to pay somebody to do it for me. What it mostly taught me was that I wanted to be successful enough that I wouldn't *have* to repair my own vehicle and *could* pay someone to do it for me, but I suppose there's a lesson in that as well.

" everything I do flows in one way or another from how my father went about his business. "

Did he enjoy what he was doing? I would say he did. He was successful, he was able to invest a little bit of his money, and he was kind of combative when he felt he needed to be. He stood up when he thought it was the right thing to do. When I was relatively young, he had me in the garage next to our home—the base of our operation—looking at empty milk bottles. Every day, one at a time, I was sorting the ones that needed replacement, that were chipped or discolored or damaged in some way. He would set them aside, because he was trying to get the dairy he bought from to get new bottles. He didn't think the bottles were up to his standards, and we wound up filling the garage with these empties. The dairy wound up discovering they were out of bottles, and lo and behold there they were, in our garage. The bottle count reached into the thousands. There were probably a couple hundred cases of empties, twelve to a case. It was my father's own little protest, designed to ensure that his customers got their milk in clear, chip-free bottles. He got a meeting with the owner of the dairy, and he got them to agree to replace the bottles.

Another time, in the late 1950s, there was a big milk strike in the city and all the local dairies were shut down. My father decided to store and freeze a bunch of milk so he could have it for his customers. He turned it into a kind of public relations stunt. There was a picture of him in the *New York Daily News* pouring a glass of milk for one of his customers' kids. His customers were the only ones who had milk delivery during the strike. He was very happy about that. I don't even know if freezing the milk was legal, in terms of the Department of Agriculture rules, but nobody complained. His customers were thrilled that their deliveries were uninterrupted. He was an enterprising guy. He got that great free publicity in the paper.

When I was little, we lived in a three-room flat in Brooklyn that my father had inherited from his dad. He put the plumbing in himself, and he rented out two floors. I had two sisters, so it was quite crammed until we moved to Long Island, but it allowed him to save some money and bankroll the rent he was collecting. He wound up investing in the stock market. I had no idea how much money he'd set aside until after he died. I still remember having to pry open the refrigerator with a screwdriver because the handle had come off. But the refrigeration element worked fine, so there was no need to replace it. That's how frugal he was about certain things.

And yet when he died in the early 1980s, there was just short of $1 million in his estate. To me the great lesson of his life was the conservative way he lived. We never took vacations, and he never spent his money, just what we needed to get by. What was left over, he invested. In the end I don't think he really got the most out of his money, or that he enjoyed his life to the fullest. But his personality and the way he conducted his business came back to me later on. They're what make me tick.

Everything I do flows in one way or another from how my father went about his business. Either I model my approach after him, or I learned how I *didn't* want to go about things by watching how he was a little too set in his ways for my tastes. He was a real people person, driven by the idea of keeping his customers happy, and my gravitation toward people is on the positive side of what I learned from him. He had tremendous confidence: dealing with business issues, fighting with the dairies, fighting for licensing, and ultimately expanding from retail to wholesale. Really, I couldn't have had a better introduction to the world of business than riding that milk truck with my father on those long Saturdays when I was a boy.

John Antioco

somebody's always watching

EDDIE ARMSTRONG
CORPORATE EXECUTIVE, FORMER YOUTH OF THE YEAR, BOYS & GIRLS CLUBS OF AMERICA

There was a man named Jim Weatherington who was executive director of the Boys & Girls Club in North Little Rock, Arkansas, where I grew up. He'd been involved in the club since before I was born. In fact, Mr. Weatherington had sponsored more Youth of the Year winners than any other executive director in the country, and I think it was because he was so effective in getting kids to reach their potential.

I was 16 and just about finished with high school when it came back to me that Mr. Weatherington had been paying close attention to me during my time at the club. I had no direct dealings with him, although I knew who he was and where his office was. But he knew me. He pulled me into his office one day, sat me down, and walked me through the basics of the Youth of the Year program, what was involved, what it entailed. He said, "I think you stand a good chance."

He gave me a long list of things to do to get myself prepared for it, letters of recommendation I had to obtain from church leaders and community leaders and teachers, an application I had to fill out, an essay I had to start thinking about writing. I'd come to Mr. Weatherington's attention, I guess, because of some of the other initiatives that were taking place in my community at the time. I was involved in a number of positive things and he started to pay attention, and this started our brief journey together.

I call it a lifelong journey now, because what he taught me has stayed with me and set me on my present course. But I only knew him a short time. The reason was because Mr. Weatherington was about to lose a battle with cancer. He never talked about it, and I never knew.

We went to Washington, D.C., after the regionals and the state Youth of the Year competitions, and each time out he would work with me on my speech, helping me to tailor it to each level of the competition, helping to prepare me for whatever I would face in the next round. He was like a godsend, and he seemed to take such joy in helping me to realize this goal I never even knew I had until he set it for me.

To this day, I'm still not sure why Mr. Weatherington had his eye on me. I still can't put my hands around how and what made him and me come together like that, because my story was no different from a lot of kids in the club. We'd moved to North Little Rock from Memphis, Tennessee, just a few years earlier. There was me, my mom and my sister, and that was it. My father was involved with drugs and alcohol, and my parents struggled to keep their marriage together for a while, but eventually we had to move on. I wasn't a terrible kid, but I was a kid with some rough edges, and I was looking for a place to fit myself in.

In my speech I talked about how amazing it was to take a modest $5 investment—the cost of a year's club membership—which I didn't have at the time (I had to borrow it from my mother) and watch it grow into a lifetime of dreams. I talked about how I had my own game room and swimming pool and basketball court and more friends than I could count. And it was heartfelt. I meant every word.

Mr. Weatherington, he just kept cheering me on like he couldn't think of anything else more important than seeing me get that honor and the scholarship that came with it. I had the chance to meet the president and all these other wonderful opportunities that have since come my way as a result.

> " God or our spirits have a peculiar way of putting particular people in our lives at particular times for particular reasons— and you never know when or how that's going to come about, but you'd best be open to it. "

There was a man named Archie Shaffer who turned up a few years later and introduced himself to me when I was working in the Washington, D.C. office of the Boys & Girls Clubs doing government relations. He worked at Tyson Foods back in Arkansas, and he said he'd been keeping an eye on me too, and some of the things I'd accomplished in college. And that's where I'm working now, at Tyson Foods, in their governmental affairs division.

The message I took in was someone's always watching. God or our spirits have a peculiar way of putting particular people in our lives at particular times for particular reasons. And you never know when or how that's going to come about, but you'd best be open to it.

I'm living proof that folks are watching. It was my mom's duty to look after me. I could have gotten involved in gangs or selling drugs, and she was fully aware of what was going on in our neighborhood. Archie Shaffer didn't have to take an interest in me, but he did. And Mr. Weatherington, reaching out to me like that, at a time when he was so sick with cancer that he knew he was dying? That one I'll never understand.

Eddie Armstrong

getting better, each time out
NOTAH BEGAY III
PGA TOUR GOLFER

My father was one of my first coaches. Basketball and soccer, mostly, but I guess you could say he taught me golf too. In the beginning, anyway. How to stand, what direction to hit the ball—the basics. I picked up enough to see that he and his friends weren't very good, and that I probably could do better.

It became a challenge to go with him to the municipal course during the summer, to try to do better. When I showed a talent for it, he sent me to a local junior camp so I could get some proper training.

He was a good athlete, though. He really knew his basketball, and he coached a group of us at the peewee level. Soccer he'd never played, but he picked up what he could. He would study soccer coaching cards he bought at a local sporting goods store, and we made good with what we had. He was new to the game and so were we, but we got better. Each time out, we got better.

45

The Chuska Warriors, that was our team. We were named for a mountain range on the Navajo reservation, and we wore bright orange and white uniforms that we paid for with a bunch of bake sales and other fundraisers. It's funny now to look back at some old team pictures, but we were proud of those uniforms. We were the only all-Indian soccer team in the state at that time, as far as any of us knew. Indian kids didn't play soccer back then, but we used to pile into the back of my dad's '69 Chevy pickup and head out to the field like we didn't want to be anyplace else. He'd get off work early, and the whole team would pile into the back of his truck. It was a great, great time in our lives. We lived on the Isleta reservation, but the players on the team were from all over. It was unheard of to see all these Native American kids running around playing soccer. There weren't even any other Indian players in our league, let alone whole teams. My dad told us to play hard and to present ourselves in a positive fashion.

We weren't very good when we started out, but we got better. My dad was very stern, a second-generation Marine. He had a real focused, disciplined outlook on life—how things should be done, how to carry yourself, how to press on in a tough spot. He was harder on his own kids than he was on the rest of the team, but that was OK. That was just my dad. He expected us to adhere to a certain standard, to persevere. All of us. Just to keep at it, you know. That's how he coached, and I get a lot of my competition and my drive from him.

It has served me well, his drive, and become my own. Whenever I'm in a tough spot, I think back to those days with the Chuska Warriors, with the discipline and focus my dad tried to instill—the determination and desire to present myself in a positive way. It's a part of me out there on the course.

In the 2000 Hartford Open, I was coming down the stretch and had four holes to play with a two-shot lead. I was playing with Mark Calcavecchia, who was only two shots behind—and it was the fourth and final round of the tournament. We came to a short par four. It was drivable, and we both drove the green. I three-putted for par, and Mark drove the green and made his putt for an eagle.

Suddenly we were tied. It was a huge turn of events because I'd been pretty much in control of the golf tournament up until that point. I know a lot of players who would have wilted in that situation, who would have felt the tournament had gotten away from them on that last hole. But I just dug deeper and knew the last three holes were for the tournament. It was still my tournament to win. It was just a matter of persevering and seeing it through—of getting better each time out.

> " Indian kids didn't play soccer back then, but we used to pile into the back of my dad's '69 chevy pickup and head out to the field like we didn't want to be anyplace else. "

We tied the following two holes, and it came down to the final hole. Four rounds of play, and it came down to this final hole, head-to-head. Thirty thousand people watching. Championship on the line. We were both looking at 30-, 35-foot putts, and he left his short, so it fell to me. Last hole, last shot, my tournament to win, and somehow I did. I thought back to those great days piling out of my dad's pickup to play soccer and I found a way to make that putt. Two shots up and now down to even. Some people would have felt they had to make that putt, so I guess there was pressure, but I wouldn't let myself feel any pressure. I just had a job to do and I got it done.

Funny thing is after one or two years the Chuska Warriors let anyone play. We started out as an all-Indian team, but if a kid had an interest my dad would let him play. After a while you could tell that these non-Indian kids were the ones who loved it the most. They're the ones I still hear from. They're the ones who, when I run into them, ask how my dad is doing, tell me what a great sense of accomplishment and structure they got from those days, and the joy they picked up from how we played the game. They tell me how important it was to come together from two completely different backgrounds and to find some common ground, some way to work together to get things done. It's a great, great thing to hear someone talk like that about your dad. These are all successful guys from all walks of life and they stay in touch. They call my dad and let him know how special that time was in their lives. And it was.

Notah Begay III

passing it on

When people ask if anyone really helped me in my career, really made a difference, that's easy. I always say Bill Dickey. He was a great teacher, real patient and kind. He was also one of the greatest catchers ever. That's probably why our manager, Casey Stengel, asked him to come out of retirement in spring 1949 to work with me.

I was a terrible catcher then. I was 23 and had played two years in the majors. I played some outfield, but I was kind of a tanglefoot out there. The main thing is, I loved to hit and I could hit a ball long and hard. But the Yankees felt if I stayed in the bigs, it had to be as a catcher. I thought it might be a big mistake because I was so lousy at it. Like in the 1947 World Series, my rookie year, Jackie Robinson and the Dodgers ran on me pretty much at will. I had a good arm, but my throws sailed. I wasn't good at calling a game or blocking pitches or even catching pop-ups. I got frustrated at times, which isn't a good thing because a good catcher always has to have a clear mind. He's doing most of the thinking for the most important guy in the game: the pitcher.

In his day Bill Dickey played with Babe Ruth and Lou Gehrig and Joe DiMaggio, and he handled pitchers better than anyone. During the 1930s and early 1940s he was the top all-around catcher in baseball. He was the backbone of those great Yankee teams. In 1943, he left the Yankees to enlist in World War II and served two years in the Pacific.

Before March 1949, Bill was home in Arkansas living a life of leisure. One of Casey's first moves when he became manager was getting Bill to join the coaching staff. Dickey's real job, they said, was to teach me how to be a major league catcher. When the papers asked me about it, I said Dickey was learning me all of his experience. I can see why it sounded funny, but to me it was true. All that mattered was that Bill was working with me as hard as he could, and he worked my butt off. He never quit on me and he made sure I never quit on myself. Hour after hour, day after day, all the time he worked with me, he kept building up my confidence.

"Catching is the best job in baseball," he kept telling me. "There are never enough good catchers to go around. Look how long catchers last. They're so scarce that a catcher who can hit .220 is practically guaranteed a job for 10 years. A young fellow like you who can hit with anybody in the league can have a great career as a catcher. All you have to do is learn how to handle yourself well enough to get by back there, and you'll have it made."

I had an awful lot to learn. Bill saw right away my biggest trouble was how I kept shifting my feet when I got ready to catch the ball or throw it. So he kept working on my footwork, telling me to stay closer to the hitter, how to get up on my toes before I threw. Soon I began to feel like I knew where the ball was going when I threw it.

Bill worked with me for a couple of hours every day and fixed all my awkwardness. He worked with me on handling pitchers, how to get the best out of them, how to get them to trust me. He taught me how to study the hitters, how to watch all their habits, how to position our fielders.

I tried my best to do whatever Bill wanted me to. There were still a lot of writers and God knows how many fans who thought I would never make a catcher. But Bill was always talking me up, telling the newspaper guys they were flat-out wrong. "Give him two years," he said, "and Yogi will be the best catcher around by a long shot."

I was a different player in 1949. Mostly I played with more confidence. I remember Casey saying I was the reason our pitchers were doing so well. "There's nobody that has the pitchers' trust like Mr. Berra," he said. "Nobody's running on him."

> " hour after hour, day after day,
> all the time he worked with me,
> he kept building up my confidence. "

I felt real good that season, except when I got hurt. In one game I got hit in the head, and the newspapers said, "X-rays of Berra's head showed nothing." I also fractured my thumb that season, but Bill was always encouraging me and I learned to play hurt. I came back and was elected to the All-Star team for the first time that season, and made it every year thereafter. We beat the Dodgers in the World Series in 1949, the first of our five straight world championships, which had never been done.

Bill Dickey was a great man, a great teacher, and years later he did for Elston Howard what he did for me. I'll never forget him. I owe him my success. When I was inducted into the Hall of Fame in 1972, I thanked Bill in my speech for all he did. I sure wouldn't have made it there without him.

Yogi Berra

happy town
CHICK BIG CROW
EXECUTIVE DIRECTOR,
SUANNE BIG CROW BOYS & GIRLS CLUB

You don't expect much from the outside world. I never did. Not until my daughter SuAnne taught me differently.

I was born and raised on the Pine Ridge reservation. Living on the reservation you face a lot of prejudice and racism, and you tend to give it back. I was waiting for my youngest daughter to grow up and get through college so I could leave. But she would say, "Mom, you can't leave; this is our home. If we don't like it we have to change it."

She went to the state basketball tournament during South Dakota's centennial year. I told her, "SuAnne, go out there and play your heart out. Try your best. But you know South Dakota is not going to let an Indian team be its centennial champion."

She just said, "Watch me, Mom. Watch me." And that year they won the state championship.

She was 17 when she was killed in a car accident. When she died, all these people came forward—people she had helped or touched in some way. She really made an impact. She could always get what she wanted. If she wanted a tomato and you had two tomatoes, she'd talk you out of one. People were drawn to her. She would always cheer them up. She would tell them, "I'm going away to college, but when I come back I'm going to build a Happy Town, and you're not going to have to worry about that here."

She had a big job ahead of her. Growing up here is tough. It really is a hard life. Your own people are the hardest on you. But it was SuAnne's home. She was always saying, "If we don't do something about it, nobody will." She was determined to make a difference.

SuAnne was always talking about her Happy Town. It was a place where everyone got along, supported each other, and was proud of each other's accomplishments. Most of all it was drug-, alcohol-, and racism-free. That was her dream. And she walked her talk. She never said, "Don't do this" or "Don't do that." If somebody said, "SuAnne, you had a good game," she'd just say, "Yeah, and I do it drug- and alcohol-free."

SuAnne did more than I'll ever do. She played softball and volleyball. She ran cross-country—set a state track record—and she was a cheerleader. And she traveled all over the world: Russia, Lithuania, Finland, Australia, New Zealand, Hawaii. Everywhere she went, she made an impact.

> " if we don't do something
> about it, nobody will. "

Everyone was dumbfounded when she died, but we knew what we wanted to do for her. We did what she would have done. We remodeled an old building and started the SuAnne Big Crow Youth Center. After that we became the first Boys & Girls Club in Indian country. Now we serve almost 900 kids. This year, we're putting in a skate park, a soccer field, and a sand volleyball court. We were going to start landscaping last year, but the prairie dogs moved in, and they're on the endangered species list, so they kind of homesteaded here. We couldn't get rid of them, but now they're gone so we can get to work.

Everybody wants something for nothing. It's become ingrained in the native people. We tell them, "No, what you want you work for." It's taken generations for us to get where we are, so it's going to take generations to get out of it. That's what we're up against. I don't know if drug and alcohol use is declining, but the kids we're serving are the ones who are going to make a difference. One or two of these kids, they'll be the spark. That's all you need.

All these federal programs and monies tend to be for the kids who are losing in life, but we also have kids who are winning, and there's no money in the government system for the kids who are succeeding or kids whose families expect them to succeed. Usually you have to get into trouble to get any attention, but out here you don't.

SuAnne kind of built this place. She just used me to help her because I was still here. Everything we do here, it's in SuAnne's memory. We're guided by her.

Leatrice "Chick" Big Crow

a career decision
GEORGE BODENHEIMER
PRESIDENT, ESPN AND ABC SPORTS

The worst thing my father could tell me when I was growing up, doing all the things schoolboys were doing, was that I'd disappointed him. He treated me with great respect, and he expected great respect in return. That was always a big thing—treating people how you want to be treated.

When I started at ESPN, in the mail room, there were plenty of people who wanted to base the level of respect or courtesy they'd give you on your position. I'd see people who couldn't act appropriately, simply because I was delivering their mail or moving a box for them from one office to the next.

You learn a lot about people working your way up, and my father's words stuck with me: "Treat people with respect." He was a retail store manager, but he spent time with everybody. He asked after their families. My mother was a bank teller, and she was the same way and it had a big impact on me.

The best advice my father ever gave me was career advice. When I graduated from Denison University, a small liberal arts school in Ohio, he sat me down at our dining room table to have a talk. I wanted to be in the entertainment business, and I loved sports, and together we came up with the idea of writing to the owners of every major league baseball team. At the time there were 28 teams, and my father brought me 28 envelopes and 28 stamps and sat with me while I wrote out 28 separate letters, longhand, right there on our dining room table.

The gist of the letters was that they needed me in their front office, that I would work hard for them, that I loved the game of baseball. I got back 27 no-thank-yous. But Bill Giles of the Philadelphia Phillies happened to be a Denison alum and was kind enough to invite me down for an interview. Bill told me that baseball front offices were small, family-run operations and that if I really wanted to get into baseball I should fire up my letter-writing campaign and start reaching out to minor league franchises.

Eventually I turned my attention to arenas, like Madison Square Garden in New York City and the Superdome in New Orleans. I could barely get an application for employment at the arenas, much less an interview. When I looked up one day, nine months had gone by since graduation.

I was living at home, in Greenwich, Connecticut, bartending at night, trying to figure out my next move. My parents were very supportive. They knew I was struggling and despairing, but they didn't put any pressure on me. They talked about it when I wanted to talk about it and they left it alone when it needed to be left alone.

One night I came home and declared I was going to move to Colorado and bartend for a year. My father discouraged me on the theory that if I did, I would let a whole other group of graduating seniors into the workforce—and the competition for a good position would be that much harder. He was right about that, so I stayed home and kept looking.

A friend of my father's who worked at CBS finally pointed me in the right direction. He said that if I wanted to get into television, I should consider cable. This was back in 1980, long before cable television was broadly distributed, and certainly long before ESPN was on the map, but I was open to anything at this point. This man knew we lived in Connecticut, so he put me in touch with someone at ESPN, which was also based in

Connecticut. I sent off a letter and didn't think anything of it until I got an interview.

I met with this contact for about two minutes. He basically just shook my hand and walked me down to the director of human resources where I had another two-minute interview. This guy looked at my resume and told me he thought I'd be qualified to be a driver, which was what we called our mail room positions at the time and still do. He asked me if I would mind shoveling snow, and I said I wouldn't. When I left, he promised to let me know something by the following week.

> " when you're starting out or starting over, make a career decision, not a money decision. "

I drove back to Greenwich thinking, "What am I going to tell my father?" Here I was looking at working in the mail room, for less money than it had cost for a year's tuition at Denison. I was desperate for a job, but I wasn't feeling too good about this. When I got home I laid it out for my father and he could see my concern. He said, "Let's go out for a beer and talk about it." We went to a famous old restaurant in Greenwich called The Clam Box, and we had a beer and some chowder and talked about the job.

He said that if I was offered the job, and that if sports television was a career I'd like to pursue, I should probably take it. "You're making a career decision, not a money decision," he said. He told me I could always live at the house if money was tight, and reminded me that I could probably find a roommate to share expenses. And once again he was right, and I've since given the same advice to thousands of young people. When you're starting out or starting over, make a career decision, not a money decision.

Sure enough, the call came in and I got the job. The starting salary was $8,300, which even in 1980 was terribly low, but I took it. I moved closer to Bristol right away, but all I could afford was a room at the New Britain YMCA. It was a bit of an eye-opener, but as my father predicted, I found a roommate after about two weeks, another guy who had started at ESPN around the same time, and it was fantastic.

It's been a great 25-year ride. It seems to have worked out pretty well.

George W. Bodenheimer

by example
DAVID BOIES
ATTORNEY

My father, who was a high school history teacher, taught me almost everything I needed to know about American history—including the constitutional principles I argued in *Bush v. Gore*. By both word and example, he taught me almost everything I ever needed to know about almost anything else, too. We talked often when I was young, and again when he was old. He always had advice, most of which was good, and some of which I took. But his most valuable lessons were not in what he said but in what he did and how he did it.

To supplement his teacher's salary, he worked at a series of second jobs, from selling *World Book* encyclopedias to working in the credit department at Sears to driving a bakery truck. He would have preferred to be at home with his family or preparing his lessons, but he always managed to find something of interest, some challenge, and something of value in every job he did, however routine or boring it might seem. Those lessons served me well as a trial lawyer, where days and weeks of preparatory drudgery are required for every hour of glamorous performance.

At home my parents managed to raise five children. Both by their own choices and by the freedom they gave us, they encouraged us to dream, to take chances, and to try to learn both from the choices that turned out well and those that did not. My parents (and their parents and grandparents) had lived in Illinois all their lives, except when my father was in the army during the Second World War. During the war he had passed through California and concluded it was the promised land. In June of 1954, my parents loaded their furniture into a moving van and their then four children into their station wagon and set out for Los Angeles. They had already sold their house, and the fact that they had neither a house nor a job waiting for them may have concerned but did not deter them.

> " by their own choices and by the freedom they gave us, they encouraged us to dream, to take chances, and to try to learn both from the choices that turned out well and those that did not. "

More than 40 years later, when I left the large firm where I had been for three decades to start my own firm in a loft, I thought of my father's even more venturesome decision. Both our choices worked out well, but in exercising the freedom our parents gave us we were not always so fortunate. There were no disasters and we managed to both recover and learn from our mistakes, but there were many times our choices proved hard for us and harder for our parents. The balance between allowing children to be independent while at the same time protecting them from serious harm is a difficult one, and I have not always been able to draw the line in the right place in raising my own six children. But the patience and perspective necessary to try to teach and lead while not controlling or managing our children is one of the most important lessons our parents taught us.

The one area in which my father permitted no leeway was his demand that we treat every person with respect. The lesson he drew from the biblical description of the Good Samaritan was that every person was entitled not only to God's love and indulgences but to ours as well. My father had been appalled by the racism he had seen in the service and in the Southern towns he had visited. Years before *Brown v. Board of Education* he taught his students that segregation was wrong and unconstitutional. When I traveled to Mississippi after law school as a civil rights volunteer in the middle 1960s, I think my father wondered why it had taken me so long.

I've been fortunate to have many mentors in my life, but none has been as important as my father. Whether it was how to work, how to raise a family, or how to treat others, his example is what made the difference in my life.

David Boies

the aura of a queen
JIMMY CARTER
39TH PRESIDENT OF THE UNITED STATES

There was a woman who lived on our farm when I was a boy—her name
was Rachel Clark—and she took me under her wing. She was married to a
man named Jack Clark who was in charge of our barn and our mules and our
livestock on the farm. Jack did all the hard work that we boys most admired,
but it was Rachel who shone. She had the aura of a queen. She was light tan
in color and small in stature, but everyone in town, black and white, knew
that somehow or other Rachel was an exalted person. She was philosophical.
She was very wise. She was kind and gentle. During the segregation years,
when there was a sharp distinction between black and white and white was
supreme, for some reason white women refrained from asking Rachel to
serve in menial duties inside the home such as cooking or ironing. But she
would volunteer to do so anytime she learned the need was real.

She was the best worker in the field; I remember that most of all. She could pick more cotton and shake more peanuts than any other person in Georgia. I could pick 150 pounds of cotton, but Rachel could pick near twice as much. At sundown we would tie what we had picked in burlap sheets and watch the foreman weigh our haul and see for ourselves that Rachel had us beat. She would put more peanuts on the stacks, hoe more weeds, shell more corn.

When my mother and father would go off on vacation—or sometimes when my mother, who was a registered nurse, had to work a long shift at the hospital in Plains or 24 hours a day in private homes—I would spend the night in Rachel's house. I slept on the floor on a pallet, we called it, a thin mattress filled with corn shucks, and during the winter Rachel would let me drag the pallet near the fireplace. I remember those nights, but mostly I remember those days, working at Rachel's side, trying to match her every move.

When the work was done or a heavy rain made the fields too wet to hoe or plow, she would take me fishing. I would follow her like a puppy dog, sometimes walking five or six miles to a creek, and fish all day with Rachel. She set out seven poles. Never six. Never eight. Always seven. She caught about five fish to my one, but she would slip a few fish into my bag. For bait we used crawfish, lizards, crickets, worms—whatever Rachel decided. We fished for perch, catfish, and bass, which we always called trout.

We used empty flour sacks to bring our fish home, and on the way Rachel would reminisce about her beliefs in God, the duties of people to one another, and the advantages of always telling the truth, taking care of the out of doors, and being kind to those in need. She talked about equality and what it meant in our community. On these long walks, over these long days, she planted in my mind the basic philosophies of life.

" everyone in town . . . knew that somehow or other Rachel was an exalted person. "

It wasn't until many years later, when I was on the submarine force, that I changed my attitude towards racial equality. I had grown up accepting "separate but equal" as the law of the land, just as Rachel appeared to have accepted it. Nobody questioned that there were no black activists, no white idealists, no lawyers, no members of the Supreme Court, no members of

Congress who challenged that law, which was effective in our country for almost 100 years, from the Civil War until the Lyndon Johnson years.

But in 1948 Harry Truman ordained, unilaterally and with extreme courage, that racial discrimination in the military forces would end. This was a remarkable act, and it took place five years before Rosa Parks sat in the front seat of a Montgomery bus, and five years before Martin Luther King Jr.'s name was even known. And Harry Truman did it. I was on a submarine, and Harry Truman was my commander in chief, and he changed the way white people and black people related to each other in the Marines, in the Navy, in the Air Force, in the Army. And it put me in mind of Rachel Clark, and the dignified way she carried herself all those years ago.

Jimmy Carter

always there
SWIN CASH
PROFESSIONAL BASKETBALL PLAYER

I talk all the time about my mom and what a strong person she's been in my life. But there's someone else behind the scenes who's also played a significant role. His name is Mr. Robert Gallagher. Everyone calls him Bob. I don't talk too much about him, because it's private, but he's been a real inspiration to me since I was about 11 years old.

I grew up in public housing in a suburb of Pittsburgh called McKeesport. It was just me and my mom for a long time. She'd been a big-time basketball player in high school. She was offered a full scholarship to play in college, but she got pregnant with me her senior year and that was that. She had to give up that scholarship. She and my dad were high school sweethearts, but they separated and my dad went off to the Marines.

We didn't have much when I was a kid. My mom was on welfare, working two jobs, doing what she could. She also was working on getting her degree, working on getting a better life going—you know, working on getting back what she might have lost by getting pregnant so young like she did and turning down that chance to go to college.

The first time I met Bob was at an AAU basketball tournament he put on through a nonprofit organization that he runs. He was really big in women's basketball in western Pennsylvania. He wasn't a coach—he got involved when his niece was killed in a car accident at an early age. She had been involved in sports, particularly basketball, and he started the Western Pennsylvania Girls Basketball Association in her memory. It was a pretty big deal when I was growing up and he ran it. Soon after I started playing he singled me out. We kind of gravitated to each other. I think he took a lot of heat for taking an interest in me because I was one of the better players. But he was just being a nice person to me and my family.

One time I was invited to a basketball camp in Terre Haute, Indiana. At the time my mom was so busy doing everything she was doing, and I had told her I needed a bus ticket to Indianapolis. I must have been about 12. I don't know how I came up with Indianapolis, but that's what I told her. So my mom went ahead and got the bus ticket. She just knew I'd be picked up at the bus terminal and taken to the camp. But it turned out I was supposed to go straight to Terre Haute, not Indianapolis. When I got to the bus terminal, there was no one there to meet me.

There I was, 12 years old, looking around, and I started to get upset. I ended up walking to this hotel, and I told the people there was no one there to pick me up and I didn't have a phone and I didn't have any money. It was one of those horrifying stories, because when I finally reached my mom she felt so bad that she hadn't checked on all the other arrangements.

So she called Bob. I remember talking to him on the phone and telling him this would never happen again. I told him it was my fault. I told him how upset my mom was. He said not to worry and that he would help me out. He ended up sending a car service to take me to the camp. After that I flew back home to Pittsburgh instead of taking the bus, and from that point on he's been like a grandfather to me. A real confidant, a great friend.

I started calling him my "Paps." He's an older guy, 6 foot 3, white, and here I am this young black girl calling him my Paps. My grandfather passed away when I was too young to remember, so for me he was really like a grandfather figure in my life. It was funny when I started to go to different camps and stuff, and I'd say, "Oh, my Paps will be here in a little bit to pick me up." And he'd show up and people would do this double take. They didn't understand.

You see so many people nowadays trying to get close to younger athletes, thinking it's their ticket into something else. But Bob is not one of those people. He's never, ever tried to get involved in anything else. He's always in the background, always just a great cheerleader and supporter.

> " he'd say, "Swin, you don't want to go down that road" . . . and he was right. You know, you have to keep focused; you have to learn from the missteps of others. "

He helped me pick a college, helped me understand what I needed to do academically. He jumped in the car with us—me and my mom and my godmom—and drove those seven hours up to Connecticut when I started college. He was always telling me to experience everything life has to offer, to never settle, to always be inspired, and to give back—that was his big thing.

To this day, he's never asked me for anything. He inspired me to start my own charity, to work with kids, to touch other lives the way he's touched mine. Without Bob, I don't believe I could have done the things I've done.

He is always so genuine, so sincere. He's a very spiritual person and my family is very spiritual. He's Catholic. We're Methodists. But we're not that different.

He had a hard time being so close to me and my mom. Some of the parents of the other players were jealous. He helped a lot of girls, providing an opportunity for them to play, but they always thought he was showing favoritism to me and my mom. It didn't matter how many people were negative. He just kept it positive.

We had a spiritual connection with him. He was always telling me to give back, always preaching about breaking the cycle of poverty and bad decisions and hardship. We talked about my mom and what she had to give up in order to have me. And he'd say, "Swin, you don't want to go down that road. Break the cycle." He kept telling me how important that was, and he was right. You know, you have to keep focused; you have to learn from the missteps of others. You have to keep it positive.

My mom is a great person. She taught me a lot. She's a fighter and a lot of what I have in me is because of her. She taught me to be strong. It's even in my name, Swintayla, which means "astounding woman." My godmom came up with that. So there was always a strong, positive example at home.

I don't want to give the impression that I was all about basketball when I was younger. My mom encouraged me to do a lot of things. I was a cheerleader. I played the cello. I loved track and field, but going into high school it was difficult with all these schools recruiting me. I had it in my head that I had to perfect my craft. Basketball was my craft, so I had to cut out a lot of these other activities. It made me sad, but you have to make sacrifices sometimes. I'm glad I did, because my family didn't have a whole lot of money, and at the end of the day if dribbling a ball is going to get you a full scholarship, it's something you can't pass up.

Bob was underneath all of this. He was always there, always supportive, and looking back it's a great, refreshing thing. We talk about coaches trying to get the next NBA star or the next WNBA star. Bob never had an agenda other than to help me become the person, the basketball player, and the woman I am today. That's something amazing.

There's so much that comes down to race in our society today. But a beautiful story like this one—a white man reaching out to help a young African-American girl—had nothing to do with the color of our skin. It had more to do with the person and with humility. It was about being a human being. I feel like he's my family, my Paps.

the red bridge club
GEN. WESLEY CLARK, USA (RET)
FORMER SUPREME COMMANDER, NATO

I want to talk about these two characters at the Little Rock Boys Club that influenced my life, and they're sort of the yin and yang of my experience there. One was Jimmy Miller, the swimming coach and camp director, and the other was J.W. "Billy" Mitchell, who was the director of the place.

Miller was from southern Arkansas, a former soldier in the South Pacific, probably in his early 30s at that point. He was a leader and an organizer. He knew how to inspire you, how to intimidate you, how to move you forward.

Mitchell, on the other hand, was a much older guy, a Texas A&M graduate, former All-American in football and basketball, and he got along with all the businessmen in town. He was more buttoned-down. He knew all the right standards, how to maintain propriety, how to keep the place going, and I guess he saw in me a kid who exemplified what the Boys Club should be about.

I fit somewhere between the two, but both men played a pivotal role in my young life. My mother was a secretary at a bank in downtown Little Rock. We didn't have any money, but people didn't feel poor if they had a home and a car and a steady job. It was just that you didn't spend money.

Billy Mitchell had a couple bankers on the Boys Club board, and he would have me make appearances and talk to people. I was always near the top of my class in school, and he brought me around as the product, to sell the club. I got to see the business world and the not-for-profit world. People around town started to know me because of this, and it gave me a lot of poise—a lot of understanding about how the adult world worked. It was a big factor in my growth as a person.

Jimmy Miller was an entirely different kind of influence. I was a swimmer, and in the eighth grade I joined Jimmy's swimming team. I'd go down there three nights a week for swimming workouts from 6:30 to 8 at night. We'd take trips on Saturdays and Sundays as a team several times a year. The first of those trips, there were four of us hoping to go along, but you couldn't just sign up for it. You had to earn it.

Miller assigned each one of us a time we had to swim in order to qualify for the trip. That was his way to get us to work hard. Each of us had a different time according to our abilities. I wasn't as good at swimming as this other kid, Mike, but Miller told me I had to do a 1:12.4 in the 100-yard freestyle, and he told Mike he had to do a 1:12.5. So we did the time trials, and Mike got his 1:12.5, but I swam a 1:13.5, so I got 11 pops with the towel, one for each tenth of a second I missed the time. In those days we didn't wear suits in the pool. They said it was for sanitary reasons, but that wasn't it. The presumption was that these poor kids couldn't afford bathing suits, so Miller was popping me on my bare rear end with a wet towel. My parents never disciplined me for anything like that. I never failed anything before. It stung and it hurt my feelings. It was embarrassing and humiliating. But this was Miller's way.

After he was through popping me with the towel, Miller said, "Your biggest problem is you. You don't believe enough in who you are."

I said, "But you gave me a faster time to swim than Mike."

And he said, "That's because you can be a better swimmer than Mike."

What a powerful lesson. That was how Jimmy Miller motivated people, and in my case it worked. The next week he let me go at it again, and this time I swam a 1:11.7, so I made the trip. It was a lesson I never forgot.

And here's another: The next summer I wanted to be a counselor at the camp, and you had to go to counselor school. I was really happy about it, because at 14 I was still young enough to be a camper and it wasn't everybody who got to be a counselor. So every Saturday for three hours you sat upstairs with Miller in this tiny cubbyhole office up in the attic, and he talked to you about leadership and first aid and water safety and how to take care of people and how to motivate them. And he gave you his secrets, the lessons he learned growing up in south Arkansas, plus some of the Army experiences he'd had.

" your biggest problem is you. You don't believe enough in who you are. "

In April of that year—it was one of these warm weekends—we went to what they called Clean-Up Camp. The log cabins had no windows, so they took everything out of them in the wintertime and stored it all in the rec hall. We had to get it all back and set up the cabins. This was part of our test, to see if we could make it as counselors. We worked all day Saturday and slept that night in one of the cabins we'd set up, and on Sunday morning we got some time off. We all went down to this wide spot of the creek. It wasn't exactly on-limits, but it was near camp and we all knew where it was because there was a big red iron bridge over the creek at that point. I had these two plastic model boats with little electric motors in them, and the idea was we would wade around in the water and run the boats.

As luck would have it, Miller drove by later that morning. I guess he was headed to the store or something, and he saw the group of us in the creek, and he said, "You guys are off-limits. Get on back to camp." And we said, "Yes, sir," but as he drove off we realized he hadn't exactly told us *when* we needed to get back to camp, so we stayed on and continued to run the boats. When Miller came back our way over the bridge, he saw we were still there. He wasn't too happy about it. He got out of his car and told us what our punishment was for not following his orders: We would all have to become members of the Red Bridge Club or lose our status as counselors.

To become a member of the Red Bridge Club you had to climb to the top girder of the trestle bridge and jump off. The thing that made it tricky was the girder was only about 10 inches wide, like a balance beam, hung 20-some feet above the roadway and 42 feet above the water. Furthermore, the water right under the bridge was only a couple feet deep, so you had to do a standing broad jump from the trestle in order to reach deeper water.

There were 10 of us caught running boats in the creek, but six weren't up to it and they walked back to camp. They'd have to come back as campers that summer. The other four of us shinnied up to the top of the bridge.

We went in order of age, so I was third in line. None of us had any clothes on. The first guy stood up and tried to find the courage to jump, but he couldn't bring himself to go. He kept saying, "Coach, I don't want to do this." And, "Coach, there's not enough water." And, "Coach, I don't have a bathing suit on. I'm gonna get hurt."

Miller just said, "I'm gonna count to three and you're gonna go."

But he didn't go, so Miller counted off again. Still the kid still didn't go, and it looked like he was getting ready to climb back down in defeat.

Then I heard gravel popping down the road. I looked out from where we were all lying on the girder like a line of tadpoles and saw a pickup truck coming. There were three women in the cab, probably going to church. I could see the ribbons of their hats flying in the open window of the truck. The approaching road was about level with the top girder of the bridge. So pretty soon these women were looking right at us, and we were looking right at them. What cajoling and intimidating and inspiring couldn't do for this first kid, embarrassment finally did. He jumped.

None of us thought he would jump. I don't even think Miller thought he'd jump at this point, but he jumped. After that, the second guy stood up and he argued for a while, but he eventually jumped. Then I stood up and started to argue, but Miller counted to three and I jumped, followed by the fourth guy. All four of us passed Miller's test and we got to stay on as counselors.

Miller and Mitchell fought like cats and dogs. It seemed like Mitchell couldn't stand Miller. He considered him an embarrassment and a roughneck. And I'm sure he wouldn't have liked the way Miller treated us on that bridge or the way he popped us with wet towels. But that's why I call them the yin and yang of my experience. They each had their own ways and their own approaches, and each had their merits.

Today you wouldn't get away with popping kids with towels or sending them jumping off a 40-foot bridge, but I guess kids now find other ways to establish themselves and prove themselves and grow into adulthood. And counselors and teachers and leaders find other ways to motivate their charges. At least I hope they do, because you need these lessons in life—lessons about believing in yourself and having courage. You need to push yourself, and to test limits, because that's what it takes to grow up.

Wes Clark

paying attention
BILL CLINTON
42ND PRESIDENT OF THE UNITED STATES

My great-uncle, Oren Grisham, who everyone called Buddy, was, along with my grandfather, the dominant male influence of my early childhood. He was my grandmother's brother, and I bet he had an IQ of 180. Everyone on that side of my family was really smart, but they were country people. They had no education. I think Buddy got to the 10th grade, and he never really made any money. He was a farmer and a fireman. And he was tough. He had a cancerous lung removed in 1974 and lived another 20 years. That was Buddy, one of the 15 percent of people with lung cancer who made it.

Buddy taught me, by example and instruction, to appreciate all kinds of people and to pay attention to everybody. Just pay attention. I remember when I was writing my book, my editor said he didn't believe I actually remembered the names of everybody I ever met. He also said readers wouldn't care what happened to their children and grandchildren, and I said, "Well, that's the way I was raised." Then after I sent him two hundred pages of the book he said, "Did you know any sane people when you were a child?" I replied that all childhoods are populated with zany people; I was just paying attention.

I was raised by that last generation of Americans where a high school diploma was still a rarity. Folks couldn't afford to take vacations and their main source of entertainment was around meals; hunting and fishing, talking, and eating. Our meals were full of conversations about ordinary people. When my uncle talked about their lives and loves, triumphs and foulups, they were fascinating. He taught us that everyone has a story and the more of others you understand, the better your grasp of human nature, a gift given great weight in my family. I didn't have a television until I was 10 years old, so my early years were marked by these strong older people, by not being distracted, by listening to their stories and learning to tell some of my own.

Even after we moved from Hope when I was 7, my mother often put me on the Trailways bus for the 2½-hour ride back from Hot Springs to Hope to visit Buddy and his wife, Ollie. I always looked forward to the meals. They had an old ice cream maker in Buddy's house, and a buttermilk churner, and they'd put me to work, churning or turning the crank on the ice cream maker, or shelling peas. All the time I'd listen, constantly astonished at what my uncle Buddy knew about people, what he remembered, how he could see somebody and recall, verbatim, their conversations from years back. When he got older, one of his daughters ran a little ice cream parlor in Hope, and he'd go in there and tell stories to the kids. He could remember the names of the bird dogs he had 60 years earlier, what they looked like, and how they chased after birds.

I remember back in '78 when I ran for governor the first time, we had a really heated senate race between the governor and two congressmen. I asked Buddy who he was for and he said, "I don't care. I wouldn't care who was gonna be governor if you weren't my nephew." Then he said, "You've got to remember something about guys like me. All we want to do is to have clean water to fish and run our feet in, and we want you to keep the Game and Fish Commissioner straightened out, and don't mess with our pickups."

That was it. And when I was beaten for reelection in 1980 after I raised the car and truck license fees to finance a large highway improvement project, Buddy reminded me that he was the first person who told me I would lose. Our conversation went something like this: He said, "Bill, I told you not to mess with our pickups."

I said, "Well, Buddy, we have to have some money for the roads."

He said, "I don't care. Go borrow it. They're gonna beat you with this." And he was right. In our state, you renew your car license on your birthday, so we made somebody mad every day and when you make a new group of people mad every day for a year, nobody has a chance to get over it and lots of people are still hot about it on Election Day. When all the pollsters and advisors still thought I couldn't be defeated, Buddy was telling me I was going to lose.

> " I often wonder how many people out there scrubbing out a living on those farms would have been doctors or scientists or Lord only knows what if only they'd had half the chances I had. "

The most memorable encounter I ever had with him was a few years later, after I was reelected governor. His wife got Alzheimer's a couple years before she died. They lived in an old home with a gas-heated stove, and she'd often forget to turn the stove off. He was afraid she was going to blow the place up. Finally, he had to move her into this little nursing home that was attached to the hospital in Hope. She was well cared for, but as the Alzheimer's progressed, she still knew who Buddy was for about 15 minutes each day. When she was clearheaded, she'd get on the phone and say, "Oren, we've been married for 57 years. Why in the living hell would you leave me out here in this strange place? Come get me right this minute." He'd get in his car and drive over, but by the time he'd get there she wouldn't know him. It happened over and over again.

One night during this period, I was down in Hope giving a talk, and I went to see him. We talked until it was getting dark and I said, "Buddy, I've got to get back to Little Rock." He'd been telling jokes the whole time, but I knew what he was going through with his wife. As I was on my way out the door, he grabbed me. When I turned around, I could see that he was crying.

It was the only time he ever cried in front of me, and I said, "This is really hard, isn't it?"

Buddy said, "Yeah, it is." Then he smiled and said, "But I signed on for the whole load, and most of it was pretty good."

That was Buddy's philosophy of life, compressed into one sentence. It's a moment that's stayed with me. My family likes to joke that none of us are perfect, but we're all stickers. My mother was like that too. I was taught that no matter what happens, you just get up, go on, and hang on.

I was really blessed to have Buddy and my grandfather and a number of other older people who took an interest in me when I was young. They didn't have any money or formal education, but they were smart. I've often wondered how many people were out there scrubbing out a living on those farms who would have been doctors or scientists or Lord only knows what if they'd had half the chances I had.

But they were rich with good hearts, open minds, and a desire to teach and learn. So I learned the importance of respecting all people, and not making judgments about them based on their income or their position in life or what kind of clothes they wore or what degrees they had hanging on the wall or what the color of their skin was. I really believe one of the principal reasons I became president is that in my childhood, I learned to keep my eyes and ears open, to soak everything in before judging a person, a situation, or a complex issue. If I'd been born 10 years later, and been watching all that television and been in an upper middle-class home, or if I'd been born 30 years later and falling in love with my computer, I would probably not have had the life I have had. I'm thrilled that young people today have access to more information and activities than ever before, but I wish for all of them an Uncle Buddy too, to open their eyes to other people's core: their fears and pain, hopes and dreams, and their stories. It was a great gift.

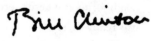

the second-fastest runner in orlando

JOHNNY DAMON
PROFESSIONAL BASEBALL PLAYER

My brother James was the fastest runner in Orlando. He was two and a half years older than me and of course I looked up to him. I used to tag along with him and his friends, and when I was old enough, they'd want me to play with them—football, baseball, even some basketball. We grew up in a neighborhood where there were a lot of kids—black, white, Spanish, Asian. It was really diverse and it was special, and every day we'd be out there playing.

There was always a game going. Whatever the season was, that's what we played. It's how we stayed out of trouble—although to be honest, I still managed to get into a little bit of trouble. For a while I ran with a group of kids my own age and we'd go pool hopping all around the community or running over the tops of cars. We were a little wild.

Not James though. He kept me mostly in line. He's the reason I'm where I'm at today. My parents were working, so they didn't have the time to look after us. James took it on himself. He looked after both of us. My father held two or three jobs at a time. He was a security guard. My mother cleaned offices and hotels. They worked hard and there was always food on the table, but James and I pretty much had to take care of ourselves. James was the responsible one. James was the parent.

When James got to high school, he started playing baseball with a group of older kids in an organized league. He was 16 and he played in the 16- to 18-year-old group, but at that age it was tough to get enough kids to show up for the games. Kids had jobs and other responsibilities.

One day I went and said I was my brother. James couldn't go for some reason. So I played and I went three-for-three. I remember pulling up at first base and talking to the other team's first baseman. He said something like, "Hey, you gonna get drafted this year?" A lot of these players were hoping to play college ball, hoping to get recruited, you know. And I said, "Oh, I'm not sure, we'll see how things go." Something like that. I was only 13, but I didn't say anything about my age. The other team's pitcher was probably going to be drafted in the first couple rounds, and I was taking it to him—playing a pretty decent center field and taking it to him.

<blockquote>" James took it on himself.
He looked after both of us. "</blockquote>

Football, I didn't love it. I think my brother started to notice my athletic gifts on the football field, though, because I'd get hit pretty hard and then stand up as if nothing happened. They wanted me to be a defensive back. They said I could go far, go to college, possibly play in the NFL. But that wasn't what I wanted. I wanted to catch touchdowns. I wanted one of those glamour positions, but that wasn't what they wanted me to do. So when I got to high school, I played baseball and ran track.

Baseball was a team game with some opportunities to show your individuality. In track it was you against everybody else. I was fast.

Freshman year it was me and this other guy in the 100 meters, a real battle. But after that I was number one in the 100 meters and the 200 meters.

No one could catch me. And that was a big deal to my brother James. See, he'd always been fast. The kind of fast that people talked about. It was a real important moment in my athletic career, and I guess also in his, when I finally got to high school to join him on the track team. I was a freshman; he was a senior. The first day of practice we were racing and I blew him away in the 100 meters—just blew him away. And James instantly quit the track team, right then and there, because his legacy of being the fastest guy in Orlando was over.

I took it to him, and he was like, *"Oh, my goodness!"* He didn't want to be the second-fastest guy in Orlando, so he quit. But I think he was proud of me—proud and probably a little pissed too, but that was James. If he had to take second place to anybody, it might as well be me, but he wasn't interested in second place. He was probably the best defensive back in high school and had some scholarship offers to play football. But he got a hairline fracture in his ankle and that really hurt his chances. So after a while he stopped playing any kind of competitive ball and decided he would just root for me.

And he's still rooting for me, although when he comes out to the stadium he's afraid to watch. It's funny, but he doesn't like it when I mess up or when the fans start to boo. My wife always says that when he's there he's not really there, he's just roaming around the stadium looking, but I guess he's still looking out for me, keeping me out of trouble.

that constant voice
DOMINIQUE DAWES
ACTRESS, FORMER
OLYMPIC GYMNAST

Kelli Hill was my coach from the time I was about 6 years old until I was 23, and I really owe my success as a gymnast to her. And it wasn't just about gymnastics. She helped me to develop my confidence, my character, and my perseverance to strive after goals.

The funny thing is that it was almost by chance that I started working with her. I was a real energetic kid. My sister and I were tearing up the furniture at home and gymnastics was something for us to do. I lived in Silver Springs, Maryland, and my mother signed us up for dance and tap lessons and all kinds of different things. She noticed Kelli's gym one day on her way to the mall and figured she'd have us try it. Gymnastics wasn't anything we'd expressed a particular interest in. But it was across the street from the mall and my mother liked to shop, so it was convenient.

Kelli didn't have a name at all at that time. Now, of course, people come from all over the world to train with her at her gym in Gaithersburg, Maryland, and whole families relocate just so their daughters can be nearby. But back then she just had this little gym in Wheaton that she had purchased when she was about 20 years old and started from scratch. She was only about 22 when I started working with her, but after about a year or two Kelli noticed something in me, something special. I'm sure the first impression I made was that I was stubborn, but I hung in there long enough and liked it well enough to get her thinking there was something there. Kelli saw that I was strong, that I wanted to keep trying things again and again until I got them right, that I liked challenges, that I could jump high—things that were advantageous in the sport.

In the beginning I went to Kelli's gym just once a week and then I guess I started going two or three times a week. When I was about 10 years old, I moved in with her. The more serious I got, the more work I had to do, and when I had to start going to practices at 6 in the morning it got to be too much for my parents. It wasn't so convenient anymore.

My dad was working from 3 in the morning until almost 8 at night, and my mom was busy taking care of my older sister and my younger brother and running them around to everything they had to do. So we all made the decision that I would move in with Kelli during the week and it would be a lot easier. I would still go home on the weekends, and I'd go back and forth to school from Kelli's house instead of mine, that's all. That lasted for a couple years and then I moved back home for a while. But then I moved back in with Kelli and her husband and two little boys when I was in high school, because she knew the intensity would have to pick up before my second Olympic games.

In gymnastics it's common to work with one coach until you reach a certain level. You get good with your first coach, who may be unknown, and then you look to someone like Bela Karolyi and—well, pretty much Bela Karolyi. A lot of girls would go to him to get that extra oomph of motivation, that extra polish, but I didn't think that was necessary for me. I thought I could get everything I needed from Kelli and I really enjoyed working with her. I didn't think, "Oh well, she's never coached a girl to the Olympics before." We had this neat kind of mother-daughter thing going, and I knew I could be the best I could be at her facility.

The routine, for the most part, was practice from 6 to 8 each morning, school from 8:30 until about 2:30, and then back to practice from 3 in the afternoon until 8 or so at night. After that I had dinner, homework, and curfew at 11. That's the grueling life of a gymnast, but you don't find it grueling when you're in the midst of it. I didn't. I was doing something I loved. I wasn't interested in dating. I didn't have a social life. I didn't hang out. You see these kids who have the fire in their eyes, or the kids who want to be the best they can be, and they tend to have no problem sacrificing those things. And look what I got back. I was able to travel the world and compete in three Olympics. If I hadn't been a gymnast, I wouldn't have been able to see the things I've seen or do the things I've done.

" she must really think a lot of me. I don't know what's wrong with her. "

With Kelli, I would set a goal and then she would set it higher. I would look at her like she was crazy—like, "Oh, my God, she must really think a lot of me. I don't know what's wrong with her." And then all of a sudden you start believing it, because she makes sure you put the work and the attitude and the energy into it. Perfect example: I was 23 and sitting in my economics class at the University of Maryland. I was really bored and I thought that I might have a few more flips in me. I'd been away from the sport for a year and a half. I had basically hung up my leotard at the ripe old age of 21 and I was pretty much done with my gymnastics career. It's not uncommon for a gymnast to finish up after high school, at 17 or so. I'd hung on for a little bit longer than most, but I hadn't been training. It's not that I was out of shape or anything, but I'd been eating a good deal and in gymnastics you have to be very particular about certain things.

Anyway I got it in my head that this was something I wanted to try. I'd been to Barcelona in '92 and to Atlanta in '96, and I wanted to see if I could get to Sydney in 2000. Right there in economics class that became my goal. So I got out of class and jumped in the car and called Kelli on my cell phone. I said, "Hey, Kelli, I just had this really odd thought." I really just wanted to get her thought on it. All she said was, "Well, then I expect to see your butt in my gym tomorrow morning."

Kelli doesn't shoot down your goals. She hears them and helps you make them a reality. If I could have a little pocket Kelli with me 24/7, it probably would be a big help. To this day I still hear her voice. I do a good deal of motivational speaking and I try to inspire kids to achieve their dreams. When I give my talks, everything I say comes from things Kelli tried to instill in me. I'm always listening for her voice. It's been a real constant for me, even away from gymnastics. When I had an opportunity to appear on Broadway in *Grease*, Kelli was one of the first people I called. It always had been a dream of mine to sing and dance on Broadway, but I worried that people would laugh at me. Obviously, I was never trained and I had no idea what people would think, so I went to Kelli and we talked about it and she said, "Oh, don't give up on that." So I went for it and got the part.

I still see Kelli as a mentor. If I need that extra little boost or a kick in the butt, I can go to Kelli and she'll give it to me. I don't see her as regularly as I used to, but I still hear her voice in my head. She's still telling me what to do.

Dominique Dawes

setting goals

SOCRATES DE LA CRUZ
CRIMINAL DEFENSE ATTORNEY,
FORMER YOUTH OF THE YEAR,
BOYS & GIRLS CLUBS OF AMERICA

God has been so good to me. He's placed so many influential people in my life, and I want to mention three who are dear to my heart: my grandmother, who's since passed; my mom, a single mother who raised me; and a very dear friend who was my basketball coach from first grade through eighth grade and who's been my mentor and friend ever since. I'll start with him.

His name is Steve Kelly and he's the closest thing I know to an angel. I met him when I was 7 years old. My mother and grandmother took me down to the Boys Club in Lawrence, Massachusetts. We were living in the housing projects right around the club, and to this day if you walk around those projects and mention Steve's name, everyone knows who you're talking about. He's helped a lot of people.

When I first met Steve, I was a product of the housing projects, a product of a single-parent home looking for guidance and attention. I was in and out of trouble. One day Steve took me aside and said, "Do you know what the word 'goal' means?" I knew what a goal was in hockey or soccer and I knew what a field goal was in basketball, but when he started talking about setting goals and trying to achieve goals, it was like he was speaking Chinese. He said this to me on the basketball court one day. I had missed school, and because I had missed school I couldn't practice. So he sat me down and this is what he said to me. It was my introduction to the way I live my life now, to setting goals and trying to achieve them.

He said, "Listen, Soc, if you're a leader, you can't keep running around in circles."

He told me I could be a positive influence in other people's lives, that I had potential, but that I wasn't steering myself in the right direction. He said that it was because I didn't know how to set goals. And he was right. I was only about 11 years old then, and of course I hadn't set any goals.

" do you know what the word 'goal' means? "

He asked me if I thought about high school or college. He asked me if I thought I could play basketball at the college level. I'd never really thought about that, but it sounded like something I wanted to try. So he said, "OK, if you think you can do that, that means you've set a goal. You've set out something in the future that you one day hope to achieve. And if you do that, then every day you have to wake up and do something, little by little, that will help you get to that point."

It was just one conversation, one afternoon on the basketball court, but it opened a door in my life. I didn't have a dad around, my mom only spoke Spanish, and until then I'd only had other street kids as models. We were all running around, going nowhere. But I realized, "Wow, this guy is right," and I instantly started setting other small goals, like getting to school early and doing my homework. From then on, I had structure and focus.

I always kept goal-setting in mind, playing high school basketball, and I won a scholarship to a boarding school, Kimball Union Academy in New Hampshire, and I played basketball there. Then I won a basketball scholarship to Holy Cross, in Worcester, Massachusetts, and I owed it all to Steve.

I broke my leg during my sophomore year, but again Steve's advice came into play. I realized I wasn't going to be a professional basketball player and that I had to decide what I wanted to do. I set the goal of becoming an attorney. I did everything I could to get good grades and to get into a good law school, and that's what I did. It all started because Steve Kelly taught me how to set goals and structure myself and guide myself through life.

Have I thanked him? Every day. I still call him all the time, whenever I need advice, and he's always there for me. And the thing is, he does the same thing for thousands of other kids—thousands. He's unbelievable.

My mother walks on water. She raised me and my older brother, who played football at Boston College. She raised both of us alone from the time I was 6 and my brother was about 7. My dad skipped out, but my mom held two jobs, sometimes three—cleaning people's houses, doing factory work, doing physical, hard-core jobs. She's from the Dominican Republic and she didn't speak English. Now she speaks it some and understands it totally.

She worked hard. She struggled. I used to hear her in her room, when my brother and I were in our room supposedly sleeping. I'd hear her crying. I'd see her get emotionally and physically beaten up, but she kept going. She never gave up. She never complained. And she never took it out on us kids. That's something I have from my mom inside me. No matter what I go through, I pick myself up and keep going.

I remember the day we had to move out of our house. My dad had left and we'd gone into some serious hardship and couldn't make the rent. The owner of the house came and asked us to leave. We had no place to go, so the sheriff's office came and took our stuff out of the house. My mom didn't know where to go or what to do, so we went to my grandmother's apartment in the housing projects. There were about six of us staying there, and when we were settled my mother took me and my brother aside and said, "Things happen. Sometimes you can't make ends meet, but as long as you wake up the following day and keep going, things will get better."

She never complained. Ever. And I can't imagine anyone ever feeling any lower than she did that day. And do you know what? She was right. Things did get better, and she managed to see us to two college graduations and one law school graduation, so it wasn't so bad.

My grandmother is another star. Everyone she knew who wanted to come to this country from the Dominican Republic, she helped them get here—friend, cousin, third cousin, it didn't matter. She took anyone and everyone in and helped everyone out. When we were living in her apartment, one of my cousins also was living there and she set fire to her bed because she was upset about something. The entire apartment went up in flames.

The night that fire happened, my grandmother had just bought me and my brother some brand-new sneakers: Pro Keds. At the time there couldn't be anything better. And then the fire happened. Everything burned up, but in our minds the most important things we'd lost were those sneakers. The fire department showed up and put out the fire and shoveled our stuff through the windows. We stood outside and watched our stuff coming out the third-floor windows, falling to the ground. We just stood there looking.

I caught my grandmother looking too, but she didn't seem worried or upset. She was very much in control of the situation and her emotions. I remember going up to her and crying about my sneakers. I remember being mad at our cousin. But my grandmother just calmly sat everyone down and told us to gather everything that was salvageable and box it up and give it to our new cousins who were due to arrive from the Dominican Republic the next week. I think about that all the time, because she never came out and said this was the lesson she wanted us to take away from this experience. Even when she was in a time of need, she was thinking about other people.

We moved back in two weeks later. The place wasn't furnished for a while because she didn't want to take furniture from other people. Folks wanted to help her, but she wanted to fix it back up herself. That's how she was. She'd been a nurse in the Dominican Republic and she was a nurse here, and she was determined to make ends meet.

That's where my mom got it from, I think, because as soon as she could she moved us out of my grandmother's apartment into a place of our own in the same projects. I look back now, all these years later, and think of the role these three people played in my life. I have my own criminal defense practice. A lot of my clients are in seriously bad shape, and I listen to their stories and I think, "There but for the grace of God and Steve Kelly and my mother and grandmother go I."

second banana
JAMIE FARR
ACTOR

I used to read *Theatre Arts Magazine* when I was a kid, and I saw an ad for the Pasadena Playhouse that somehow left me thinking I'd like to study acting. My parents couldn't afford to send me to acting school in California. My dad had a little corner grocery store and we lived in all these duplexes—always on the second floor. When my mother hung clothes out to dry, the soot from the factories would get them dirtier than they had been before she washed them.

This was back during World War II, and everywhere you looked they were selling war stamps. It cost 10 cents for a stamp. If you filled up a book it was worth $18.75 and in 10 years you'd get $25. Every Tuesday I had to buy a stamp, because I didn't want to be unpatriotic, and when I graduated high school I cashed in those stamps and that's how I got the money to go to the Pasadena Playhouse.

I was only able to go there for one year, but by that time I had screen-tested for an MGM movie called *Blackboard Jungle*. As soon as I finished it, I did a television pilot for CBS that didn't sell for some reason. Sherwood Schwartz, Red Skelton's head writer at CBS, saw the pilot and decided to pluck two characters from the script for Red's show. There was Cookie the Sailor, who would be played by Red, and there was Schnorkle, who had such a nose on him he could smell anything. That was my character, and the next thing I knew I was doing Red's show, live, on coast-to-coast television.

What a thrill! I was 19 or 20 years old and I'd grown up listening to Red Skelton's radio show on a crystal set under the covers, because it came on so late on a school night. He was such a big hero to me, and I was cast as his sidekick. Whatever I could have hoped to learn at the Pasadena Playhouse was nothing next to the chance to work with Red Skelton. He had all these great characters: Clem Kadiddlehopper, Sheriff Deadeye, Willie Lump Lump, Cauliflower McPugg, Freddie the Freeloader. And for whatever reason, these two characters went over very well and we kind of clicked.

" I'd grown up listening to Red Skelton … and I was cast as his sidekick. "

Red was the only one that had cue cards and he would always ad-lib. The rest of us had to know where we were so that we could bring him back into the script—this was live television. I was just a kid, but I could bring him back, so the producers liked me and the network liked me. Oh, it was seat-of-the-pants stuff, but it really was a wonderful education and a great opportunity. I got to work with Peter Lorre, Buster Crabbe, Boris Karloff, George Raft, Jayne Mansfield, Vincent Price. It was unbelievable. I was like a kid in a candy store, but the real treat of course was working with Red.

Red Skelton was the most influential person in my life, even when I got drafted into the Army and served in Korea and Japan. When Red decided he wanted to entertain the troops, he requested me from the State Department. I was a mere private with Armed Forces Radio, but I got VIP status and flew in a United Nations airplane and entertained with Red all the way up to the 38th Parallel. "When you get out," he told me, "you come back and see me."

When I was dischargedfrom the Army, I went back to California to restart my career. But my father died and we had no money, so I was about ready to give up the business and go back to Toledo to support my mom. I'd given this acting thing a shot, but I had a responsibility back home. When I stopped in at CBS to say goodbye to Red, he refused to let me go. He put me under contract and pressed some money in my hand to send home to my mother that afternoon.

I reported to his house the next morning, and we were together for the next year or so, traveling all over to all the nightclubs, doing his television show, all his personal appearances, everything. I was his second banana and almost like a road manager as well. But he helped me a whole lot more than I could have ever helped him.

Every day with him was an education. He taught me how to deal with people, how to be respectful of people, how to be respectful of the business. Red was someone who really loved and respected show business. A lot of young performers today don't have that respect; they take it for granted. But it was sacred to Red, and he never, ever took it for granted.

That was such an important lesson. He was just a kind, wonderful man, a holdover from another era, and I was lucky to be able to learn from him. And he in turn learned from people like Ed Wynn and a wonderful writer named Gene Fowler. Fowler wrote *Goodnight, Sweet Prince* and *Schnozzola*, and he was like a father to Red, so I was in their company too. It was Ed Wynn who took me aside one day and offered three words of advice that turned out to be very valuable. He said to me, "If you're gonna stay in this business, save your money."

It's one of the great ironies of my life, to grow up listening to Red on the radio under the covers and to have him become like a second father to me.

Jamie Farr

finding fish
ANTWONE FISHER
SCREENWRITER

The people who helped me the most were only around for a moment or two. You have to understand, I had it hard. I was born to an unwed mother who was in prison at the time. I was raised in institutions, but I eventually went to live with a foster family and that too was hard.

The real inspiration, I think, came from where I was. I grew up in the Glenville area of Cleveland, and it was an interesting neighborhood. So many successful people came from that neighborhood: Bob Hope, Jesse Owens, John Glenn. The two guys who created "Superman" were in art class in Glenville High School when they came up with the idea. That's the type of place it was: home to people who became famous and made a difference and did something positive with their lives.

And they never forgot where they came from. Every summer Bob Hope would come through the neighborhood. All these people, they'd keep ties to the community. There was a singing group, The Dramatics, and their thing was to bring a big barrel of sandals and leave it out on the street. All the kids would come out and get brand-new sandals. One time I had mismatched sandals and I wore them all summer.

There's a big mall in the center of town, at 105th and St. Claire, where the Glenville Development Corporation set up our own community's little Hall of Fame filled with all these names, all these plaques, all these great people from that part of Cleveland who'd gone on to accomplish great things. It's a street I practically grew up walking on, and I used to think, "If they can make it big, so can I."

A lot of times when I was a little kid, I'd be afraid of something and have to run back home and I'd go by that Hall of Fame. It was comforting and reassuring to walk past all those great names. The people on that wall were like gods. They kept me safe. It never once occurred to me that one day my community would think about me in the same way. I just wanted to make something of myself.

" if they can make it big, so can I. "

A lot of stuff happened to me back there in Cleveland, some tragic. But I never associated those things with the city. Cleveland was a proud place, a righteous place, a special place. And one of the special things about it was this Hall of Fame. All these names symbolized all these great opportunities. When I finally made my way out to Los Angeles and started writing screenplays and working as a security guard at the studios, I kept thinking about all those people who had made it. I kept thinking, "If they can make it big, so can I." That was its own kind of inspiration.

I met Denzel Washington on the lot at Sony Pictures, and he was always pleasant. It never occurred to me that we would one day work together, but he found out about my story. I'd written it as a screenplay and it was bouncing around at the studio. It was called *Finding Fish*. It was about how I was abandoned, then a foster kid, then living on the streets, and finally enlisting in the Navy and finding myself. Denzel got hold of it and wanted to direct it. He ended up changing the title to *Antwone Fisher*, but I was thinking that didn't even sound like a movie.

I think it was the honesty of my story, really, that attracted Denzel to it. I made myself vulnerable and he didn't judge me. He made me feel so comfortable. Throughout the whole process—from rewriting to going off and selling the movie, traveling around the country—he was always incredibly supportive. If I live for a thousand years, I'll never have the chance to thank him enough.

After we made the movie, people seemed to respond to it. One day I got a letter from the Glenville Development Corporation. They wanted to put my name up on that wall. I was blown away when I saw that letter. I got myself out to Cleveland as soon as I could to check out the Hall of Fame and to see my name on that wall. The first time I went I was by myself and I couldn't find my name. I actually left without finding it, because there are a lot of names, and I just couldn't see it. I told my friend about it and he said, "Oh yeah, it's there."

So I went back and there it was, right in front of me: "Antwone Fisher." I was pretty emotional seeing my name up there on the wall with people like Jesse Owens who did so much to inspire so many people. And a part of me was thinking they made a mistake. You know, as soon as they figure out my name's up there, they'll take it down.

But then I thought, "If they can make it big, so can I."

the fundamental things
DANNY GLOVER
ACTOR

My third-grade teacher was Miss Lumber from Beaumont, Texas. She was a very authoritarian, strict teacher. If you used an improper word, she'd have you wash your mouth out with soap. At the same time she rewarded those who were good students. One of her rewards was being able to serve graham crackers during the milk and graham cracker break. She always spoke about raising good citizens. That was her phrase. She'd say, "Good students are good citizens." And it meant something to us. It truly did.

Miss Lumber had a big impact on my life because she realized that I had problems reading. No one knew how to diagnose dyslexia in those days, but Miss Lumber recognized that I was struggling. At the same time, she recognized that I had this enormous facility for numbers. I loved math and I loved numbers. Miss Lumber encouraged me in that way and certainly it played a major role in my life. Had I not felt in some way that I had ownership of numbers as a child, I don't know what would have happened to me, because it was a real struggle for me to read. A real struggle.

Of course my real role models were my mother and father. I loved my parents. From the first moment I knew I felt something special for them to the day they left here, I didn't miss a beat. They instructed me simply by being decent, honest, good, sweet, funny people.

We lived in what we called the projects, in the southeastern end of San Francisco. My dad worked in the post office. My mom did too, handling mail. She worked the day shift, he worked the night shift, and they would pass each other on the way. They were the main people in my life, but that's a given, you know. If you come from a solid family, that's a given.

But someone like Miss Lumber—you don't expect to come across someone like that. You don't really know that reading is a problem until about the second or third grade, and Miss Lumber took that special interest. She was my teacher in second grade and in third grade, and it was an important relationship. In many ways it was the first relationship I had with another adult in that short period of time when you leave the protection of your parents, the nurturing of your parents, and you're out there in the world on your own. Miss Lumber could see I was struggling. She realized I had this facility for math, and she encouraged me in that.

So things could have gone another way for me, because back in those days dyslexia didn't have a name. I never had a diagnosis. And as I went on in school, I'd come across students who I later realized were dyslexic and they were thought to be not as smart as the other kids or slow learners. Sometimes they'd even say retarded—that was the word they used.

When you don't understand something, you label it and condemn it, so it was not an easy time. Unfortunately I don't think Miss Lumber had the technical tools to help me compensate, but she understood. Even though I didn't do well in reading, she upheld what I did do well, and that was the most important and instructive thing. She encouraged me in math and didn't dwell on what I couldn't do well.

Later on, as a college student, I began to tutor kids, and one of the things I learned was that children have a variety of ways of learning. The best thing you can do as a teacher is provide a space where they feel good about themselves, comfortable about themselves, and that's what Miss Lumber did for me.

I never did have a chance to thank her. She retired and moved back to Beaumont, Texas. I still have some friends who were in that class and some of them stayed in touch with her, and I learned not too long ago that she had passed away. But I also learned that she was among the first group of teachers to visit China after Nixon had opened up relations there. That was something. You know, you think about her life, coming from a small town like that, probably going to a small southern college, getting accredited to teach in California and heading to San Francisco to teach elementary school. That says a lot.

> " when you don't understand something,
> you label it and condemn it,
> but Miss Lumber understood. "

I still struggle with my reading. The scripts, I don't have problems with that. It's a different part of the brain, I guess. But once you get to a certain age, you are what you are, you got what you got. Sometimes when I do one of those award shows and they have a teleprompter, I've had some difficulty. I invert the letters or the words or something like that, and I laugh to myself and think, "It's just the dyslexia kicking in." And then I remember Miss Lumber, and her great kindness and compassion, and I work to get it right.

a kick in the stomach
WHOOPI GOLDBERG
ACTRESS AND COMEDIAN

In grammar school there was a boy in my class named Robert. He wasn't particularly popular and I wasn't particularly popular either, and we were friends. We were 8 or 9 years old and we were not in the crew. We were our own little world.

One day we went on an outing with the rest of our school. On that day somehow I was running with the popular folks. You know how that is. Every now and then, there are satellite groups hovering around the popular folks, and on that day I was one of the satellites. I was in the crew. Robert was not. And I didn't treat Robert very well. At all. It wasn't overt. We weren't hitting him or making fun of him. He just didn't exist. It's like I left him behind.

I remember getting home and my mother was kind of cool to me. I asked her about it because she seemed kind of distant. I said, "What's wrong?"

"Nothing," she said. "How was the day? Tell me about the trip."

"Oh, the trip was great," I said. "We had a great time."

She said, "Do you think *everybody* had a great time?" in a leading kind of way, like she knew something. She always knew when something was up.

I kind of shrugged and said, "Oh yeah, it was just so great."

"What about Robert?" she said. "Did he have a great time?"

I kind of shrugged again, I guess because I realized where she was going with all this and because I had left my friend behind.

And she said, "Well, you were one of the popular people today, huh? Everyone was your friend?"

"Yes," I said.

"But they're not like that every day, are they?" she said.

"No," I said.

"And do you remember how you feel when they're not like that?"

I nodded.

"Like you made Robert feel today?"

It was like being kicked in the stomach. It never occurred to me that I had done to my friend what these folks had always done to me. That on this day at least I was part of that group of kids who could on occasion make me cry, just by the way they treated me. It really messed me up. I went to school the next day and talked to Robert. I made sure he knew that I knew I'd messed up. I apologized, but it was a kid apology.

A kid apology is different from an adult apology. A kid apology is, "Yo, let's go over here and get some pretzels." An adult apology would be, "Oh, I realize the ramifications of our relationship have changed …" and blah, blah, blah. But he was cool about it and that was the end of it. I guess it might have taken him a while to trust me, but for the most part that was the end of it.

> " it never occurred to me that I had done to my friend what these folks had always done to me. "

Over the years it's stayed with me, what I put Robert through. From that day forward I've been really, really careful about all my friendships and really, really conscious of other people's feelings. If I mess up I try to cop to it. I'm a human being, so I make lots of mistakes. But if I've unknowingly been neglectful or cruel or hurtful to someone, I try to rectify it as soon as I'm aware of it.

I appeared on *The View* not very long ago, and we were talking about fame and how kids these days seem to want to be famous. I began to talk about the fact that you don't have to have talent anymore to become famous. People can eat a bug on some reality show and become famous. I didn't realize that the young lady on the show had come from one of those reality shows. That was her claim to fame. And it wrecked me once I realized how I must have made her feel. So I apologized and I apologized, and the next day I sent over some chocolate, because that's what you do when you mess up and call someone out in front of millions of people: You send over some chocolate. We're human, right? We say things and we don't really realize what we're saying, but we've all got to do a better job. We've got to carry it, you know. That's what I learned from my mom.

the giant within
TONY GONZALEZ
PROFESSIONAL FOOTBALL PLAYER

I wouldn't even have played sports if it weren't for my older brother, Chris. He was almost two years older than me and he loved football way more than I did. It's weird how I became the professional football player, because he used to have to drag me out to play.

We grew up in Huntington Beach, in Southern California. It was just the two of us, but then we picked up some siblings along the way. We basically adopted these two other guys. I call them my brothers today. One of them had a mother who died when he was real young, so he came to live with us. The other one was kicked out of his house in high school and he came to live with us as well. But until we were older, it was just the two of us, and Chris was big into football.

I pretty much played everything, but even when we were kids he was the one who kept pushing me. And he's still pushing me. He's the one telling me like it is. If my head's getting too big or if I'm not playing well, he'll tell me the truth. He watches all my games. He'll get film and break it down with me. I always tell him he should go into coaching. He really knows what he's talking about, and I trust his opinion more than anybody's. He's not trying to blow smoke.

There's another buddy from that same group—Donnie—who might as well be a brother too. He calls my mom "Mom" and my dad "Dad." After my second year in the league, he reached out to me. I was having the worst year of my career. I'd dropped about 17 balls that season and I was just getting killed in the Kansas City papers. The Chiefs fans were starting to get on me too. I'd been a first-round draft pick the year before and I'd had a pretty decent rookie year, so my second year in the league there were all these expectations. People were talking about me being a Pro Bowl pick before we even played our first game, so I really wasn't living up to expectations.

Donnie, from out of nowhere, sent me a letter. It was all my attitude, he said, and he knew me well enough to say it. It wasn't my talent that was holding me back, it was me. He sent me a book of quotes by Vince Lombardi and in the accompanying letter he said, "Hey, Tony. I've noticed some things in your game." And he went right into it.

You know, we weren't seeing each other on any kind of day-to-day basis at that point, and I'm sure there were a lot of people wanting to tell me what I was doing wrong, but I guess you tune out the people you're closest to after a while. But I read the letter and I really took it to heart. Then I read the book, and there was one quote that popped out about what it takes to be a champion: the dedication, the mental part of the game, which of course is just as important as any physical talent. And it set me on the path that I'm still on today.

> " the blueprint for success, I've learned,
> comes down to character, and for me
> character is everything coming together. "

Thanks to that one book, I read books all the time. I'm reading two or three at a time now—a lot of self-improvement and empowerment books mostly. I think all this reading really turned my career around and put me in a direction I'm glad I'm going.

I never was much of a reader and I certainly never read these types of books before, but if you've had some success in the world of sports and you've written a book about that success, I'll want to hear what you have to say. Michael Jordan. Pat Riley. Lou Holtz. Phil Jackson. And it's not just sports. Deepak Chopra. Dr. Wayne Dyer. Anthony Robbins. All these books help me try to figure out what works best for me.

My brother Chris is not a person who read all that much. He was like me. But now I've got him reading, and there's been a change in his life too. A change for the good.

When we were kids, he was the one dragging me out onto the football field, and now I'm the one dragging him to the bookstore. He used to say to me, "Why do you keep reading the same books over and over?" And he's right, I guess. Self-improvement is self-improvement. But then I tell him it's like going to church. "Why do you go to church every week and read the same Bible?" I say. It's because we want it to become a part of us.

So that's what I do. If I believe in what someone has to say, I'll follow their little tips and suggestions. I do daily affirmations. I keep lists, just to remind myself where I want to go in life. I do a lot of writing. I do a lot of stuff people might think is corny, but I try to stick to it. It's a good thing I do, because when I talk to kids and I tell them about reading and trying to improve themselves, trying to get better, it comes from a very real place. It's a part of who I am.

Chris used to kind of force football on me, but I've tried not to force all this self-improvement and motivational stuff on him. I'm sure I used to be annoying to him. You know, like when you first learn something and you're so excited you want to share it with everybody, but then you realize people just aren't on the same page. They're not ready to commit to that thing the way you've committed to it. You can't change people. The only thing you can do is inspire people to make a better decision. So I don't overtalk Chris anymore. I don't oversell him on this stuff. I tell him what I think he needs to hear and the rest is up to him, the same way he tells me what he thinks I need to do about my game, then leaves it up to me to do something about it.

You know, it's funny. When I was a kid the talent was there, but I just never had the attitude for it. No one was telling me what it took. I was pretty good on the playground, but once you start playing organized ball, you can't just go out there and play. A lot of people think they're working hard because they go to practice and bust their butts, but to me that's what you're supposed to do, especially at the professional level. That's what we get paid for. What are you doing extra? That's what counts. That's when you're working hard—when you're going above and over what's expected of you.

Going above and over, that's what made me the player I am today. Because the truth is, when I first started playing Pop Warner football I was the worst kid on the team. Literally. I was terrible. Back then, it cost a certain amount of money to sign up for a team, and to pay for your uniform and the league fees. In exchange for that money, you were guaranteed to get six plays a game. That was the deal.

And yet many times I didn't get my six plays a game. Some games I didn't get to play at all, because I didn't have anybody advocating for me. Other kids, their dads or moms were watching them play, but I never had that, so these coaches were happy not to play me. I didn't deserve to play. I wasn't aggressive. I was just the worst.

I quit during the middle of my first year, but Chris pushed me back to try it again for a second season, and this time around I stuck it out. At the awards ceremony at the end of the year, this one coach called me out and said, "He might have been a better athlete if he wasn't running on eggshells every time he touched the ball." I'll never forget that. He said that in front of all these people and it stuck with me. So I really come from a humble beginning as far as football and I were concerned.

But what finally turned things around for me was a change in attitude. I got bullied as a kid. My eighth grade year, there were two guys from high school who used to come down and kick my butt every day. I used to run, every single day, just to avoid them. My parents knew about it. My brother knew about it. He said, "Why don't you just fight these guys and get it over with?" He tried to stick up for me, but he didn't go to the same high school as these other kids and he wasn't really able to help me out.

Meanwhile I was the biggest dork in the school, because everybody knew as soon as the bell rang I'd be out the door, running home to sit in front of the television. I missed all the school dances. I didn't hang out in the park after school. I was just so scared of these two guys that I hid out at home.

That was how I dealt with the problem—by running away from it. It all came to a head at graduation that year. I went to graduation, my whole family was there, but at the end of the ceremony I didn't throw my hat in the air like everyone else. I saw one of these kids somewhere in the crowd, and I ducked out and hid behind a wall. For a long time, no one in my family could find me. It was like a scene out of a movie, and they were all walking around looking for me. They were all like, "Hey, where's Tony?" They all found me at pretty much the same time, cowering behind this wall.

It was pretty humiliating. I can still see the looks on their faces. My brother especially, he shot me this look like I was just a huge disappointment. And my mother? She didn't say anything. She just flashed me this stern, cold look, and I could tell she was really disappointed in me, and she was the most loving person you could imagine.

It was a low moment, but I made a promise to myself that I would never have to see those looks on their faces again. I would never disappoint them again. If I was going to get my butt kicked, I would get my butt kicked. So be it. But I wasn't going to run from a confrontation or a challenge any more. And that changed my attitude—not just in sports but in everything.

The blueprint for success, I've learned, comes down to character, and for me character is everything coming together. It's a bunch of things really. It's working hard. It's never being complacent. There are guys I know who work really hard on the football field, but they might be a selfish person and that's what's holding them back from being great. That's what I'm interested in: character and performance. I want to be great at what I do, the best that I can be.

When I talk to kids, I tell them it's how they practice that makes all the difference in how they play. I tell them they shouldn't just practice to play, they should practice to dominate. That's the mindset you need to be great. That's the attitude. That's what I've picked up in all these books.

escape **the norm**
OMAR GOODING
ACTOR

I've always liked escaping reality. We grew up through some hard times: sleeping in cars, living in hotels. It was rough and I grabbed onto acting because of the adventure, the escape.

I was always an adventurous kid. I liked escaping the norm. OK, we don't have any money. Boom! In my world I could be a soldier or a fireman. That's why I like movies. I can escape reality. I don't like reality shows. I loved movies like *The Wizard of Oz, Star Wars, Godzilla*—fantasy, science fiction-type films.

My brother Cuba played a huge part in my life. He's always been there if I need some advice or to help me figure out a direction for a particular role. But I was a kid in elementary school doing plays and talent shows long before he got his first big break, so I was headed this way on my own. He was out there taking classes and studying. He knew what he wanted to do and how he wanted to go about it.

For me, it just kind of happened. It's just who I was, and it was going to happen whether or not the road was paved for me. I never took any formal drama classes or lessons other than play production and drama at North Hollywood High School. That's where I met the first person who really broke it down for me: Diana Horne. When we were doing Shakespeare's *A Midsummer Night's Dream,* Ms. Horne was a big, big help, working with me to understand the material. I played Bottom. He turns into a donkey, then he comes back out of that—there was a lot going on. It was a comedic role and it was hard trying to do comedy and speak Shakespeare, trying to get it across to people who didn't understand it. The language is tough for a lot of people to understand. It's amazing how Ms. Horne got us all to sit still and learn and understand the material and break it down so we could say it.

She was my brother's teacher too. He graduated from the same high school nine years before me. His break was *Boyz N The Hood*. John Singleton, in 1989. I was only 11. I started in the business when I was about 10 with small-scale, independent films, commercials, and stuff. My first professional role was in an industrial film—*McGruff the Crime Dog*. It was shot at a house, and there were a bunch of kids running around. It was really comfortable and relaxed and at one point I caught myself thinking, "Hey, yo, I can do this. This is all right." I thought maybe I got something. You know, it wasn't really acting—just me being me, running around with a bunch of other kids saying "Don't do drugs" and stuff like that, but it was cool.

When I was 13, I landed my first regular series on Nickelodeon. Something called *Wild and Crazy Kids*. And from there I went and did *Smart Guy*. Eight straight years of sitcoms.

" this guy is really good at seeing talent inside a person and bringing it out. "

That's where John Singleton came back in. He's the other pivotal person in my career, just like he was a pivotal person in my brother's career. He gave me a call one day—I'd just finished this three-year run on *Smart Guy*—and he said he had a script for me, a movie called *Baby Boy*. Once I read it, it was just mind-boggling to me. I'm like, "How did he see me in *that* role? Playing a tough guy, a gangster, just out of prison?" All he'd seen me in was a sitcom, doing cheesy stuff, but this guy is really good at seeing talent inside a person and bringing it out.

He said, "I know you can do this." He told me he'd seen me in this little bit part and remembered I'd made this one expression. That's what he was basing it on. He said, "I could look in your face and see the depth in your eyes."

I trusted him. He trusted me. I hit the gym, and three months later and 20 pounds lighter I was doing one of the breakout roles of my career, playing Sweetpea in *Baby Boy*. After that my career just kind of took off. I was taken seriously for dramatic roles as well as comedy roles, and I really have to dig up John Singleton for seeing something in me. If it weren't for him, I don't know what I'd be doing.

baby, run on
GLENDA HATCHETT
RETIRED JUVENILE COURT JUDGE, SYNDICATED TELEVISION PERSONALITY

I'm a "daddy's girl."

Even though my father has passed on, I don't believe it's humanly possible for a daughter to love her father any more than I loved my dad. He was constantly telling me I could do anything in the world, and that made all the difference to me when I was growing up. Because of my father, being born a little colored girl in the Deep South was not a curse but a blessing. Because of my father, I knew that I had to believe in myself to be able to move forward. Academically, professionally, personally—my dad made me believe that there was nothing in the world I couldn't do.

I'm enormously blessed to have had a Paul Hatchett who said, "I believe in you." *I believe in you*. And he did.

Here's an example: The afternoon I had to post my acceptance letter to college, people were calling from this college and that college and I just couldn't decide. My father turned to me and said, "Glenda, we just have to get in the car." We went for a drive in our bronze-colored Delta 88. He said, "When you're ready, you tell me and we'll go to the post office." We drove and drove. We didn't talk much, but there was a lot to consider. I was having trouble deciding between Radcliffe and Mount Holyoke. I had a full scholarship to Emory, but I didn't really want to stay at home. I also was accepted at Spelman, Duke, Agnes Scott, and Vanderbilt, but it came down to Radcliffe and Mount Holyoke. All were wonderful options. And all along my father kept telling me, "You just get in and we'll get you out. Your mother and I will figure out where to get the money, and we'll make it work." It was a huge financial sacrifice for my parents, but I took them at their word that the money shouldn't be part of the equation, so we drove around for a while until finally I said, "OK, I'm ready."

We headed for the old post office by the Federal Building downtown, and I half-expected my father to pull over so we could talk about my decision one final time. But he never did. He just pulled up to the mailbox and I reached out and put the envelope in, and even then he didn't say anything. I waited for a while as we pulled away until I finally said, "Aren't you going to ask me which school I chose?"

And he said, "When you're ready to tell me, I'm sure you will."

It sounds simple, but it was such a vote of confidence. He didn't stop me or second-guess me or question me. He just let me send it off without saying a word. As a parent, I now realize how difficult it must have been to let me make a decision like that entirely on my own. As a parent, *I* couldn't do that. Put me in a car with one of my children and I'd make us go around the corner and park for a minute and have a little sidebar and say, "Let's talk about this one more time before it's too late." But not my dad. He just pulled up to the mailbox and let me roll down my window and slip the envelope inside. That's just one example, but he consistently did things and said things that told me, "I believe in you."

It wasn't *just* my father. My mother also has been huge in my life, and so has my community. Community is essential. I stand on the shoulders of generations of men and women who made many sacrifices for me that have allowed me to succeed. Most of those people I will never know. I credit all the people who came before me in our segregated society, folks who didn't have the opportunities I have had but who nevertheless prayed that there would be a generation that would realize its dreams and accomplish great things. I'm a product of that. I'm always mindful of it and grateful to have had all these people cheering me on.

> " if you really believe in yourself, the rest is just hard work. "

For example, the Sunday before I left for school, one of the church elders, Odessa Duncan, pulled me aside. Mother Duncan knew me from the day I was born. My parents joined the church as a young couple. I was christened in that church. She knew I was going off to school and she knew what it meant to me and my family, and it meant something to her as well. So she came up and gave me a handkerchief. It was one of those white lace handkerchiefs with little flowers embroidered along the sides, and I'm sure she'd had it forever. Before she left for church that morning she very patiently tied four silver half-dollars into it, one in each corner. When she saw me she pressed the handkerchief into my hand and closed my hand around it and said, "Baby, run on! You run on."

I now understand that "Baby, run on!" meant that was the way I was to repay her—by moving forward, by making strides. Of course, there's no way I could ever repay her for her confidence in me—that was a gift beyond measure. But the way I repay it is to pay it forward, with my commitment to my community and in my calling to try to help young people.

This is the community piece I'm talking about, and it's all tied together. Mother Duncan probably didn't get very far in school. Her gift to me wasn't those four coins so much as it was a mandate, from her generation to mine, to go forward and to take advantage of opportunities available to me that hadn't been available to them. I was heading off to college for all of them, that whole community, that whole generation. I don't think I realized it at the time, but it was upon their shoulders that my father also stood before I stood on his. I look back now and worry that today's generation of young people doesn't connect the dots in quite the same way.

The world has changed. I see so many young people who are drifting, and if I can have one wish for them it would be that my dad could put his hands on them, that he could encourage them to believe in themselves the way he taught me to believe in myself. I also wish that they could feel a part of a community and know that people like Mother Odessa Duncan are cheering for them, because that's where hope comes from. That was the seed of hope for me—knowing that if you really believe in yourself, then the rest is just hard work.

I think too many young people end up in my courtroom because they don't have any hope. They can't see past today. There's no one cheering for them. Even when you hit tough places in your life, you need to have someone to tell you, "This trouble won't last." Someone needs to help you regroup and get you believing there's something better and more hopeful down the road. Otherwise, why keep going?

Three seasons ago we did an intervention on our show for a 16-year-old kid, real hard-core. He was running a prostitution ring. He was into drugs. You name it, he was doing it, and I tried to get him to understand that he came from greatness. He didn't get it, so we sent him off to sit with the Reverend C. T. Vivian. C. T. Vivian was one of the great leaders in the civil rights movement, appointed by Martin Luther King Jr. to a top position in the Southern Christian Leadership Conference. It was Rev. Vivian who was famously beaten by the county sheriff on the steps of the Selma County courthouse in 1965 in a seminal standoff on voting rights. We set it up so that this hard-core kid had to sit with Rev. Vivian and watch some old news footage of that incident. At the end of the tape, Rev. Vivian turned to this kid and said, "I took that beating so you wouldn't have to, and now I hear what you're up to and I have to ask whether it was worth it."

It was a powerful moment, because if you don't feel linked to greatness it's hard for you to see greatness. But this one kid, he finally heard it. He'd already spent two years in jail and he was looking at another long stretch, but he was able to connect the dots and get his life going. He went back to school and earned his GED. He became the primary caretaker for his sick grandmother. This was a kid who didn't give a damn about anybody, but all he needed was to see that link to greatness to find those seeds of hope. Whatever I had from my father, from my community, he desperately needed, and he needed to trust it and make it his own.

my skips
CHAMIQUE HOLDSCLAW
PROFESSIONAL BASKETBALL PLAYER

I have to talk about my grandmother, June Holdsclaw—my mom's mom. When my parents went through a difficult time, she took my brother and me in. I appreciated that. After raising all her kids and sending them through college, here she takes on these two young kids.

I was 11 years old, my brother was 8, and she had to do everything all over again. Even something simple like shopping for sneakers wasn't so simple anymore. I was like, "Oh my God, I want the Jordans!" And I wouldn't shut up. My grandmother said, "I'm not buying you *those*." She took one look at the price and couldn't believe it. She ended up buying me some knockoffs and all the kids made fun of me. I was like, "Grandma, you've got me wearing skips. I can't wear these."

But of course that's what I wore. That's what we could afford. All the girls at school were looking at my shoes. I caught a lady on the school staff looking one day, and she said, "What kind of shoes are those?" All I could tell her was, "Oh, my grandmother bought me these."

We lived in Astoria, Queens, in the projects. My grandmother always stressed schoolwork. All her kids graduated from college, and she used to say it's not where you're from that's important. You have to want to better yourself and work hard. She was real tough on me about doing as well as I could academically.

She made sure I wasn't hanging around getting into trouble. She used to volunteer at the church to feed the homeless every Wednesday and Friday, and she would have me meet her there. She would set things up like that. She was a very religious woman, a spiritual woman. The first thing I had to do every day right after school was my homework. Until I was done with my homework, there was no going outside, no nothing.

My parents went through a difficult time. They had it tough. They were both alcoholics, both battling pretty hard. They went through a period when they didn't know if they were going or coming, but thank God, they've been in recovery since I was about 11 or 12 years old.

At some point early on, my brother went back to live with my mom when she was doing a little better, but I chose to stay on with my grandmother. That's where I felt that I belonged. I was embarrassed and hurt to have my parents struggling and dealing with their illness, but my grandmother made me realize they actually had an illness. She had us go to Alateen, and she would go to Al-Anon. She kept telling me a lot of people have different issues with their families and said it was nothing to be ashamed of. She took care to explain it all.

Basketball was my outlet. You could look out the window and see the courts. They were lit, so you could play at night. My grandmother, when it was getting late, she'd yell out the window that it was time for me to head on in. I was out there all the time, but I didn't play on a team until I was older.

My grandmother knew how much I loved to play and how much I practiced, so she went outside and talked to this coach who was putting together a team. She told him all about me and convinced him to let me try out. When she came back and told me, I didn't want to go. I mean, how embarrassing is that, to have your grandmother arrange a tryout? But at the same time I wanted to go. It was a great opportunity.

So I went down and played with the guys. I was better than most of them, but they gathered in a circle afterward and voted on whether they wanted a girl on the team, and they voted against it. I was shut out. After that, my grandmother sat me down and talked to me. She said, "You've got to keep trying. Don't let it get you down." Next season, another team came along. This time they took me on, and I was really, really good. I led the team in scoring and everything, and every time I'd see the coach of that other team, I'd say, "See, I told you I could play."

" Chamique, one day I'm not gonna be here, and the only thing I want is for you to establish a relationship with your mom, because when I'm gone, the only thing you'll have is each other. "

I kept at it all through high school. At some point my aunt and uncle took me shopping for sneakers. They bought me some cool basketball shoes, gym shorts, my own ball, all that stuff. Growing up in the city, you had to have your own ball, and I took mine with me everywhere I went. Everywhere you go, you're dribbling—walking up the street, dribbling your basketball. We'd walk miles and miles to get up a game, that's how pure it was. And it was mostly me playing with the guys. It wasn't until I got to high school that I started playing on girls teams. Eventually I went to Christ the King, which had the best girls high school basketball program in the city. Eventually. At first my grandmother wouldn't let me go because it was too far from home and she worried I wouldn't be able to do all my work, traveling back and forth to school.

She was with me every step of the way, all through the recruiting process. She learned all about it and helped me make the best decision. We both really liked Tennessee, which is where I ended up going, but we went on visits to the University of Virginia, and Penn State, and the University of Connecticut. At Tennessee, Coach Summitt will tell you how important it was to my grandmother for me to go to a school with a high graduation rate for its athletes. That was first and foremost. The University of Tennessee was an elite program with a one hundred percent graduation rate and the best coach in women's college basketball. But I was still dragging my grandmother all over, looking at these other schools.

She couldn't understand why I just didn't settle on Tennessee, so I played a trick on her on the way back from one of our recruiting visits. I'd already committed to Tennessee, but I hadn't told my grandmother yet. As we were flying back I said, "Grandma, I think I'm gonna go to UVA." And oh my God, I thought she'd die. I knew how much she liked Coach Summitt, how much she liked the school, but I had to make it fun, right?

My grandmother was always very proud of me and always very supportive, but the most important thing to her was setting things right with me and my parents. I had a lot of anger toward my parents, but when my parents were finally doing well my grandmother sat me down and talked to me. She said, "Chamique, one day I'm not gonna be here, and the only thing I want is for you to establish a relationship with your mom. Because when I'm gone, the only thing you'll have is each other."

Now that my grandmother has passed on, I really understand what she meant. My mom now is a blessing in my life, one of my best friends, but I don't think I would have taken that step without my grandmother. There was a lot of resentment and hurt inside me. I remember that my sophomore year in college was the first time in a long time I told my mother I loved her. It was on the phone. I can remember crying and crying. Afterward I called my grandmother and told her what happened. I told her I'd done what she said, and that I would work on our relationship. My grandmother couldn't have been more pleased and proud.

the middle path
PHIL JACKSON
PROFESSIONAL BASKETBALL COACH, RETIRED PROFESSIONAL BASKETBALL PLAYER

Red Holzman, the head scout for the New York Knicks, was my first Buddhist teacher. He walked the middle path: Don't be an ascetic, a person who denies his body or whips himself or sits on a bed of nails. Don't do anything in excess either. Red didn't use those words but that's how he was: very consistent, very even. Red came to scout me when I was a player at the University of North Dakota. I had a mediocre performance in the first game of the tournament that year, but I scored 50 points in the next game against Illinois State. Red ended up drafting me in the second round.

So I went to New York City to meet the people in the front office and the coach, Dick McGuire. I flew in from Grand Forks, North Dakota, my first trip to New York, and I didn't know what to expect. Red and his wife, Selma, picked me up at JFK airport, and as we were driving along the Brooklyn Queens Expressway, some kids threw a stone about half the size of a brick and cracked Red's windshield. The stone came down hard and made a pretty big noise and Selma let out a little cry of surprise. Red turned to me and said, "Phil, there are many things that happen in this city that you have to live right through and bypass, and this is just one of those things." Smoke should have been coming out his ears, but Red would not allow himself to get upset. We continued on our drive and that was that.

This was 1967 and the American Basketball Association had just started, so I had an opportunity to play there as well. I thought about playing in the ABA, because it was only 300 miles from where I went to school, but ultimately the greatest challenge was in New York City with the Knicks. Red made a special trip to Fargo, North Dakota, to sign me. I was a chaplain and counselor at Boys State that year, which is kind of a big function in the world outside New York City, and he came out to meet me there. It's a weeklong government study and a gathering of promising students. That year the speaker was Mayor Lindsay of New York. When Red came out he said, "Well, I wasn't too sure about coming here, but when I heard Mayor Lindsay was coming, I decided it couldn't be that bad."

I liked his sense of humor. He used to tell people what a great life it was, coaching in the NBA. "How can it not be great?" he'd say. "We stay in the finest hotels, travel first class, get this great per diem to go on the road …" Then he'd throw up his hands and say, "But it's these games, these games, they just keep coming! They never stop. If we could only get rid of these games, it would be a great life."

He was fun to be around, but I was most impressed by his even temperament. There wasn't a whole lot that could rattle him, and he set a tremendous example. He was at all of our home games. During one of the games, middle of the fourth quarter, he caught Nate Bowman and me looking up in the stands. Time had been called. Nate was a big girl-watcher, and someone must have caught his eye and he wanted me to look up at some girl. Before I could even turn back down and get my head back in the huddle, Red was in my face. "Do you know how much time there is on the clock?" he demanded.

I said, "Yeah, there are about six minutes and thirty-four seconds to go." And Red said, "I don't mean that clock. I mean the 24-second clock."

I didn't know. Red's point was that I needed to stay tuned in. It didn't matter if I was playing or just sitting on the bench: I had to pay attention.

I became his mentee. When he took over the coaching duties in December of my rookie year, he put me in an elevated role as a presser. He liked me in that role and I ended up having a very successful second half of the season. The whole team played well under Red. We won more games than any other team in the league the second half and started to make our move as a basketball team at that time.

> " you know, Phil, the great thing about newspapers is they line parrot cages a day or two after they're published. "

He saw something in me, I guess. We communicated. And over time he encouraged me to coach. My second year in the league I was injured on a long road trip in January, and I ended up having a spinal fusion at the end of the year. Red took me under his wing when I was injured. He really included me in the team, even though I was in a lot of pain and discomfort. He kept me involved by having me keep track of things and diagram plays. Because of that I started questioning him about how he saw the game and what he looked for in a game. I was in the locker room with him before the game, and we spent a lot of time talking about basketball.

Red saw me coach the Chicago Bulls to six championships, and he called me after every single one to congratulate me. He also called me after losing one year in that tough series against the New York Knicks. I was angry about losing, but what I was most upset about was that I turned around to shake hands with Pat Riley, the opposing coach, and he was gone.

It had been a hard series. There had been a fight. But the Knicks finally beat us and went on to the finals, and I expected Pat Riley to at least stay around and shake hands. I talked about it in a book I wrote called *Maverick*. Red called me up after the book came out and said, "You know, Phil, the great thing about newspapers is they line parrot cages a day or two after they're published. Those words disappear. But your book is going to last forever." His point was, I shouldn't ever talk in a negative way about an organization I've been as close to as the New York Knicks, because I might be asked some day to come back and coach them. And Red was right. Those words have come back to haunt me, and I have to laugh about it once in a while.

There's a comment attributed to Red that says a lot about him. During the 1969-70 season, the Knicks reeled off 18 wins in a row. It set a league record. We were back in New York, at Madison Square Garden, and we finally lost. After the game someone came up to Red and asked him what he would have done had the Knicks won. He said, "Well, Selma and I would have gone home, and she would have poured me a scotch, and I probably would have had a steak and smoked a cigar." So then the person asked Red what he was going to do now that the Knicks had lost. And Red said, "Well, I'll probably go home, and Selma will pour me a scotch, and I'll have a steak and smoke a cigar." Red was a very, very consistent person. Losing and winning made a difference, but not a remarkable difference in his temperament, and it was comforting to us as players to know that.

sweat and spirit
DONNA RICHARDSON JOYNER
FITNESS EXPERT

Many people encouraged me when I was growing up. My physical education teacher was also my dance teacher, and she was the one who got me interested in dance. Ms. Wells, who now goes by Mrs. Woods, helped me to be the best I could be, and dance became a big, big part of my life. She also had us taking those presidential fitness tests. Remember those? I became so competitive about that, so focused. And the great thing was, I was competing against a standard—against myself, really—trying to be the best that I could be.

There weren't a lot of role models for women in fitness in Silver Springs, Maryland, where I grew up. I participated in all kinds of sports though. I was a baton girl when I was 5 years old, and I have to laugh at that. How did my parents even find out about baton lessons for a 5-year-old? Their idea was to keep me busy and active, so I played softball too. Swim team, track and field, dance, gymnastics—I did it all, and they supported me in everything I did. Eventually I started competing in aerobics.

But a role model? There weren't any at that time really. It wasn't until I got out of college that Jane Fonda started the whole aerobics craze. There was nothing before her back then. We were just out there on our own, doing our best.

I don't think I would have put myself out there like that if it weren't for my mother, Laverne Richardson. She was a true soccer mom even back then. I don't think she ever missed one of my events. All the way through college she was cheering me on.

Now this is going to surprise a lot of people because I'm so active, but one of my earliest inspirations other than my mom was my home economics teacher. She taught me how to cook, sew, crochet, and knit, and she was very encouraging. I became very, very good at it. This teacher encouraged me to take it to the next level. I decided I didn't really make enough money in allowance, so I went to my parents and told them I wanted to start my own business, and they supported me in this as well. I started crocheting items and having my parents take them to their jobs. I'd also sell them to friends and family members and eventually even to local gift stores and churches. My mother had a big family, and all of them and their friends and extended family had my samples. I'd get orders and fill every last one. Let me tell you, it was a very lucrative deal, better than any allowance I ever heard about.

Donna's Crocheting Specialties—that was my business from grade school to high school. Then suddenly I woke up one day and realized it wasn't cool to crochet anymore. In high school you do not crochet. You don't even tell anybody you know *how* to crochet. So I stopped. Six or seven years ago I was cleaning out my house and came across these "granny squares" from my crocheting days and I picked it up again. Lately I've been making afghans for family and special friends for Christmas gifts. I get a little backed up around the holidays. I'll stay up until six o'clock in the morning on Christmas Day finishing the last ones. I made one for my father-in-law once, and when I presented it to him he got teary-eyed. He was 84 years old.

"Donna," he said, "in all my years on this Earth, no one has ever made me anything."

Usually when you think of physical fitness, you think "workout." But my thing now is to connect the mind, body, and spirit. That's the foundation of everything I do now. Crocheting is tied in to it, because it's a great de-stresser. It relaxes me.

You might think there's a health and fitness craze sweeping the country, but 65 percent of Americans are still overweight. It's alarming. So I've targeted this large segment of the population that needs a little different inspiration to be active and healthier. That's how we came up with the "Sweating to the Spirit" program we do with churches and religious groups all across the country.

" we're in serious trouble … raising a generation of unhealthy, sedentary children. "

People go to church to get spiritually and mentally strong. While we're there we get the rest of them healthy. We call our moves "praise moves," so nobody's thinking of it like a workout. I call it an experience instead of a workout. Even better, it's a celebration, because when you're in that type of environment, you're not thinking about how many calories you're burning or your cottage cheese thighs or whether you'll fit into that bathing suit from last summer. You're in the moment.

The Bible tells us to train a child in the way he should go and when he is old he will not depart from that path. Now whenever you start quoting Scripture it makes people nervous. They go, "OK, Donna, did you have to go *there?*" But we're in serious trouble. We're raising a generation of unhealthy, sedentary children. They spend too much time in front of the television or playing video games. School districts are cutting back physical education. When the majority of your meals come through a takeout window, you're in trouble. All these unhealthy kids eventually will become unhealthy adults. Think of the skyrocketing health costs we have now and imagine what our future will be like if we don't get healthier as a society.

And do you know who my biggest supporter is after all these years? My mom. She comes on the road with me and helps me lead some of these "Sweating to the Spirit" workshops. She'll call me up and say, "Donna, when's our next gig?" She really enjoys it. She is always very energizing, very assertive.

My mother was a computer analyst, but she always found time for me. She always made sure that her career did not interfere with her being a loving and supportive mother to her young daughter participating in sports. Now we're out there together, training people to lead these experiences in churches and community groups all over the world. We go in with a starter kit, give the folks in charge the tools and guidelines to keep it going, and when we leave we've really made a difference. My mother used to say to me, "Donna, you can do all things through Christ." She used to have me repeat those words, and whenever I was about to go out there on the field or the stage, those words would kick in. I still think about them.

Back when I was competing, I'd look at the other girls and realize they were not my competition. I was competing against myself to reach a standard just like in those old presidential fitness tests. That's what my mother taught me most of all. And now it has me thinking we have to start taking better care of ourselves. I'm thrilled to have my mom at my side, still cheering me on and helping me to lead the way.

a kind of grace
JACKIE JOYNER-KERSEE
OLYMPIC TRACK STAR

A lot of folks have had a hand in my success. Nobody gets to where they want to be without a little help along the way, and that's how it's been with me.

It starts with my brother Al. We were always very close growing up. He was two years older, and he always looked out for me. We lived in East St. Louis, and I guess it was pretty tough. At the time we didn't think it was so bad; it was the environment we lived in, what we saw every day. But once you leave and your eyes open up to all these other things, you realize, wow, you're lucky you made it out of there.

He put up a basketball goal for me in our backyard. When my mother went to work, he was the babysitter. Wherever he had to go, we had to go with him, whether we wanted to or not.

He used to get me to play chess because he told me it was a mind game and he told me it would be good for me, so I started playing. I might not have wanted to play, but I had to play. He was always teaching me, always telling me how to do something better, always looking out for me.

I was part of an AAU program with the East St. Louis Railers. We won the Junior Olympics one year, and I was featured in *Sports Illustrated*. My brother was very proud of me—but he also gave me a hard time about it. That was his thing, teaching me to be tough. I guess he thought that if I could take a hard time from him, I could take a hard time from anyone.

He knew how much I loved to run and how much I loved going to practice. I think maybe some of that love and commitment rubbed off on him and got him thinking maybe he could be good too, if he went to practice the way I did. Truth is, he didn't like it, but in time he did it anyway. So maybe he learned something from me too.

There was a man named Nino Fennoy who ran our AAU team. He was one of my first track coaches, and he had a way about him. He knew how to read kids and how to get the best out of them. This was a person who made sure when I was hungry, I had something to eat.

> " as I was coming down the homestretch
> I could see Al down there along the track
> encouraging me to push it. "

We'd go to meets and tournaments. My parents didn't have the money for me to be going to these places, but Coach Fennoy would take care of me. Of course I could never say I didn't have any money. That would be too embarrassing. I'd just say I wasn't hungry, but he was wise enough to know I was, and he found a way to get me something to eat without letting on.

He also taught me about myself. He used to tell us to keep a journal, and in the beginning I thought this was just his way of being nosy, but he was really trying to get us to concentrate on our sentence structure, our communication skills, and our writing. He was preparing us for where he thought we would be one day in life. When you're younger you don't appreciate a lot of the things that people give you, because you think you're supposed to be there. But this man was volunteering his time. This man was out there because he loved working with kids, and he put it in my head to be the best that I could be.

I had another coach early on. His name was George Ward and he was really hard on me. He used to talk a lot. It wasn't until I was a little older that I realized he was trying to teach me about being focused and disciplined. His big thing was teaching us that even though we had talent, we had to be willing to listen, and be willing to be coached.

I don't think I was ready to be coached. But then I watched the Olympics on television and realized these girls were trying to do the same things I was trying to do. And I started to think, "Maybe I can go to the Olympics."

That was a big moment for me, because when I was growing up in the 1970s, women in sports weren't a celebrated thing, but I happened to think there was a kind of grace in them. There was nothing unfeminine about being a powerful athlete—just the opposite. There was something really beautiful and empowering, and the Olympics were the only showcase for female athletes. I saw myself in these girls on television at the Olympics, and that's when I really started focusing.

I went to UCLA on a basketball scholarship, but I really wanted to run track. They had all these great coaches, and track and field was something I wanted to do. I wanted to become a great athlete. I'd been to the Olympic trials as a high schooler, and I realized that these girls were no better than I was, and that if I dedicated myself and really pushed myself, I could maybe make the team in 1984.

In the meantime though, basketball was going to get me an education, so I didn't run track my freshman year. In some ways basketball was always more challenging, because you had to deal with all these other personalities and you had to fit your game into a team format. Track is much more individualized. It's on you.

Al and I ended up going to the 1984 Olympic Games together. We both made the team, so that was a nice bonus. I'd taken the year off from school to keep my focus on the Olympic team and Al had come out to California from Arkansas State to train with my husband, Bobby. It was a very exciting thing to be going to our first Olympic Games together in Los Angeles.

Al won the gold in the triple jump that year and I was running the 800 meters, the last event of the heptathlon. They'd just announced his victory on the public address system, and I heard it, but I filed it away for later because I needed to concentrate on my race. But as I was coming down the homestretch I could see Al down there along the track encouraging me to push it. I thought, "That's just like Al, to finish up in his own event and come to cheer me on."

I tried to push it, but psychologically I wasn't really there. I had dreamed about being in the Olympics, but you have to be mentally and physically ready to endure the ups and downs, the good and the bad, and figure out a way to be victorious. I thought I was ready for that, but when you walk into the Los Angeles Coliseum with 100,000 people watching you and cheering for you—wow, It just hits you. And I wasn't ready.

I ended up winning the silver medal that year, losing the gold to Glynis Nunn of Australia by just 5 points. She had 6,390 points and I had 6,385 points. Five points out of 6,000—that's all I needed!

But I wasn't disappointed. It was the greatest experience I could have had as an athlete, because it taught me an important lesson. I had a hamstring problem, but it wasn't as bad as I'd made it out to be. But by thinking it was, each time I went to the start line I didn't go thinking like a champion. I went to the start line worrying about the pain, wondering where it was, wondering why it wasn't hurting. Over two days of competition, I lost my strength and focus. I didn't replenish my fluids. I didn't eat between events. I showed that I was immature and didn't really know what I was doing. So on the one hand it would have been nice to win the gold medal in '84 to go along with Al's, but I wasn't ready for it. The whole experience put me in shape for the 1988 Olympics; that's exactly what it did. My new attitude was the missing piece.

I ended up going back to UCLA and completing my last year of eligibility on the basketball team. By this point I was running track as well, and I was totally focused on 1988, totally ready. Al didn't make the 1988 team and that was hard on all of us. I think he was fourth in the trials. But he was there looking out for me, cheering me on, and pushing me, and this time around I was ready. This time around, at the 1988 Olympic Games in Seoul, South Korea, I took the gold, and I still believe it took that narrow defeat in 1984 to get me there. I really do.

Jackie Joyner Kersee

a clear-sighted awareness

JOHN KASICH

FORMER CONGRESSMAN, FOX NEWS COMMENTATOR

The best way I can describe my father is to share a story.

I was 11 years old and trying out for Little League. There was a tryout and a draft, and as the season drew near, all my friends were being asked to join this or that team. But by opening day there were a few of us who had managed to fall through the cracks and not get selected. Looking back, I guess it's not that surprising. I was a decent enough ballplayer, but I was skinny and small and easily overlooked. Back then parents didn't advocate for their children the way they do today and getting cut was an accepted part of the deal.

I took it in stride. Anyway, I meant to. Like every other boy in McKees Rocks, Pennsylvania, I dreamed of someday playing for the Pittsburgh Pirates, but I was sidelined by the system. Even as a kid, I could see what was going on. Some kids were getting picked for teams because their fathers were coaches or because their fathers were friendly with the coaches. Some of those kids were no better than me, except they had some type of connection, some kind of *in*.

> " Johnny, I'm not going to owe anybody anything. You're going to have to earn your way onto one of these teams. "

One night a week or so into the season, I went up to my father and laid it out for him. He knew I hadn't been picked for a team, but I don't think he understood why. I told him I was as good a ballplayer as some of these kids and that he needed to go and talk to somebody. I thought that should be easy enough. My father was a mailman. He knew everyone in town. I figured there had to be someone he could talk to about getting me on a team.

My father didn't see things quite the same way. He said, "Johnny, I'm not going to owe anybody anything. You're going to have to earn your way onto one of these teams."

Man oh man, that was a tough lesson, but I tried to swallow it. I wasn't mad at my father, but I did have a hard time understanding him. I didn't see this as any kind of life lesson. I didn't see any point worth proving. All I could see was that these other kids were playing ball and I wasn't. My friends all had their uniforms and their practices, while all I had was my own ball and glove, and once the season started there wasn't even anyone around for me to have a catch with. I ended up doing a lot of tossing the ball high up into the air, over and over, or practicing up against a wall. My father would throw the ball around with me whenever he could, but he would not go with his hand out to anyone, for anything—certainly not for something like this.

After a couple weeks, some kid broke his leg and I got my shot, which meant I got to play without my father being beholden to anybody in town. It's a shame my shot had to happen as a result of someone else's misfortune, though at the time I didn't worry too much about the poor kid with the broken leg. I just grabbed my glove and raced to the field for my first practice, thrilled to finally be getting a real uniform and the chance to play for a real team. No one was happier for me than my father, mostly because he knew what it meant to me but also because it got him off the hook.

So that's my father for you. This was his stand. And in the end, what did it accomplish? Well, for one very important thing, it made an impression. Here I am a lifetime later, still telling the story. Here I am still thinking about the lesson it carries, the values it upholds, the example it sets.

"A human action becomes genuinely important when it springs from the soil of a clear-sighted awareness," the great Czech playwright Vaclav Havel writes in *Disturbing the Peace*. "It is only this awareness that can breathe any greatness into an action."

Was there greatness in such a small act as this? Probably not. Was there even a clear-sighted awareness on the part of my father that his principles were not only *his* principles but that they might soon become mine as well? I don't think so. He simply was doing what he felt was right, and he expected me to do the same.

more flies with honey
PATRICK J. KELLY
CHAIRMAN, DEPARTMENT OF
NEUROLOGICAL SURGERY,
NYU SCHOOL OF MEDICINE

There wasn't much going on in East Aurora, New York, where I grew up, but fortunately we had a Boys Club. Most of us used to go there after school and on weekends. There were basketball courts, a television, Ping Pong tables. And there were nice people there. I particularly remember the director, Mr. Whitney. We all called him Whit. He was a big bear of a man who didn't tolerate unruly behavior, foul language, or disrespect. But he was also a family man with kids of his own and it was clear that he loved being around children. He knew all of our names and seemed glad to see us when we came to the club, which was not at all like the indifference a lot of us faced at home.

Most of us came from low-income families with brawling, abusive parents. We were tough kids who settled disagreements with our fists, which of course was how things usually got worked out at home. That's why one episode with Whit stands out in memory. We were about 11 years old. Two of my friends got into an argument that degenerated into foulmouthed name-calling and then a fight. The fight became more and more vicious. Each boy looked like he was trying to kill the other. They used their fists, pool cues, chairs—whatever they could find. Whit's assistants tried to break it up, but the fight had become so violent that they were worried about getting hurt themselves, so they sent for Whit.

We expected Whit to give these kids a good thrashing and kick them out of the club. Instead, he did something that I thought at the time was incredible. He walked calmly toward the two boys, but he didn't say anything. He didn't move to break up the fight. He just stared at them with a look that seemed to be more sadness than anger. Then he put his arms around both fighters and hugged them—not the kind of hug that these days can get you fired or written up in the newspapers, but a hug of genuine affection, like a father hugging his sons. I had no idea what to make of this, but the boys calmed down. One broke into tears, and the other looked like he was spending all his energy fighting them back. Finally the two boys shook hands.

Fifteen years later, I was reminded of Whit's unusual approach. I'd joined the U.S. Navy because it was the only way I could get enough money to finish medical school. I joined the Navy and got paid enough as an ensign to get me through my final year. Vern Fitchett was the chief of surgery at the Naval Support Activity Hospital in Da Nang, where I had been assigned. He took a shine to me, thinking I was regular Navy, not realizing that I was just passing through. I had no specialized surgical training, but I had volunteered for Vietnam because I had just spent a year on a ship and was bored chasing cockroaches and treating gonorrhea in 500 otherwise healthy men, and because Hippocrates said that all those who wanted to be a surgeon should go to war.

It was clear from my very first day that I didn't know what the hell I was doing. I was an FNG. The N was for new, the G was for guy, and the F—well, I'm sure you can figure it out. All FNGs were assigned to triage—

a brutal introduction to war. The hospital was a collection of Quonset huts situated between a Vietcong-controlled village and a marine helicopter base.

My first day in triage, choppers were dropping off about 20 or 30 severely wounded men at a time. The first patient I saw was a man who was late tossing a grenade. It blew off his left arm and both legs and I took one look at him raising his left arm and staring in disbelief where his hand used to be, and then seeing his eyes sort of roll back in his head. And I remember being very, very upset about this. Vern Fitchett was trying to take care of all these other people while I was mesmerized by this scene. I should have been doing something, getting an IV started or something, but I was so upset by the sight of this poor guy that I just stood there, until Vern finally said, "Okay, P.J., war's not pretty—now get in gear."

> ## " OK, P. J., war's not pretty— now get in gear. "

So I started working and the Corpsmen helped me. Soon these two Marines came in and they'd each lost their legs in a booby trap. I was just slow as molasses and both of them died on me, because what they really needed was some competent person treating them. I went off into this little room and just cried and cried. I hadn't cried since I was 10 years old. And then I realized that the room I was in was the KIA room, killed in action, where they put all the dead bodies, and I was the only one in there alive, and I almost wished I could join them. I never felt so useless in my life.

But failure can motivate you to try harder too. So I sucked up everything I could learn from Vern and the Corpsmen. There were always major casualties, and Vern didn't always have time to teach a greenhorn the ropes, but eventually he turned me from a bad first assistant into a passable first assistant. His only words of consolation to me were the words he said that first day: "War's not pretty—now get your ass in gear."

Do the best you can; that's what I learned from Vern. We'd see these horribly mangled men, and they were all screaming in pain, and if we lost one of them, did we blame our government for getting us into that stupid war? No, we didn't. Did we blame the enemy? No, we didn't. We blamed ourselves, until all of a sudden you had the confidence to realize that you did the best you could and it really wasn't in the cards for that person to survive.

And with that confidence, I'm afraid, came a little bit of arrogance. One day Vern caught me being a little tough on the Corpsmen. I guess I thought they were incompetent, which was exactly the way I had been, but I didn't have the patience with them that Vern had had with me, and Vern came over to me and said, "P.J., you can catch more flies with honey than with vinegar."

It wasn't exactly an original line, but I got the message, and it takes me to the third part of the story. A couple years ago, I had a resident who was extremely bright, and I let him open up the bone flap of a man with a brain tumor. He was all thumbs, this resident, but he opened up the bone flap, and I'll be goddamned, when he opened up the bone flap he also cut the dura and even cut into the brain with the saw, and I was all set just to read him the riot act. Really, I was ready to excoriate this guy. But then I thought back to Vern Fitchett and his incredible patience, and then all the way back to Mr. Whitney, and the way he walked over so calmly to those two friends of mine when they were fighting. So I didn't say anything. Instead I repaired the damage and the patient did great, so there was no problem there. But I called this resident several hours after the case had finished and I said, "Look, don't be depressed. Everybody makes mistakes." I was thinking of Whit's kindness with these two brawling kids and Vern's comment about catching more flies with honey than vinegar, and this young man was just so grateful, because of course he thought I was going to fire him.

And I thought, "Well, these fellas were right." All these years afterwards. I thought, "You know what, I should call Vern and tell him that his advice meant something to me." I didn't think to call Mr. Whitney, because I had only known him a short time, but I caught myself wanting Vern to know he had an impact on me.

I found him on the Internet. It said he was retired from the Navy and working in some clinic in North Dakota where he was from. I called his office and I told them who I was and what I wanted to do and they said, "Dr. Kelly, I'm so sorry to tell you this, but Dr. Fitchett died a few years ago." So I never got a chance to tell him what his advice had meant. It might have been a cliché, but it had meant the world.

patience and perseverance
ANNA KOURNIKOVA
PROFESSIONAL TENNIS PLAYER, MODEL

I was born in Russia, obviously. In Moscow. My parents were both athletes, so I had a lot of energy when I was a child and I still do. I'm very hyper. When I was a kid and my parents were busy working, they wanted me to have a healthy lifestyle. They were very young and basically they were looking for a daycare kind of thing, so they enrolled me in the Spartak Tennis Club in Moscow. It was my second home when I was growing up.

It was by chance that I ended up there, but tennis was the sport I enjoyed the most. Every day after school, my parents or my grandparents would take me to Spartak and I would be there until maybe nine o'clock, until somebody from my family could pick me up. All we did was play tennis, eat, have fun, and hang out with the other kids and the moms and the coaches. We would do our homework there. It was basically my second family.

In that second family was a woman who was like a second mother to me, my first coach, Larissa Preobraschenskaja. Still today I refer to her as my second mother. She taught me everything I know about how to play tennis, but she's such a wonderful human being. She's kind and patient, which is not what you expect from one of the top tennis coaches in Russia. She was a top player herself, back in the Soviet days, and she was just really, really patient—and fun.

Probably she was very tough, but her whole program when I was little was based on tricking us into doing our drills. She would put candy under the targets, and we would try to hit them. The targets would fly off, and under the target there it would be. Everything was a game. If you hit a certain number of balls, you got to have an ice cream. Everything was based on bribes, but in a good way. In a positive way. The whole place was like that, not just Larissa. I couldn't have had a better coach. I couldn't have been in a better environment.

That place gave me a place of belonging. That was my life, my community. Because I had so much energy, if I was into something I was really into it. That's how it was for me with Spartak and tennis. I just loved going there every day.

Even today some of my best friends are the people I know from Spartak. We have so much history because we went through so much together at such an important time in our lives. Even as a kid, I was a people person. For me, the more people the better. It was just really, really great.

Spartak was in a forest, like a park. There were rides there and when we were older we would go out for runs. We wouldn't tell the coaches, but we would take money with us, maybe 10 cents worth, and sprint there as fast as we could so we would have the time to stop and go on the rides or have an ice cream before sprinting back.

It was just a fun place. Even when I started competing in tournaments, it was fun. There was hard work, but Larissa made it fun. She's the best coach in Russia in terms of working with children. You have to have a very specific character and patience level and tolerance level to work with small children, and she had all these things.

She really loved the kids. She was always calm. She never raised her voice, and probably some of the kids took advantage of her a little bit. But at the same time, you wanted to succeed and make her happy because she was so nice and so patient and kind. I was playing for her and for myself. I know how hard she worked with me on the court to improve my technique and my game, and it was always a pleasure to make her happy. I didn't want to let her down.

Larissa didn't want us to feel like we were working hard. It was meant to be fun. She wasn't aggressive at all with us. Yes, of course we worked hard, but we didn't notice it. To us, it was play.

My second tournament was the Moscow Championships and I won. Afterward Larissa came up to me and said, "Congratulations. Enjoy today because tomorrow it's back to hard work again."

> " it was always a pleasure to make her happy.
> I didn't want to let her down. "

That was how she was: "Tomorrow we don't discuss the win." She was always telling us to enjoy it and celebrate and have fun with any particular achievement, but to always remember there is something more you can do, something more you can achieve. That's how I heard it. Have fun but work hard, because your opponent is working hard too.

I moved to the United States in 1991 to play tennis because there wasn't really a good opportunity for that in Russia. It was hard to play tennis there if you were really serious about it. Spartak was great, but obviously the conditions weren't perfect. Winter is seven months long over there. It snows. It rains. You have to fight for court time. There were so many good kids, good players, and very little court space. We had only 12 courts back then and not a lot of tennis balls, so it was the best decision for me to come to America and play.

But of course I was sad to leave my community. Larissa was very supportive. She understood. And now, every time I go back to Russia, like four times a year to see my grandmother, I go to Spartak. We have tea. We look at all the pictures from all the birthday parties and tournaments and celebrations. It's really cool to have someone like that in my life. She's still coaching, but we don't talk much about tennis anymore. We just talk.

a hardship and a blessing

KELLY ZIMMERMAN LANE
RECRUITING AGENT,
FORMER YOUTH OF THE YEAR,
BOYS & GIRLS CLUBS OF AMERICA

I grew up in Orrville, Ohio, home of Smucker's jam and jelly, about an hour south of Cleveland. It was a small town with all kinds of pride and cheer. It really was a nice place to live, but for me things weren't always so nice at home.

My dad was in and out of the picture. He was rotten to my mother, physically and emotionally. He was abusive to me and to my sisters. He was an alcoholic, and my mother would sacrifice herself for us kids. She would put us all in a bedroom or closet and she would take the brunt of it. When we were older and able to get out of the hiding space to see what was going on, I asked her to get a divorce. That was a very hard thing. All around Orrville were these nice, middle-class homes with the white picket fence, the whole deal. That's what she wanted, and my dad didn't allow that to happen.

I was the oldest of three girls. My mother worked at least three jobs at any given time and did everything she could not only to keep food on the table but to keep us in cheerleading uniforms and gymnastics classes and all those good things as well. We were on food stamps and welfare, but we got by.

It was hard being on food stamps in a small town where everyone knew everyone. A lot of people were surprised, not because we were trying to hide anything, but because my mom always made sure everything was handled so well. Whatever we had, it was always the cleanest. She took pride in absolutely everything and made stuff out of nothing for us. It's a wonder to me how she ever found the time. She was a nursery school teacher and the custodian of our church. When she was done with that, she would go make apple dumplings at a bakery. She picked up any job she could. She even worked at Hardee's for a while on the breakfast shift.

> " whatever lessons we learned,
> we learned by example. "

I don't know what we would have done without my grandmother too. We went to stay with her many times—whenever things were very bad at home. We normally stayed for a year or so each time. Luckily she lived in the same neighborhood, so we didn't have to switch schools. There wasn't a lot of room at her place. We laid out blankets and pillows in front of the fireplace and made the best of it.

One time when we went to my grandmother's, we woke up the next morning to find all of our belongings all over her front yard. My father had just cleaned everything out. My sisters were young at the time. For them to see all their toys and stuffed animals, their clothes and everything else—all their worldly possessions—all over the yard was very disturbing.

But my mom and my grandmother handled that as well as people could. They went out, as dignified as possible, and started picking up our things. It was difficult to watch. After awhile I went out and helped. It taught me that that's the way you handle those types of situations. You do the best you can, and everything can be picked up and set right—literally, I guess.

My grandmother lived on a quiet boulevard and I'm sure her neighbors were having a heyday talking about it, but she didn't care. She took us in and did what she could to make sure we had steady activities in our lives outside of school: sports, church choir, softball down at the Boys & Girls Club. They were things that didn't change regardless of what was changing at home, when you didn't know what you were coming home to.

It was a hardship and a blessing for my grandmother to have us under her roof. She didn't have it easy. She worked as a secretary. She didn't have a lot of money. It must have broken her heart to see us struggling.

But I can't ever remember her not being there. She made me cinnamon toast every single day. She was the other parent. She was my true dad, in an odd way. When something happened—if you were hurt at school or needed to be taken to the doctor or whatever—you called Grandma.

We didn't talk a lot about our situation when I was younger. Whatever lessons we learned, we learned by example. My mother never told me I was going to college. It was understood. She never said, "You will not be a teenage mother." It was understood. We never talked about how we were going to get through this, we just got through it. We looked at my mother, working three jobs, always managing to put food on the table, always putting me and my sisters first. Sunday nights, dinner would be on the table, regardless of what it was, and we were having it and pretending it was Thanksgiving.

Her actions did her talking. We could see her struggling, and that meant we were going to college. We knew we had to act responsibly and couldn't bring another baby into the family because there wasn't any money for another mouth to feed. That wasn't what my mother was working for. She wasn't struggling to watch us go down that road. We looked at my grandmother too, taking us in, making our lives hers, and we knew it was on us to repay that in kind. Success, in whatever form my sisters and I chose it to be, was the only option. That was our responsibility.

Kelly J. Lane

the wind beneath my wings
TARA LIPINSKI
OLYMPIC FIGURE SKATER

I started competing when I was 5 years old. It was mostly just for fun. The serious competition didn't start until I was 8 or 9, and by then I was so deep into it I don't think my parents knew quite what to do with me.

They weren't into sports at all. My dad was a lawyer. My mom worked on Wall Street, but she stopped working when I was born. They really just wanted me to do well in school and be happy and well-rounded and all those other things most parents want for their children. The only reason they put me on skates was because I was such an active kid. They were just looking for a way for me to burn off all this energy.

They tried to get me out of skating a few times, the more serious it got. They didn't like the politics of the sport. They didn't like that it was so time-consuming and expensive. In order to compete, I had to live away from home with my mom for a while, and they certainly didn't like that. It was hard. It seems now like we were always on the move, always settling into some new environment. New coaches. New friends. New everything. But I loved skating and I was really good at it.

At the competitions I was usually the youngest one there. That was always intimidating. I tried not to let it show, but even that can be a wearying thing for a little kid. And that's just what I was, a little kid. At my first World Championship, I was only 13! Now they have an age restriction, but I think I was the youngest skater ever to compete at Worlds, and I just messed up everything. I fell on every jump. I was just totally distracted. I saw Midori Ito skate before I went out and thought, "Oh my God, I'm skating after Midori Ito! This is amazing!" I wasn't ready to be competing at that level.

It was a disaster. I wasn't close to my coaches at the time, so I couldn't talk to them about what I was feeling. My mom couldn't be down there on the ice with me during the competition, so I couldn't talk to her. And she didn't know anything about sports. She was completely there for me emotionally and completely supportive, but even at 13 I had to take care of the stuff on the ice. That was all me.

But I didn't think I could handle a disaster like this all on my own. I came off the ice and I was in 23rd place. I just barely made the long program for the next day. My coaches wouldn't even talk to me, they were so upset about my performance, so I wandered around for a while and I really didn't know what to do.

After a while my mom found me and together we found this little broom closet in the arena, and we went inside and closed the door behind us, just to get away from everything. And we just sat there and cried and cried. And we talked it out. After a while my coaches were outside pounding on the door, shouting, "Get out here!" But my mom shouted right back. "No," she said. "We're just going to sit here a while longer while Tara tells me everything that's on her mind."

And that was my mom. She tried to make sure I had a normal life. A lot of my skating friends weren't allowed to have sleepovers, but my mom used to let me bring my girlfriend to competitions with me, and we'd run around and have a great time. My coaches weren't too happy about it. They'd pull my mom aside and say, "You really can't have Tara run around like this. She needs to focus." And Mom would say, "She's a kid. She's supposed to have fun. This is supposed to be fun."

There used to be weigh-ins back then, and I know a lot of athletes who continue to struggle with weight issues as a result of this type of thing. They had all this pressure on them about their weight, especially skaters, but I never had any of that. I don't think I even knew they had weigh-ins, because my mom must have said to my coaches, "You say one word to Tara about her weight and she's out."

" she gave up her life for my childhood dream. "

She meant the world to me, and she still does. I didn't have any brothers or sisters, so she was able to focus her attention on me, to really be there for me, even on this rough journey I chose for myself.

I've had two wonderful opportunities to tell her what she's meant to me. One was kind of a private moment, and the other was a little public and staged but also pretty meaningful.

The first was when I won the gold medal at the Olympics in Japan. I'd been up on the podium with my medal, and I skated around the arena with it at the end of the medal ceremony. But when I was through, instead of going back up to the podium with the other skaters, I skated over to where my mom was. I gave the medal to her and said, "Mom, thank you for everything. I love you so much." It was just a few seconds, but for a couple beats everything just stopped, and we were able to be with each other and hug each other and realize that everything we did, we did together. And we got through it.

The second moment came during a television special for CBS that we shot in Canada. There was no audience and we had the rink to ourselves. The set decorators had come up with beautiful lighting, and it was really breathtaking. My mom came out onto the set and I skated for her to that Bette Midler song "Wind Beneath My Wings." We used to watch that movie all the time, *Beaches*. We loved that movie, and I knew the song would mean a lot to her.

I choreographed the program myself. At the beginning of the song I'd recorded a little voice-over telling my mother how much I loved her and how much I appreciated everything she'd done for me. I skated this whole program for her. There was no one else in the arena except for the crew, and it was cold and quiet and just beautiful. Although it was for a television special, at the same time it was an intimate, private moment. And of course, my mother was just bawling on the ice by the time I was through.

Lesson one from all of this? Well, my kids won't be doing competitive sports. My mom said she's not taking her grandchild to any rink, so they cannot skate.

The real lesson, though, is that even though it was hard, even though we sacrificed a lot and put up with a lot, my parents knew how much I loved it and were willing to make those sacrifices. I have such a different outlook on it now, and we can joke about it, but I hope that when I get around to having kids I can be like my mom. She gave up her life for my childhood dream, but in a good way, and she tried to do it on her own terms. She wouldn't let skating rule our lives.

Tara Lipinski

mental toughness
MARIO LOPEZ
ACTOR

I was a border town kid. I grew up in southern California, right on the border of Tijuana, Mexico, in a town called Chula Vista. My mom's idea was to keep me busy, to keep me out of trouble that way. There was just me and my sister, but my mom and dad both came from big families and everyone was nearby. My father worked for the city street department; he was a real blue-collar guy. My mother worked for the phone company. They set it up so we always had something to do until they came home from work.

My sister and I never got into any trouble because we were so busy. Dancing, karate, drama, wrestling—my mother had me doing everything, and I really loved it. I started dancing when I was only 2 years old.

Ricki Adney was my first dance teacher and she was a big influence. When you're two years old, you're happy to be anywhere jumping around. But when I was older I didn't really like it. The other kids started calling me names and dancing wasn't the most masculine thing in the world, but I kept at it. I wanted to make my mom happy. She was working hard to pay for these classes, so I didn't want to quit.

Then I started liking girls and I realized that girls like guys who can dance. So it's obvious, right? You keep dancing. On top of that, I started to see that it was helping me with sports, with my balance and agility and flexibility. It was all tied in, and Ricki Adney was really helpful, getting me to realize how everything was connected.

> " Mario, if you're a successful wrestler, you'll be successful in life, because the attributes you need to be a successful wrestler are the same you'll need to be successful in whatever it is you do. "

Wrestling was my other big thing. All of my uncles wrestled and I really loved it. I had two coaches at the Chula Vista Boys Club, Coach Ruiz and Coach Stone. They taught me how to be mentally tough, physically tough, and focused, which is what the sport demands. These guys taught me how to wrestle and they taught me a lot about life in general—about keeping your nose clean and focusing on school. That was always a top priority, doing well in school, especially where I grew up. All around, kids were getting into trouble and there were gangs, but I was able to stay busy and focused.

When you're a little Mexican kid in Chula Vista, there aren't many role models on television or examples of people who'd made it up and out of a tough situation. Actually there weren't any. Who was I going to look up to, Ricky Ricardo in *I Love Lucy?* I mean, that was basically it. Freddie Prinze had already passed away when I was growing up. I had to cut my own path, and I had to be disciplined and focused. That was my mother's influence: keeping busy, making school a priority. I never wanted to disappoint her.

Then drama kicked in. I was 10 years old when I landed my first professional gig, something called *Kids Incorporated*, but I'd been on stage long before that. I was just a performer, I guess. Dancing, theater, it was all connected. Even wrestling was tied in. My parents couldn't have been more supportive. They never missed a wrestling match, never missed a performance: *Scrooge, Annie, Grease,* we did all those typical high school productions and they were there at every one, cheering me on.

In high school my wrestling coach was also my drama coach. He was this great guy named Bill Virchis, and I'm in touch with him to this day. He wasn't the high school drama teacher, but I did plays for him outside of high school in community theater. Now he runs the Old World Theater in San Diego, but back then he was my wrestling coach, and he used to tell me that wrestling and acting were a lot alike. You're on the stage, you're all alone. It's a performance, but there's a skill involved. You have to keep focused. He used to say, "Mario, if you're a successful wrestler, you'll be successful in life, because the attributes you need to be a successful wrestler are the same you'll need to be successful in whatever it is you do."

I've found that to be the case most of the time. You need dedication, strong will, mental toughness. It teaches you a lot when you're out there on the mat on your own. In team sports you lean on people and there's finger-pointing and excuses. But when you're wrestling, it's all on you.

Mario Lopez

sister eleanor
REVEREND EDWARD A. "MONK" MALLOY
PRESIDENT EMERITUS, UNIVERSITY OF NOTRE DAME

There was one particular person in my life who instilled in me a love of learning and a sense of responsibility to make the most of my talents. Her name was Sister Eleanor, and she was my teacher at St. Anthony's grade school in Washington, D.C. She taught me in the fourth, fifth, and sixth grades. It was unusual to stay with the same teacher in consecutive years, but that's how it happened.

There was a nice article in the *Washington Post*, my hometown newspaper, the year I was elected president of Notre Dame. It was 1986, and two or three weeks after the article appeared I received a letter in the mail that read something like this: "Dear Father Malloy: You probably don't remember me, but I was your grade school teacher at St. Anthony's, and I wanted to tell you how proud I and the other sisters are of your accomplishments." And it went on to say a bunch of other laudatory things.

I quickly wrote back: "How can you have ever imagined I wouldn't remember who you were? I was in your class for three grades in a row. More important than that, you were one of the decisive influences in my life. I didn't have the wisdom at the time to thank you properly, so I'm pleased that you wrote me, because now I can thank you as an adult for what in retrospect was a pivotal set of possibilities that you opened up for me."

Sister Eleanor identified a few of us she believed to be the smartest in the class. Typically the smartest kids in the class were girls, but here it was three boys. It was a pivotal time in our lives. We were all going through puberty, and there were a lot of other distractions. Sister Eleanor would get together with us after class, and she would have us do additional assignments and look at things the class as a whole wasn't studying. Most of all she convinced us that we had God-given intelligence, that we were capable of doing great things, and that a lot of opportunities would open to us if we would only use our capacities to learn. She did this in a very unobtrusive, nondictatorial fashion, and she made it fun. The three of us were just delighted to have someone set us apart and encourage us in just such a fashion, and the fact that we had her three years in a row meant this went on all that time.

She gave us a tremendous amount of confidence, exposed us to some of the thrill of learning, and convinced us that we had a moral obligation to use the opportunities that were available to us. That confidence was important outside the classroom as well.

In my case I was also a determined athlete. I was lucky enough to play on some excellent teams, including the most successful high school basketball team in the history of the country. We won 55 straight games. That was something. As an athlete I had greater success in high school than I did in college, but I did manage to attend Notre Dame on an athletic scholarship. My parents could never have afforded to send me to Notre Dame, so for that I'll be eternally grateful.

I had been doing well in school prior to Sister Eleanor's extra help, but I wasn't passionate about it. Education was important in my family. Both my parents were high school educated. My father was a claim adjuster for the DC Transit Company. My mother was a sometime secretary. They sacrificed to send us to Catholic schools and to pay the tuition, but I didn't have any models in my family for going on to college. So I went from a family where my grandparents were grade school educated, and my parents were high school educated to a doctorate and the presidency of a major university. That was something too.

> " she convinced us that we had God-given intelligence, that we were capable of doing great things, and that a lot of opportunities would open up to us if we would only use our capacities to learn. "

I had a lot of great teachers and other people who were influential in my life, but Sister Eleanor was just extraordinary. She had us cultivate a more developed vocabulary. She got us interested in science projects. All the things we were studying in fourth, fifth, and sixth grades, whether it was history or geography or grammar, she supplemented. I always had been a strong reader, but with Sister Eleanor's guidance I became an enthusiastic reader. Her theory, which is now mine, is that it doesn't really matter what you're reading as long as you're reading, because if you enjoy it you'll keep passing on to more complicated and sophisticated material. You'll already have the passion and desire that makes for a real learner.

I've talked about Sister Eleanor a number of times when I've given presentations to educators, and I see a lot of heads nod, either because everybody thinks the movie *Mr. Holland's Opus*—where everybody you've ever taught comes back and creates a great symphony—could have been made about them or because they had teachers that they didn't have the wisdom to thank adequately when they received the benefits from them.

Ed 'monk' Malloy, csc

just play
WILLIE McGINEST
PROFESSIONAL FOOTBALL PLAYER

I've been lucky to play for some great coaches, starting with Don Norford, my high school football coach. I was into basketball too, but the basketball coach told me I couldn't play both and said I needed to concentrate on just basketball. Coach Norford said, "Look, I don't care what he says. Just play."

Don Norford really taught me how to play. He taught me how to be relentless on the field and how to never stop working hard. He was a track coach too, so he was involved in a lot of kids' lives. He believed that if you have talent you should use it to your highest ability—go at it 100 miles an hour. I thought I was pretty aggressive before I met him, but he helped me kick it to the next level.

In Long Beach, California, there were a lot of distractions. School came easy. I'd finish my work quickly and get bored and get into stuff. My parents fixed that by keeping me busy playing football and baseball and basketball since as far back as I can remember. I don't think I've had a summer off from playing sports since I was 7 or 8, even to this day.

Back then the park system used to give out free lunches and run all these great programs. I just kind of took to football. Coach Norford said I was a natural, and I guess I had a pretty good high school career because I was recruited by a lot of different schools. USC had just won the Rose Bowl that year, and Mark Carrier came out to talk to me. He was playing for the Chicago Bears at the time. He had been to USC and also came from my high school. It meant a lot to see someone from the same neighborhood doing well there. Plus it was good for my parents, who weren't used to traveling a lot. They could come see me play.

> " he believed that if you have talent you should use it to your highest ability— go at it 100 miles an hour. "

John Robinson at USC was the one who had me thinking I could play in the NFL. That had been my dream, but I never had any real idea if I could make it. My plan was to get my degree and get into some type of business, but I started thinking I'd give football a shot. Coach Robinson had been an NFL coach and he gave me the stepping stone I needed.

He knew what it took. He trained us like we were professionals, and I took to it pretty well. He started telling me that coaches and scouts were calling and asking about me. That really got me pumped up. Bill Belichick was coaching the Cleveland Browns at the time and they had the ninth pick. Bill Parcells was coaching the New England Patriots and they had the fourth pick. Both teams were interested in me. I spent countless hours talking to Bill Belichick. That's how they do it—the coaches come out and talk to the players they're thinking about drafting, talk to them about their program and their work ethic and see if there's a good fit. Coach Belichick told me if I was available there was a good chance that Cleveland would take me. I spent a lot of time with Coach Parcells too, and he told me there was a good chance New England would take me.

The way it turned out, Parcells took me first, with the fourth pick, so I went to New England. He had tremendous knowledge of the game. He taught us all these little tricks: how to cover guys, how to read formations, how to figure certain tendencies on players. We were just a bunch of talented, raw athletes. Bill Parcells prepared us. He's very demanding and expects a lot from his players. He taught me a lot at a young age. He really set me up for the rest of my career.

I ended up playing for Pete Carroll for a couple years, and of course he's now had all that success at USC. After that Coach Belichick came in and we've had a great run ever since. It's been a real blessing to have played under all these great coaches in all these great programs. Belichick and Parcells, Pete Carroll and John Robinson—it just doesn't get any better than that.

small town
JOHN MELLENCAMP
MUSICIAN

I grew up in a very small town in Indiana called Seymour, but it seemed to me like there were 10,000 kids. This was in the 1950s baby boom, and next door to us was a family with three kids. Next door to them was a family that had five kids, and there were five of us. There were kids everywhere, but there were no black kids in my neighborhood, no Hispanic kids, no diversity at all. Down at the Boys Club was about the only place you could find any diversity in town, and down there everybody was color-blind. It didn't matter what race you were. It only mattered if you could shoot pool or play ball.

I played a lot of ball as a kid. I played everything. I was a good athlete, but by the time I was in high school I was kicked out of everything. Back in junior high, I held all kinds of records—the 100-yard dash record, the touchdown record—but I was also into smoking and drinking and girls and guitars.

I went to football practice one day with a pack of cigarettes in my pocket, and just as I was getting dressed the cigarettes fell out right onto the floor, right in front of a coach. He took me outside the stadium, threw me against the fence, slapped me across the face, and said, "I don't care how great you think you are, Mellencamp. You're not gonna play football anymore." So that was that.

And as a kid, everybody I looked up to turned out to be a bad influence. Mentors? Well, I certainly learned from their example. My dad's older brother Joe was somebody I admired, but he was a macho womanizer. He was a rounder—a big athlete, good-looking, a smoker, a fast-car driver—and he was a role model for me. I've been trying to get rid of that crap for 50 years.

My grandpa's big advice to me was, "John, if you're gonna hit somebody, kill him." In other words, if you're going to do something, go all the way. That's the family I grew up in, and this Mellencamp gene always seems to get me in trouble.

So how did I get from there to here? Let me tell you something, I've never planned anything in my life, even to this day. Music just happened. My older brother got a guitar for Christmas one year, but after a while he didn't seem that interested in it so I started playing. I can barely play any better today than I did then, but I went to New York City thinking I was going to be an artist. I was trying to get the dough together to go to the Art Students League, and some guy came up to me and asked if I wanted to make records. That's basically how it happened. I had two hooks in the water and music came in first, so I started making records.

> " the guys I played with in bands were
> just a bunch of 12-year-olds messing around …
> just hanging on with one, two, three, four.
> Really, it was all we could do to keep time. "

I was very fortunate, I guess, when it came to music. My dad was only 19 when I was born and he used to have bongo parties in the '50s. He would get these records and that big fat hi-fi they used to have, and he and his friends would bongo to these great records and I'd listen in. I was listening to Woody Guthrie, Odetta, and the New Christy Minstrels as a young child, before I ever heard of the Beatles. First song I ever learned to play was a Woody Guthrie song called "Car Car." The guys I played with in bands were just a bunch of 12-year-olds messing around. We didn't know what was cool. We didn't know what was good. We were just hanging on with one, two, three, four. Really, it was all we could do to keep time. We could play "Walk, Don't Run," "Hang on, Sloopy," and those kinds of songs, and like I said, I'm still playing the same three chords today.

I'll say this, though, about inspiration. I once had a really famous songwriter come up to me. He was a friend of mine, and he said, "John, I'm blocked." He couldn't write a damn thing. I looked at him and said, "Look out your window. There's your influence. Inspiration is everywhere."

roll or fold
DARYL "CHILL" MITCHELL
ACTOR

November 7, 2001, I'm vacationing with my family on Warsaw Island, near Beaufort, South Carolina. My nephew asks me if I want to check out his Kawasaki Ninja 900 motorcycle. I say, "Give me the keys."

I wasn't going all that fast when I crashed. But I broke my wrist, punctured my lung, bruised my kidneys, and damaged my spinal cord so badly it left me paralyzed from the waist down. There was no other vehicle involved. No drugs. No alcohol. Just a bad curve, some bad luck, and some gravel, and I ended up in a ditch with the bike on top of me.

My story starts in that ditch. Last thing I remember, I was getting on the bike and thinking, "Aw, my new boots are gonna get all dusty." When I woke up three days later, the doctor told me there was a strong possibility I'd never walk again. You hear something like that and right away your mind starts racing. You start thinking, "What do I do now?" And what I came up with was to just keep going at it, hard—to keep doing for myself whatever I could do. "Roll or fold" became my motto—right there in that hospital room, the first day I came to.

I couldn't put it out that I was in trouble. Check that: I *could* have, but I wouldn't. It wasn't my style to ask for help, and for some reason, in those first months after the accident, I was still fussing about my style. I had to keep up appearances. I had my wife and my kids to worry about and the rest of my big family, and I couldn't let a thing like this shake me from that role. I was the one who had it going on, right? I was the one with the career and the money and the energy to make all these good things happen. I was the guy everyone else in my family turned to for help, and I had myself thinking it would take a whole lot more than a damn motorcycle accident to change who I was or what I was all about.

It was all about attitude, early on. I had to stay positive. I kept telling myself this rehabilitation business, this learning how to get by in my chair, this taking care of myself and going out on auditions and looking for work—it'd all be a piece of cake. And so I put it out that I was doing OK. I'm rolling, I told everyone. Don't worry about me. I've *still* got it going on.

After a while, thanks to Christopher Reeve, it caught up with me that it wasn't just about me. And to be honest, it kinda caught me by surprise. But that came a bit later. At first, as soon as I could, I started hauling ass to my auditions: It didn't matter what I was reading for. If there was an open part, I meant to fill it. New York, Los Angeles. It didn't matter where it was either. I was back at it, hard. First role I auditioned for from my chair was for a part on *The Wire*, for HBO, and it felt great to be back at it again. I didn't get the gig, but that wasn't the point. I was back in the game—and I was in it to win it. To matter. To get the rest of my life back.

Eventually I won myself this part on *Ed*. The show was shot in the New York area and I'd grown up on Long Island, so that was cool. It was a whole lot better to be living and working in earshot of friends and family. I threw myself into the work like nothing else mattered. My world had been rocked, but at least I was working. I had a paycheck and a place to put my focus. I was pulling my own weight—literally.

It was around this time that I got to know Christopher Reeve. He reached out. He heard about what happened and he wanted to let me know he was there for me. The first time we got together after my accident, it was at his birthday gala at the Marriott hotel in New York. It was a big event for his foundation, but he found some time for me. He made it a special point.

We went into this little room and shut the door and talked. I hadn't really seen anybody that first year. I just went to work and did my thing, but it was reassuring to be around all these people in wheelchairs in Chris' organization letting me know I was not alone. Chris really emphasized that. Then he asked me if I would represent the Christopher Reeve Foundation as a minority spokesperson. I was honored. It's like he gave me a new pair of shoes to walk with by asking me to do something like that. I'd been doing all this stuff for myself, but Chris gave me an opportunity to spread a powerful message.

> " Chris said just be, and let the world see that you're still the same person. "

That's how our friendship started. We'd meet at events and talk—really talk. He'd ask me how I was doing, what I was doing, how I was taking care of myself. And I'd ask him. We'd talk honestly. For real.

Chris made the best of it. You have to go forward, man. He talked about how we struggle so much for our friends and our family. Because as hard as it is for you to accept that you might never walk again, it's even harder for them. When they come at you looking all sorry, you're like, "Man, you're still on *that*?" Some people still treat it like it happened last week. To that he'd just say, "Daryl, you've got to let it be." Because if you couldn't accept that reaction, you wouldn't be able to be around anybody. It'd be too hard. You don't want people acting and feeling that way and looking at you funny. Chris said just be, and let the world see that you're still the same person.

Chris also told me that if being in a wheelchair was any indication of what it's like to face prejudice and bias and what it is to be a black person, then black people should have had wheelchairs a long time ago. And I thought, "Wow, that's deep." And it's dead-on.

I'm black all over again with this thing. I've gone from being the token black guy on the set to being the token guy in the wheelchair. I look at how people treat me now because I'm in the chair, and it really is like I'm black again. It went away for a while, because when you're successful folks become a little color-blind. But now it's back, although this time people are making the effort to understand what it's like for me and for others like me, because

I insist they make the effort. They catch me making the effort to live a full life, just like they caught Chris making the effort, and they can't help but fall in line.

Chris knew that you've just got to keep going. That was his thing: Keep moving. Roll or fold. Watching him maneuver in that wheelchair, watching him maintain and keep order in his organization and in his household, watching him with his son—it made me realize I can still maintain my family. I can still be a man. Chris was still the head of his household. When he said something, everybody moved.

I had been struggling with that in my own mind. How am I going to play with my kids? How am I going to discipline them? How am I going to be with my wife? Chris inspired me just by being. It wasn't what he said but what he did.

I have a picture of me and Chris on the beach at Puerto Vallarta. We were there for a fundraiser and I went to take a run on a Jet Ski. Chris couldn't believe that I'd be out there on the water like that—he said he had to come down and see that for himself. He cancelled a meeting so he could come down to the beach and check me out. The day before, when I'd first come down to the beach to practice, I couldn't get down to the shore. It was all sand. I couldn't get my chair down there. This time someone at the resort had put down some plywood so I could get down.

So could Chris. And he said, "Daryl, you see how things happen? You go and pave the way for other people."

He made me see that, yeah, we pave the way for other people. That's why you've got to keep pushing.

the complete person
JOE MORGAN
RETIRED PROFESSIONAL BASEBALL
PLAYER, ESPN COMMENTATOR

My dad was my hero. My mom and dad were both my heroes, actually, but I want to talk about my dad. His name was Leonard. That's my middle name. My first name is Joe, because of my grandfather whose name was Joe—not Joseph but Joe—and I carry my dad's name as well.

I was born in a town called Bonham, Texas, right outside Dallas, but he moved us to California when I was 6 or 7 years old. He was a supervisor for the transit company, then a shop steward for the Pacific Tire and Rubber Company. We ended up living in Oakland, and he was always so warm and loving but at the same time stern when he needed to be. It wasn't tough love. It was the love of a father doing what he had to do. He was there for each and every one of his children. There were six of us, three boys and three girls, and I was the oldest.

My dad loved baseball and he always pointed me in that direction. I was the bat boy for his team when he was playing, back when I was a little, tiny kid, before we moved to California. In those days African-Americans couldn't get to the minor leagues, let alone the big leagues, and he and my uncles and a lot of people played semipro baseball. They traveled around and played in all these different cities, and I used to go along as the bat boy.

I couldn't really tell you what kind of ballplayer he was, because I was just a kid and he was my dad and in my eyes he was Willie Mays. He was an outfielder, and I thought he was the greatest. But he wasn't one to talk about himself. I have a photo of him as a high school football coach, and I don't know anything about that. He never talked about that, but there he is in the picture.

Baseball was always a big thing between us. I used to use it as an excuse to get myself out of trouble. One time I was supposed to come home after school, but I was late and I said I was still at practice even though it was past dark. I used that because I knew he loved baseball, and anything I did in baseball he supported.

But he saw right through it. I said that we were practicing and I'd stayed late. It was a typical young person's excuse, one of those lines that if you think about it you know it's not going to work. He told me not to lie to him, told me to tell him the truth, told me that if I made a mistake to take the consequences and move on. That was a very good lesson for me.

To give you an insight into who my dad was, when they retired my number in Cincinnati, my banker came with me as one of my guests. She said to my dad at one point during the ceremony, "You must be very proud of your son." And my dad's answer was, "I'm proud of all my children." That's the kind of person he was. Even though I was a Hall of Famer and this and that, his other kids were just as important.

He gave me a lot of advice when it came to baseball. We lived in East Oakland for a few years, and the Oakland Oaks baseball team was about five blocks from our house. Every night we'd eat dinner at home with the family, and he and my oldest sister, Linda, and I would walk down to the stadium. The three of us would go every night they were in town.

We'd sit in the stands and my dad would point out things. He'd say, "Well, that guy can hit but he doesn't field," or, "That guy can field but he doesn't hit." He said, "I want you to be a complete player."

And that was how I got it in my head to be a complete player rather than the best player. And the highlight of that for me was in the 1976 *Sports Illustrated* preseason baseball issue. There was a picture of me that said, "Joe Morgan, Baseball's Most Complete Player." That meant more to me, for him, for my dad, than it did for me, because he'd made it my goal—not to be the best player but to be the most complete player.

" I'm proud of all my children. "

Don't lie, take the consequences, do the best you can, and move on. That was what I learned from my dad, in baseball and in life. My mom too. I've always said that the things that happen in sports usually parallel your life. As a player the way you approach sports and what you put into it is what you get out of it. If you're willing to work extra hard as a player, you're going to get better. If you're willing to work extra hard as a person, you will get better. Those are the parallels that I drew from being around my dad, from him telling me that it wasn't just baseball that was important, it wasn't just sports, it was everything. Education. Getting good grades. Treating people right. Being a complete person.

I can talk all day about my dad, but my mom was just as important. She was the rock at home. We were one of the first African-American families to move into a neighborhood in Oakland. I came home one day and I was really mad. This kid down the street had done something to me, and my mother could see that I was angry. She said, "What happened?"

I said, "Well, that white kid down the street did something to me."

She said, "What did you just say?"

I repeated myself. I said: "That white kid down the street did something to me."

She said, "Would it have made you mad if a black kid did the same thing?"

I said, "Yeah."

She said, "Well then, why did you say it was a white kid? We don't talk like that around here. People are just people. If we expect them to treat us that way, then we have to treat them the same way."

I was about 8 years old, and I still remember that. I guess the message took. My parents taught me a lot about life and dealing with people and who people really are. That was the thing they wanted us to know. Find out who a person is before you make a decision on what you think of him. That's been with me throughout my life. I've always thought I could read people really well because I started reading people at an early age. I watched how they treated each other and I watched how I treated them.

Jackie Robinson and Nellie Fox were my idols growing up, but my parents were my role models and my dad was my hero. I hear a lot of people talk about their dads being their best friends. In fact just the other day I heard Tiger Woods in an interview talking about his dad being his best friend. Well, my dad wasn't my best friend. He was my dad. My dad taught me responsibility and he taught me how to be a man. My friends are my friends, and my dad was my dad. I understand that a lot of people think that way about their father, but I never did. He was my dad. He had a responsibility to me and I had one to him, and I don't always find that with friendships. I always had the belief that he was above my friends. And he was.

Timothy Greenfield-Sanders

the perfect seam
TONI MORRISON
NOVELIST

When I was 12 or 13 years old, I had an encounter with my father that made an enormous impression on me. I was working after school as a cleaner in a woman's house and not doing a very good job. I didn't know how. I scrubbed floors on my knees, and she had a mop. I had never seen a vacuum cleaner. The money was small, but it was everything, and at some point I complained to my mother about the woman who had hired me. My mother said I should quit, but obviously I wanted those few coins so I didn't. And yet when I spoke to my father he just looked at me and said, "Listen, you don't live there, you live here."

Now a lot of times people say simple things and it's not so much what they say as what you hear. I heard, "Do your work well, not for who hires you but for yourself." I heard, "You make the job, it doesn't make you." I heard, "You are not the work, you are not the job, you are the person." My father's words affected me all my life, because I was always interested in doing first-rate work, and I was always interested in knowing that I could not be defined by the work I did. I didn't have to say, "I'm a teacher, I'm an editor, I'm a housecleaner, I'm a waitress." Those were occupations, but there was a person back there, and I think it was the person who was enabled, ultimately, to begin to write books much later in life.

" you don't live there, you live here. "

My father was a welder on a shipyard during World War II, and I remember him coming home one day and telling me that he had welded a perfect seam. And he seemed so pleased. It was so flawless, he said, he had welded his initials in it. And I said, "Well, nobody's going to see it." And he said, "Yes, but I know it's there." He always took pride in his work, everything from the way you opened a box to how you washed the dishes. It was all very elegant, and I heard his comment and thought it was very much like the way he approached his own work.

I don't think I appreciated it at the time, but I also had the great privilege of having the money I earned mean something. In the 1930s and '40s, children were needed. Not just loved, but *needed* because they could earn money or help take care of other children. Nobody needs children now. Of course they love them and they care for them and they dote on them, but it's not that desperate need that families had during the Depression. When I got $2, half of it was translated into something like milk or something I could see, and the adults were pleased with my contribution. The other half? I wanted to play with it. Maybe a dollar could get me into 16 movies. That's how I measured it.

And so I went back to work that next day and my employer was no longer a villain. I was able to look at her as someone who was critical of my chores, but not hostile to me personally. Because my personhood was not involved. Because I didn't *live* there. I ended up working for this woman another year and a half, and when I did something wrong and she corrected me, I just got better at it. I learned the right way to clean a four-burner gas stove. The first time I cleaned it, I didn't even go near the oven, but now I knew how.

awake and sing
LEONARD NIMOY
ACTOR

I grew up in a tenement district in Boston, and I spent a lot of time at the
Elizabeth Peabody Playhouse in my neighborhood. It was founded in honor
of the lady who started the kindergarten program in the United States,
Elizabeth Peabody, and in those days it used to be known as a settlement
house. Its mission was to help immigrants learn how to integrate into the
American democratic society and how to function within that society in
various ways. It offered classes on how to keep a kitchen sterile, how to
heat your home properly, how to take care of your hair and bodily needs.
And of course this was an immigrant neighborhood—Italians, Irish, Jews,
and so forth.

The place had a gym and a sports program and a science lab where young
people could go and do experiments. A lot of people, including my brother,

spent a lot of time there and eventually went to the New York World's Fair in 1939 as presenters from this settlement house.

But most important to me was a 375-seat legitimate theater in the building. It originally had been used for plays presented for and by various minorities in the neighborhood. Eventually it came into rather popular use doing Gilbert & Sullivan operettas and that sort of thing. One afternoon when I was about 8 years old I was asked if I could sing a song for someone at the playhouse where I was hanging around, and I did. The next thing I knew I was cast as Hansel in a production of *Hansel and Gretel*. It was my first time on the stage. I continued to do children's theater at this place and it became a terribly important part of my life.

When I was 17, a young guy named Boris Sagal was directing plays at the playhouse—adult plays—and I went to audition for him. He was a law student at Harvard who had been given a guest room to live in at the playhouse. In return for this guest room, he was directing plays there. The playhouse was across the river from Harvard, so he could get over to school quickly on the subway for 10 cents and it was a good deal all around. He cast me in a Clifford Odets play called *Awake and Sing*, and it had a profound effect on me. Boris Sagal's direction had a profound effect on me as well.

That *Awake and Sing* production was a major, major event for me. It was the first time that I was playing in an adult piece of theater for an adult audience, and I was portraying the juvenile in a family much like my own. I related totally to this character. It was about a Jewish family in the Bronx. Mine happened to be a Jewish family in Boston. It was three generations living in an apartment, same as me. It was an ensemble piece, and I was playing this kid who was struggling with the same issues I was struggling with: How do you discover who you are? How do you figure out how to get a decent job? How do you find the right girl? And how do you work your way through the dynamics of these family issues and dramas and tensions, which were very much like my own?

Ironically the grandfather who lived in this apartment with this family was a barber, and my father was also a barber, so there were all these points of identification for me. My grandfather was a leather-cutter for a luggage factory and my grandmother stayed at home. She never learned to speak English. I had to learn to speak Yiddish in order to communicate with her, and there were just so many similarities between the life of the character I was playing and my own life.

It was a profound experience to realize that there was theater that could be done that reflected the human condition. I decided that if I could be involved in this kind of theater it would be a blessing to me. I didn't realize the profundity of it at the time, but I knew that something terribly important was sitting there for me, a wonderful touchpoint, and I decided to grab it. It was a crucial turning point, and I decided to become a professional actor. I began to look for parts.

Meanwhile, I was acting under the direction of another young guy who would go on to become a successful television and film director, Elliot Silverstein. Elliot directed me in a play called *John Loves Mary*, which was a rather popular commercial play of the period. He was a student at Boston College in the drama department at the time, so he invited a Jesuit priest from the school to come down to see the play. His name was John Bonn. This was in the spring of 1949, and after the play John Bonn came to the dressing room and was shaking hands all around. When he came to me he said, "What are you doing this summer?" I said, "I don't have any plans." And he said, "Well, you do now." And he offered me a half-scholarship to a summer theater program at Boston College.

> " keep in mind, there's always
> room for one more good one. "

Now as I said, my dad was a barber. My folks were not interested in encouraging me to spend money on an acting career. The last thing in the world they wanted was for me to become an actor. But this was an eight-week summer program, and this priest had offered a half-scholarship.

It was an exciting opportunity, so I went to another settlement house where I was active—a place called the West End House—and reached out to the director there, a man named Jack Burns. I didn't know him well—there were hundreds of kids attached to this place—but I told him about the offer of the half-scholarship and he said, "You have the rest of the money."

He gave me the other half of the money necessary to go to Boston College that summer. It wasn't the money that was important; it was the validation. Sure, it was wonderful to have someone say, "Don't worry about the money."

But the validation was terribly important to me at the time, especially because there was no endorsement at home.

I still needed a job, so I found work that summer selling vacuum cleaners. I saved the money necessary to pay for my first year's tuition at the Pasadena Playhouse in California. I bought myself a $100 train ticket, sat in a coach seat for three days and three nights across the country, and stepped off the train and started studying theater. That was the beginning of my career, in a sense. It wasn't one moment or one individual who sent me on my way, but it was all these things and all these people together.

There was, however, one incredible piece of advice that came to me fairly early on in Los Angeles. It was 1956, and I was just out of the Army. I had joined the service in December 1953, and during that time I'd gotten married and had my first child. When I came out in December 1955, I'd left behind only a little bit of a career. There were no threads to pick up except an agent I'd been working with. So I started driving a taxi cab in Los Angeles to make ends meet.

One day I got a call to go to a Bel-Air hotel to pick up a Mr. Kennedy. That fare turned out to be Senator Jack Kennedy, who needed a ride to the Beverly Hilton where he was speaking for Adlai Stevenson that night. This was before Senator Kennedy had any national prominence. It was later that year, at the Democratic Convention, that he was almost nominated for the vice presidency and made a speech that earned him some national attention. But of course, being from Boston I recognized him.

I introduced myself, and he was very interested to hear from someone from Massachusetts, and he asked me what I was doing in Los Angeles. I explained that I was a hopeful actor, and we chatted a bit about acting and politics. At one point he said, "Your business is the same as mine. There's a lot of competition." And we laughed about that, and then he said, "But keep in mind, there's always room for one more good one."

And I took those words very much to heart.

sweepin' the clouds away

HOLLY ROBINSON PEETE
ACTRESS

My dad was a writer for television shows in Philadelphia. When I was little he got a job as a producer for *Sesame Street* and ended up playing one of the main characters. He was Matt Robinson and he played Gordon. Anyone who grew up with a television set at that time knew who he was. He was an integral part of the first four years of *Sesame Street*. The frustrating thing for me was that he didn't want me to be on the set, yet at the same time all these kids from Philly were being bused to New York to be on the show. They were looking for a lot of extras. Everybody we knew was calling my dad and he was helping them get their kids on the show and I was stuck at home.

Finally—I must have been 6 or 7 years old—I went up to him and said, "Dad, this is ridiculous. My friends are going on the show and you won't let me go on. It's not fair."

He thought it was unhealthy for me to be around that kind of show business environment. It wasn't what he wanted for me, so he kept me away. But I kept at it, and he finally let me come to New York a couple times to be on the set. I got to meet Big Bird and Oscar and all that great stuff. But that just made it worse. He even let me be on the show, instead of just behind the scenes, but I blew my one line. I was supposed to walk down the street and say, "Hi, Gordon!" But I kept messing up and saying "Hi, Dad" instead. So they cut my line. I did make one appearance on the show, though, walking down the street holding Big Bird's hand. That was my television debut.

My dad wasn't emotionally available to me as a kid. I loved him and I loved hanging out with him, but he wasn't the most affectionate man in the world. I was jealous of the little girl who played his daughter on the show. I'd see Gordon on television, being all affectionate with his pseudo family, and I couldn't understand it. It didn't match how he was at home with me.

I don't think he ever told me he loved me when I was a little girl. It just wasn't in his vocabulary. I was constantly trying to please him, trying to get him to tell me he loved me. I don't set this out as a criticism; that's just how he was.

Later when I was in college, I stumbled across a letter written by a cousin that mapped out my dad's childhood. My dad's older sister died when she was about 7 years old. She had scarlet fever and she died because they took her to the white hospital in Philadelphia and they wouldn't treat her. They could have saved her, but they didn't because of the color of her skin.

“ we cried together, and from that moment on we were able to have a great father-daughter relationship. ”

And as a result of that tragedy, my father's father—an amazing writer in his own right—just kind of shut down. He used to write for the Negro newspapers. He couldn't get into the mainstream press because of the times, but he was a brilliant man. When his daughter died, he literally went into the living room, pulled the blinds, and stayed there for the rest of his life. He was completely unavailable to his two sons after that.

My grandmother reacted in the opposite way. She became this over-the-top, mothering-type person. "Don't ride your bike. Be careful." Really overprotective, almost smothering. So my dad spent most of his childhood with a father who was shut out and a mother who was overprotective almost to the point of craziness. It must have been a weird, tense combination. Not getting enough love from one parent and too much from the other. When he became a father, he had a hard time expressing his love. I think it was the residue of how he grew up.

I didn't know any of this as a kid. I had no idea why he was so distant, so unreachable. He wasn't like the other fathers I saw on television. Heck, he wasn't like *he* was on television. I knew he loved me, but I wanted him to be available to me, to open up. When I finally came across that letter I went up to him and said, "Why didn't you tell me?" And he said, "Well, it's just such an ugly memory." And then he cried. We cried together, and from that moment on we were able to have a really great father-daughter relationship and he was able to tell me he loved me at every turn. After going 20 years without ever saying those words, he really made up for lost time.

Unfortunately my father was diagnosed with Parkinson's disease when he was just 43 years old. He used to think it was some perverse karma, living his life this way, unable to tell his own kids that he loved them, and then when he finally learned how to open up he was diagnosed with Parkinson's. He lived another 20 years, but the disease slowly ate at him. It's great we were able to get all that other stuff out of the way before his illness. That would have just been the worst, if he'd have died before we had a chance to figure each other out. But we found a way to talk about it and to set it right. We had an incredible second chance.

What it taught me was forgiveness. It taught me that when people present themselves in a certain way, there's probably some back story or issue or reason for the way they are. It's not you. It's them. And a lot of times, it's about something that's completely out of their control. So it was really such a wonderful life lesson for me and it opened me up to this great relationship. I went from thinking it was my fault that my father was so cold and distant to knowing it wasn't anything I had done. That was the most freeing realization. It was a blessing, really. That's the best way to put it.

Holly Robinson Peete

fortunate son
BILL PEROCCHI
CHIEF EXECUTIVE OFFICER,
PEBBLE BEACH RESORTS

Lawrence, Massachusetts, is a tough city. It's the poorest city in New England, the 12th poorest city in the United States. The high school dropout rate sits near 60 percent, so it's not the easiest place to raise children, although there are a lot of good things going on now, a lot of positive developments helping the city to recover.

I grew up in the Lawrence Stadium projects, and we had a hard time of it. My mother passed away when I was 9 and my father had a drinking problem, so it was a real difficult environment.

I had two older siblings and they were out of the house pretty quickly. That left me with my dad and a younger brother. I started going to the Lawrence Boys & Girls Club when I was about 9 years old—fourth or fifth grade, somewhere in there. We were in South Lawrence and the club was in North Lawrence and there used to be a bus that would take us.

The club became a second home to me—a place to go where people really cared about you. My younger brother didn't take to it. I don't really know why. I guess it wasn't for him, but it was certainly for me. I was very athletic, very involved in sports and in those days the club's focus was much more on sports, especially basketball. We used to run out some pretty competitive teams. Today it focuses more on the whole individual: schoolwork, getting a hot meal, those types of things.

Our basketball coach was Steve Kelly. He was a kid back then, probably in his early 20s, and he's someone I looked up to from the beginning. He was just a real positive influence, and a great coach and leader. The thing I remember about Steve is how we'd never had a chance to go into Boston to see the Celtics play, and he'd get six or seven of us crammed into his car and he'd take us in to see a Celtics game, and that was the biggest thing in the world to us. He knew what it meant too. He really encouraged me to work hard, to study, to make something of myself. He knew what was going on at home, but I think he saw I had some potential. My athletic abilities were just average, even though I just loved sports. We could all see it wasn't going to be my ticket out of the projects. But I think he saw I was a good kid, an intelligent kid, a goal-oriented kid. I asked a lot of questions.

" he let me know that drinking like that wasn't what I should be doing, and at that point the respect I had for him was so great, it had a tremendous impact. "

Steve was a savior for me. The other savior was Brooks, where I ended up going to high school. I went to Lawrence High School my freshman year, but I ended up getting suspended from the basketball team for two weeks for drinking. Steve Kelly heard about it and made a special point to get me straightened out. I was afraid I'd let him down and didn't really want to talk to him about it. They kept it quiet, so my father never found out. The club didn't tell him. The school didn't tell him. What I ended up doing after that, with Steve's encouragement, was applying to this private school, Brooks, in Andover, Massachusetts. My uncle was a football coach there, and he encouraged me as well. I was able to get in with virtually 100 percent financial aid, which was important because we couldn't have afforded it.

We didn't have a lot of money. My father was disabled. He had worked for the city of Lawrence, but there was a major hurricane in the area before I was born, and he was severely hurt—hit by a tree. He ended up with a plate in his head and a severe limp. He didn't work after that. My mother was in a car accident when I was about 9, and she died like a year later, so it was just awful. If I hadn't had the Boys & Girls Club and later on the good people at Brooks, I don't know what would have happened to me.

I could have gone another way. My siblings all had it tough. We didn't always make the best choices. I was the lucky one, really. I made it out OK. One of my brothers ended up spending time in jail. All of them struggled at one time or another, in one way or another. Getting caught drinking was a turning point for me. Steve Kelly took me aside and he let me know he was disappointed, and that he thought I was better than that. He let me know that drinking like that wasn't what I should be doing, and at that point the respect I had for him was so great, it had a tremendous impact. There was something about him. You just don't want to disappoint Steve Kelly.

He's gone on to have that same tremendous impact on hundreds and hundreds of kids. It's a remarkable club, the Lawrence Boys & Girls Club, in large part due to Steve. They're constructing a building named in Steve's honor, and that says a lot. He's a very, very humble guy. He really downplays his role, but he's the real reason kids come out of that club and do well. They've had a couple "Youth of the Year" winners in the past few years, which is remarkable for a small club in a difficult city.

In fact there's one young man, Socrates de la Cruz, who's now working in Lawrence as a criminal defense attorney, who also singles out Steve as a very positive influence in his life. Steve's impact doesn't end with me. It didn't start with me either. And I certainly don't want to give the impression that it was just that one talk with Steve after I got busted for drinking that set me right immediately. But it got me headed down the right road. That's all you can ask. The road is not going to get you where you're going right away, but it gets you pointed in the right direction.

Bill Perocchi

one hundred percent
MATTHEW F. POTTINGER
2ND LIEUTENANT, U.S. MARINE CORPS

A few months ago, at the ripe old age of 32, I decided to leave Beijing, China, where I worked as a reporter for the *Wall Street Journal,* and try to become an officer in the U.S. Marine Corps. Like most Americans, I grew up in the States, but after learning to speak Chinese in school and working on a college newspaper, I headed toward journalism and a career abroad.

When you live in a foreign country—especially an undemocratic country—you learn things about your own country you can't see when you're home. Despite the things we need to do to improve ourselves, you come to realize that the U.S. holds the greatest hope for us and many people in the world. It felt as if it was time for me to get more directly involved. Although there are many ways to do that, my way was to join the Marines.

The problem was I was 32 years old and completely out of shape. When I visited an officer-selection officer for the Marines, the first thing he asked wasn't about my views of the world, my education, or my experience, but "How's your endurance?" I thought: "Well, I can sit at my desk for 12 hours straight—14 if I have a bag of Reese's." Obviously I wasn't ready for prime time in the Marines, and I had big doubts that I ever would be.

A few months later, while reporting for the *Wall Street Journal* on the horrible Asian tsunami of December 2004, I found myself in Lumpini Park, in downtown Bangkok, with a little free time on my hands. I was still impressed by seeing the Marines save so many lives in the tsunami zone, so I decided to work out and see what kind of shape I really was in. I started running around the park only to be beaten by a monitor lizard. When I came panting up to an abandoned jungle gym, I couldn't do more than half a pull-up. I was pathetic. Why I didn't give up right then and there I'll never know. But that's when a helping hand came my way.

Shortly after returning to Beijing from Thailand, I met a 29-year-old captain in the Marine Corps named Cedric Lee who was on a fellowship studying for a master's degree in China. After jogging with him for a few weeks, I finally got up the nerve to tell him I was thinking of trying to become a Marine officer myself. To my surprise, instead of laughing me off, he offered to help. Before long he was running with me several days a week and pushing me hard.

> " get the pain out of your system now.
> Cut a corner and you'll pay for it later. "

Running in Beijing in the winter isn't an easy thing to do. Aside from the bitter cold, the air pollution, and the darkness, there's no culture of running the way there is in the United States. Cars run you off the street onto the sidewalk where a thousand bicyclists are equally happy to run you down. You have to work at finding a way to work out.

Captain Lee didn't need somebody like me to overload his busy schedule, and yet he never failed to help. More than once I would have been happy to stay in bed at 5:30 in the morning, but he'd call me up and tell me to get moving. "One hundred percent" is all he'd say before hanging up, and I'd roll out of bed.

"One hundred percent" was his motto, and before long I began to understand what it meant. He'd do pull-ups first, then when it was my turn, he'd shout into my ear that I could do them too. Somehow his confidence found its way into my muscle and I started improving. He led the two of us in wind sprints, and just as we were recovering, he'd make us do another, then another, until I couldn't move. What made him effective was that he always led by example. When I wanted to cut a lap because of the rain, heat, or coal dust, he'd do the lap himself and say, "Get the pain out of your system now. Cut a corner and you'll pay for it later." Some of his advice seems obvious, but when you're puking your guts out you don't want to hear it.

After a few months of working out, I started getting into shape and learning things I needed to know about getting through Officer Candidate School. Captain Lee said the training was at its worst when you had to maintain your intensity. When a drill instructor was in your face yelling that you were a disgrace to the Marines, that's when you had to get motivated. When an instructor said you didn't have what it took to lead a goat on a leash, that's when you had to maintain your bearing. When you had to pick a fellow officer candidate off the ground, put him over your shoulder, and sprint a hundred yards, that's when you had to think: "One hundred percent."

One day when I was crawling on my back across a half-frozen swamp with only my nose and weapon above the surface, I thought about the Great Wall and Captain Lee's phrase: "One hundred percent."

The Great Wall had special meaning for me because of something that happened there one July. The captain and I took a 12-mile hike on the Great Wall on a day that turned out to be the hottest of the year. I was wearing a heavy backpack, boots, and the captain's flak jacket. We'd come to stone steps that were as vertical as a ladder, so you had to get on your hands and knees to climb. We finished the hike after several hours, but by then I was so exhausted and overhydrated from drinking too much water that I developed a condition called hyponatremia. When I got out of the hospital the next day, Captain Lee said, "If you could survive that, Pottinger, I think you've got a shot at OCS."

The idea of pushing yourself beyond what you think you can do was drilled into me in those training sessions, but Captain Lee also taught me things about leadership and survival in general. When you're under stress, total commitment is a way of thinking in the Marines, he said. Without that mindset, you're going to have a hard time making it.

When I started Officer Candidate School at Quantico, Virginia, the real fun began. We lived on four hours of sleep a night, which I wasn't sure I could handle because I like my sleep, and the training was unusually intense and occasionally extreme. But that's when Captain Lee's coaching paid off. Despite my age I managed to reach a level of physical and mental toughness I wouldn't have had without his help. Most of my sergeant instructors were younger than I was, and most of them seemed skeptical that a guy my age could make it. More than once, so was I.

My company at OCS started with 307 candidates and ended with 187. Those who dropped out did so for a variety of reasons—illness, injury, fear, or an inability to "take it." But most of them dropped because they were physically and mentally unprepared. When I graduated from OCS and received my commission, I wrote Captain Lee and thanked him for his help. He said I would have made it regardless, but I disagree. His training and inspiration were the tools I needed at every make-or-break fork in the road. His attitude kicked in and his confidence became my own.

it takes a tribe
GEN. COLIN L. POWELL, USA (RET)
FORMER CHAIRMAN OF THE JOINT CHIEFS OF STAFF, FORMER U.S. SECRETARY OF STATE

So many people intersected in my life as a child, they created almost a tribal framework that kept me in play. I had an extended network of aunts, uncles, and cousins, and we all lived in the same neighborhood. Eventually we started to break up and move on to other boroughs of New York, but when I was a kid I had an aunt in almost every other house on every block from my school to my home. You can talk about the Internet all you want, but it is nothing compared with the speed of the Auntnet in the South Bronx. All these aunts were hanging out the windows, looking down on the street, watching out for us kids.

We lived in Hunts Point, in a neighborhood called Banana Kelly, because one of the Kelly Street blocks was curved in such a way that it looked like a banana. We lived in 952. My Aunt Laurice lived in 935 and my Aunt Evadne lived in 936, and another set of aunts lived in 920, I think. Everybody was considered an aunt, whether they were a real aunt or not. You couldn't get into trouble without getting caught by this network of aunts and uncles and cousins, and when you were caught, the speed of the Auntnet brought it to your parents for retribution before you even made it home.

That's unless they didn't want to wait, in which case they would punish you before your parents came home. They essentially had an attitude that said, "We came to this country with nothing. We're working hard. We didn't come to this country for our children to get lost, to be allowed to fail, to be allowed to drop out of school, or be allowed to shame the family. That's not what we're about, and by God, this family and this tribe doesn't work any other way."

It worked. There isn't a failure among the cousins. Very few divorces. Nobody went to jail. Nobody was a drug addict. Nobody failed to become *something*. I was one of the more troubling cousins because I didn't want to be an engineer or a lawyer or a doctor. I didn't seem to have any particular skills or interests that the family could encourage me in, but fortunately I found the Army through ROTC and a new set of mentors, a new set of possibilities, entered into my life.

There's an old African proverb—the one Hillary Rodham Clinton used for her book—that says, "It takes a village to raise a child." My experience has been an extension of that. I say it takes a tribe to raise a child. You have to have people who are interacting with each other to raise a child, people who are connected to that child.

A child is born knowing very little and has to wait for adults to pass on the experience of the last hundred generations—just like a lion mother does to her cubs or a cat for her kittens. If you don't have this tribe or this pack or this pride to pass on accumulated wisdom and experience, where does the child get it? You have to get it from somewhere. If you don't get it from family and tribe, you're going to get it from the street, and that usually means from the worst influences on the street.

The mentors in my life early on were all these assorted people, and on top of that there was my church. The Episcopal church with its high Anglican traditions was part of the imprinting tribal process as well, to pass on the faith of my father and my mother and the faith of the Church of England. I give enormous credit to the public school system of New York City. From all these influences I took in the message that said, "We're going to keep you in play. You are not going to be allowed to do anything but succeed. It's not even a choice for you to make. This is none of your business. This is our business. You're going to make something of yourself."

It goes beyond even family and church and school. A wonderful Jewish gentleman by the name of Jay Sickser lived in our neighborhood and owned a children's furniture store three blocks from my house on the way to the post office. One day when I was about 14 years old I was walking by his store and Mr. Sickser called out to me in his thick Russian accent and said, "Kid, you want to make a few bucks?" I said, "Sure."

He asked me to come into his store and help unload a truck, and I spent the whole afternoon unloading baby furniture and cribs and toys and whatnot, putting them in the warehouse that was behind the store. I did it to the best of my ability, and I worked hard, and he gave me a few dollars and said, "You're a good worker. Do you want to do some more tomorrow?"

That began a relationship that lasted seven years, on and off all the way through college. Summers and Christmastime, when it was the busy season, I was there all the time. I learned a great deal from Mr. Sickser about hard work, about how he dealt with his family and how he dealt with his customers. He was a wonderful man.

When I was about 18, he called me aside and said, "You're a part of the family. We love you. You've been here for years. I don't want you to be confused though. You can never have a future in this business. This business will go to my family, and you have more potential than to be just a worker in a store. So you get your education and you do something with your life."

Of course I never had any intention of staying in the store. Nevertheless that this man would stop and worry about what I was thinking, and give me that kind of guidance, was just remarkable. It reinforces my point that it does take a tribe. It's not just your immediate family or even your extended family. It's all the people around you who know you and care about you.

The footnote to this story about the children's furniture store is that Mr. Sickser's son-in-law inherited the store and eventually sold it and retired to Florida. Many years go by, decades go by, and one day this son-in-law picks up a newspaper and sees that this kid has been named national security adviser under President Reagan. He looks at the name and the face and says, "That's the kid. That's the kid from the store!" He got in touch with me, we reconnected after decades, and we're still in touch. He tells me he loves walking around Palm Beach telling everybody, "You see that kid? You know that kid, the general? I made him!"

> " don't just sit around waiting for someone unique or special to come touch you. There are mentors and positive influences in every direction you look. "

I'll share an example of how the Auntnet worked in my family so you understand its impact. When I was 15 or 16 years old, I got thrown out of church camp for drinking beer. We were in upstate New York, and my father was the senior warden of the church back in the Bronx. We were just kids horsing around, away from home, and we snuck out and bought some beer. We got back and hid the beer in the toilet tank where it would be chilled at the same time it was being hidden. It was the cheapest beer on the market, which was what we could afford. And we got caught. The priest found out about it and we were all summarily assembled the next day. The priest said, "OK, we found the beer. Now whose is it and who did it?"

We all stared at each other for a while, and finally I stood up and admitted that I was one of the ones who bought the beer. Then two other guys who were with me admitted it as well. We were kicked out of camp and told to get on the train and find our way home, which we did.

I got back to Kelly Street, and of course word had already preceded me. It got back to the church and back to my family. I can still recall the deadly, agonizing moment of watching my mother come home from work, walking up the street as I sat on the stoop in front of my house. She looked at me and said, "What you've done to this family, you've shamed us."

That was about the worst thing you could say to me or one of my cousins. I thought, "Beat me, but don't tell me I shamed the family. Just beat me."

But everybody knew about it and everybody was talking about it, and I was feeling as low as I could possibly feel. Then the priest called to talk to my parents about it and he laid it out for them. At the end he said, "But he stood up like a man and admitted it and took his punishment." So I went from somebody being on his way to prison to being some kind of hero because I'd stood up and admitted what I had done.

That's a part of it too: being accountable. There were drugs in Banana Kelly. It was the beginning of the marijuana and heroin age in my neighborhood, and we had some guys who fell to it and overdosed in the hallways, but I never went anywhere near it. I had a few other buddies who managed to steer clear too, and when I look back, I realize we all had that same strong family background, that tribal background, and we all fed off each other and kept each other straight.

You never know who's going to touch your life or how. Mr. Sickser, my family, my buddies in the neighborhood. The important message to our children is that they're being mentored every day by somebody. A teacher. A neighbor. Somebody who gets up to stand at a bus stop to go do a hard day's work to support their family. Look all around and you'll see people who are living good lives, who are making a difference, maybe not in the world but in their family, in their community. Learn from them. Don't just sit around waiting for someone unique or special to come touch you. There are mentors and positive influences in every direction you look.

manna from heaven
BONNIE RAITT
MUSICIAN

My folks, I guess. That's a place to start. I had a lot of influences in terms of music, activism, and social awareness, but it all flows from my parents.

My mother was my dad's accompanist and music director, and I fell in love with piano through her incredible talent and love of playing. One of her greatest gifts to me was not making me take music lessons, just letting me come to it by her example. She made it so appealing, so natural and joyful that I wanted to get to the point where I could enjoy playing for myself, as she did for hours. And with my mom and dad performing all through my childhood, I knew the love, the sheer joy of playing music, and the thrill of it. I got to see the backstage life of the theater, the rehearsals, and the warming up, and I developed a great love and respect for it all—and for knowing that in order to be really good at something you had to stick with it and practice.

My brothers and I were naturally good singers, but we learned from our parents the love of music, social activism, and the need to take care of yourself. I love that they never succumbed to the flashy and shallow "show biz" lifestyle, either in the usual addictive excesses or in the shallow values that you see in people out to just get famous or make a lot of money.

I think my folks' greatest gift besides music was in showing us that it's important to help others and give something back. They were both athletes who took great care of themselves, and that wended its way into my life. From them I learned that when you're on the road you really have to work at it. You have to watch what you eat, get enough rest and exercise, and you have to work on your relationships with your family and life at home. And you have to apply yourself to get good at your musical instrument and your singing. It doesn't just fall out of the sky. A lot of work goes into what looks on stage to be just so much fun.

" when you're a kid, one artist or one album can change your life. "

Musical influences? For me, they start with Joan Baez. I didn't pick up a guitar until I went away to summer camp. That's where I fell in love with the folk guitar. From about 1958 until about 1962, those formative, influencing years for me, whenever one of those counselors picked up a guitar and sang around the campfire, that was it for me. They were the ones who aimed me to Joan Baez, and she became my first hero, both for her gorgeous voice and her beautiful playing, but also because she was a Quaker, part Scottish, and from California, like me. And because she was also a peace and civil-rights activist, I idolized her. Really, she's stayed a touchstone for me since before I knew her. And now we've been friends for a long time, and have become like sisters in our causes and in song.

When you're a kid, one artist or one album can change your life. For me, it was Ray Charles and the country blues. We had a friend of the family who sold sound and TV equipment, and he got lots of promo records. I guess he must have thought, "Hey, Bonnie's musical, maybe she'll like these." So I had these Ray Charles albums, so unusual for a kid to have at age 12, and I just listened to them over and over. They were a huge part of how I learned about singing and music with soul. I hope you can hear Ray in there.

The slide guitar thing happened from another fortuitous gift of a record—*Blues at Newport '63* on Vanguard. That record was like manna from heaven, my first exposure to country folk blues. It had Mississippi John Hurt, Brownie McGhee, John Lee Hooker, and lots of others. I was just gone for it and worked hard at teaching myself nearly every song on the record.

One of the cuts was by an artist named John Hammond. I looked at the picture and saw that he wasn't a really old black guy but another middle-class white kid who just loved the blues. He sounded so cool and was playing something called "bottleneck guitar." I just loved that sound and had to figure out how to get it myself. I remembered playing hymns with my grandpa on his Hawaiian lap steel guitar when I was little, sliding a metal bar over the strings to make the chords. I'd never seen anyone play blues bottleneck, but I figured out I could soak the label off a glass Coricidin® cold-medicine bottle, tune the guitar to an open chord, and maybe that would work. I slipped the bottle on my third finger and somehow got it to sound like I wanted. Years later, when I switched to a wine bottleneck, I still used that third finger, and that was how I taught myself to play.

My dad, though, he's probably been the most important influence. Not just in his music, but in the way he lived his life and the integrity with which he made decisions. For example, he really wanted to be there for us kids, and so he probably turned down work here and there that could have furthered his career and made him more money. But both he and my mom felt it was important to spend time together as a family. They made sure to spend every Christmas, Thanksgiving, and Easter vacation camping with family friends, in the desert or on the Colorado River, because they knew they'd be working away from home all summer in summer stock. He did it for 25 straight years, so the rest of the time he made the most of it. Really, his commitment to family and friends was a great model for me.

I look now at the decisions he made, and the roles he took, and I realize he could have furthered his career making an album of slick songs, or different types of arrangements that were more "with it," and he could have played Vegas or done other more lucrative things. But he didn't like to be around smokers or hecklers or people who were drinking.

He would rather take a great show to the hinterlands and play for less money than play in a mediocre script on Broadway. That was his attitude. Slow and steady wins the race. I'll tell you, that guy made every

BONNIE RAITT: MANNA FROM HEAVEN

night opening night, and he made every show and every audience equally important. And they never deserted him. His fans really appreciated that he was out there, year after year, in more leading roles than any other leading man in history. That was his thing, you know? Rather than take over a role that was originated by someone else on Broadway, he'd go play *Pajama Game* in St. Paul, Minnesota, only it wasn't an ego thing with him. He truly felt that the people in St. Paul deserved to see that kind of show.

He never criticized me for my lifestyle and choices. He led by example. I remember he once told me that if I wanted my voice and health to stay stronger out on the road, I had to take better care of myself. As easy as that. Well, it took a while for that to sink in, but I saw that it worked for him, and he was hardly ever sick and never lost his voice. He lived his principles in his actions, and was the most positive person I ever met. He never complained, and he never spoke badly about anyone. It's what everyone remarked about at his memorial, and that's been an incredible lesson for me. It's why, whenever I find myself whining or complaining, I think about my dad and how he just chose to be happy and not stressed.

It really is a choice. Every day, no matter how bad his arthritis got or whether he lost a part or something set him back, he'd just pick himself up and said, "Let's just stay busy and move on down the road." He was an evolved, spiritual guy, my dad, and I loved him for being a great father and friend to us kids, but also for how he lived his life. It was this ability to be in the moment and stay positive, and watching him deal with his illness and his passing—these are also some of his greatest gifts to me.

I look back and think, "It's been a hard year." It really has. I lost my mom and my dad, both in the same year, and I had to take some time off. I was grief-stricken. I needed time to heal before I went back on the road. But now that I'm back out there touring again, it feels like I've finally got it right. It had always been my dream to get my home life as satisfying and fulfilling as my road life, and I've only lately managed to do it.

That's another unexpected gift of my parents' passing. It's forced me to really make a conscious effort to nurture the friendships and relationships in my life, to start making the right choices for the right reasons, and it's so exciting to be thinking about coming home, instead of thinking of it as a place to do your laundry. Really, this is absolutely the best time of my life, and it's so much due to my parents' inspiration. It truly is.

the next time
AHMAD RASHAD
RETIRED PROFESSIONAL FOOTBALL PLAYER, SPORTSCASTER

Playing sports has never been my number one focus in life. It was just something I loved. I enjoyed school as much as sports. And I played everything. Football, basketball, baseball. Even as a kid, I think I recognized that sports aren't really about winning and losing. They're about learning how to win and how to lose, and how to do it as a team, and those are the things you need in life to be successful. It's all about working with others.

I'll tell you what else sports can teach you. It can teach you to never quit, never give up. I was fortunate to learn that lesson very early on. When I was a kid, I played ball at the South End Boys Club in Tacoma, Washington. That's where I spent most of my time and where I feel like I came into my own as a person. It's a place where I learned responsibility, where I learned how to interact with people, where I learned the concept of teamwork, where I learned about respect—all the things that make you a successful human being. The confidence I got spending all that time at the club was so important. Leadership, determination, perseverance, discipline, the desire to succeed … all of that I learned at the club.

Sometimes I took in those life lessons in the negative. For example, I can remember when I started playing football I was a third-string tackle. I went to every practice and never got into a game. I could have gone one of two ways with that: I could have quit and never shown up again, or I could have displayed some resolve and gone on to show this coach what I could do.

The philosophy of the club at the time was that every kid got to play, no matter how bad you were. So I really wasn't prepared to sit out like that. This football coach was probably a good guy in every other respect, but his son played my position and of course his son played. I kept going to every practice, and every game, and still I never got in. And I learned something at that point. I learned that it's not about whether you get in the game: It's about coming back and trying harder and finding some way to do better or work harder to get what you want.

So I felt from that time on that I had something to prove to this man, to show him what kind of person I was, what kind of player I would be. Years later I was still thinking about this coach and showing him what I could do. I mean, I had been a third-string tackle, never coming off the bench, and here I am an All-American, here I am an All-Pro, years later, wanting to prove this guy wrong. Any time in my life when things got tough, I thought about this coach, about having to go to every single practice and never getting in the game and how down I felt. To this day I think about it. But it's always about the next time. It's not about the last time, it's about the next time.

That coach eventually gave me my chance to play, and I scored a ton of touchdowns and the rest was history. Every time I saw this guy after that he always acted like he was responsible for whatever success I had on the football field. And you know in a way he was, but not in the way he thought. I was successful despite him. For the rest of his life, he'd see me play on television and claim he was the guy who gave me my start, and let's let him go on believing that. Because there's no denying he was an inspiration. Not the inspiration he claims to be, but an inspiration just the same.

the only way I know
CAL RIPKEN JR.
RETIRED PROFESSIONAL
BASEBALL PLAYER

For the first 14 years of my life my father was a minor league manager. He worked all over for the Baltimore Orioles organization, a real company guy. I can't even remember every place he managed. Asheville, North Carolina. Rochester, New York. Dallas-Fort Worth. Elmira, New York. Miami. He'd jump from one town to the next almost every year, but he stayed in Asheville for three years, and that was a long time.

We were in school, of course, but when school let out for the summer we'd pick up and go to wherever he was. We'd pack up the car and a trailer and head out, sometimes clear across the country—South Dakota, Washington, wherever he happened to be that season. We'd spend the summer with my father and we'd come home in time for school to start in September. That's what it was like growing up in a baseball family.

Even when we hooked up with my father, the baseball games were always at night, and half the time he was traveling on road trips. When the team was home he'd leave for the ballpark for a night game about one o'clock in the afternoon, so that left very little time to see him. I found out early on that if I wanted to spend any time with my dad, I'd have to go to work with him, so to speak.

Because he made all the rules, he was able to put me in a little uniform and send me to the outfield to shag flies. If the ball came out to me, I was supposed to let it hit the ground or hit the wall, then pick it up and throw it back in. At 8 or 9 years old, that's what he had me doing.

> " knowing you had that regular time, that was a real key. If there was a tough subject you wanted to talk about, you could. "

I was a sponge, soaking up as much as I could. I had the Encyclopedia of Baseball for a dad, and all these other real-life editions of the encyclopedia whom I could ask for instructions. And I'd come back and measure what these other guys said with my dad's advice. I'd say, "Doug DeCinces told me to put my butt down and get my hands out front and my head up. Is that right?" And Dad would say, "That's exactly right." So I learned to trust what Doug said. Then I'd say, "Well, this outfielder told me to catch the ball one-handed, 'cause it looks better." Then Dad would say, "No, that's not right." So I would cross that guy off my list.

Dad was the hitting coach, the pitching coach, and the infield coach. He warmed pitchers up, hit fungoes, threw the batting practice. The truth was, he had very little time for me. The only time was at the end of the day. That was the best part. There'd be 15 or 20 minutes when we could talk about our day. The drive back and forth to the ballpark together was our time, just me and him. And that time became very valuable to me.

It's something I hold on to as a parent. I take my kids to school. We could carpool, but that time in the car is essential. When I was playing, no matter how tired I was, if I got in from a game at three o'clock in the morning from Texas, let's say, I'd set the alarm, get up, and take the kids to school, then go back home and go back to sleep. That all goes back to that time I had with Dad in the car. And sometimes it was totally quiet. It wasn't forced. But knowing you had that regular time, that was a real key. If there was a tough subject you wanted to talk about, you could.

From when I was 8 years old until I was 18, Dad probably saw a total of two of my games. He wasn't there because of his lifestyle. He couldn't come and watch a game. My mom was there all the time, but he couldn't be there.

So I had to explain to him in pretty great detail what had happened in my games. I had to paint the picture for him in place of him being able to witness them himself. But that was always pretty special, to go back and get the approval of Dad. I'd tell him what happened, what I did, what the situation was, why I made this or that decision.

I was always a *why* kid. That was what those drives home were always all about, for me to download my whys. Why'd you do this? Why'd you do that? And that's what these sessions were like after one of my games. It was a valuable exercise. I would have preferred to have him watch the games, but because he wasn't there, as a side benefit, I was able to examine and learn the game better. I had to so I could communicate it to him.

I graduated from high school in 1978, and dad was already in the bigs as a coach. I was drafted in June 1978 and went to the minor leagues. I played in Bluefield, West Virginia; Miami; Charlotte; and then the big leagues. The Orioles had the 24th pick in that draft, and they had three or four second-round picks all told because of free agent compensation, and a lot of the scouts who had come out to see me play said they were thinking of drafting me in the first round. So the reality was I didn't think the Orioles would have a chance to draft me, and I was trying to get comfortable with that.

In truth, though, I really wanted to be an Oriole. I had grown up in the organization and Dad was part of the organization, so I kept my fingers crossed. Sure enough, everyone passed on me in the first round and I was one of those picks in the second round.

Dad welcomed me to the organization in his very professional way. It didn't even seem like family, just like it was part of his job, and then I finally earned my way in, after my third year in the minors.

In 1981 I went to spring training. That was the first time I was protected on the roster, and it felt really good to be one of the invited players. Of course I was one of the first cuts out of spring training. I had no real chance to make the club. Earl Weaver was the manager at the time, and he cut me at the very first opportunity so I could go back down and get in my at bats.

Later that year after the strike was over, I was called up for good, but I knew the situation in spring training. Doug DeCinces was playing third base, and that's where they had me playing, so the writing was on the wall that he had the job. Dad framed it for me by saying my job was to go back down to AAA and continue doing what I was doing. To get ready. That was always his thing: to be ready in case the manager needed you. So it wasn't a big surprise.

The first time I was called up for good, it dawned on me what a really big stage it was to play in the major leagues. And with my dad being there, I don't think I realized how special it was at the time, although there were special moments when I did—special moments between me and my dad.

Moments like my first big-league home run. It was Opening Day, 1982. Dad was in the third-base coaching box. I was so juiced. It was my first at bat of the season, and we were already down by one run. Kansas City had scored early. Ken Singleton had walked in front of me, and I hit a two-run home run to give us the lead. The crowd went nuts. I ran so fast around the bases, I had to slow myself down or I would have passed Ken Singleton in front of me. I was right on his tail.

To have that brief moment on the field with your dad, when you're rounding third—there aren't too many ballplayers who get to experience something like that. I'm sure it was as exciting for Dad as it was for me, but he wasn't someone who expressed his love in ways that more modern fathers do. His generation was kind of closed, but you could tell by the way he looked at you, by the way he shook hands with you or patted you on the back, that he was really proud of you. And that's what it felt like at just that moment. He said something like "Attaboy!" or "Way to go!" And he patted me on the butt as I went by.

That was my first big moment as a big leaguer, and he was there. He was there for a lot of my big moments—most of them really. He got to see my consecutive game streak play itself out. I consulted him when I took a day off, when I ended the streak at 2,632 consecutive games. I wanted to let him know how I was planning to do it and get his thoughts on the best way to go.

He died the next spring, but he was there for all of it. And of course he was there at the ballpark for the 2,131st consecutive game, the night I broke Lou Gehrig's record in 1995. That was a great, great night, but what a lot of people don't realize about that streak was that for me it was never about the streak. It was about your job as a baseball player and who you were as a baseball player.

It was all about my dad really. It was his honest and hardworking approach to the game. Dad's expectation for every baseball player was that you need to be prepared and be ready to play, and you came to the ballpark and you put yourself in the hands of the manager. It's the manager's job to make out the lineup and help you to win. If he chooses you, you play. No questions asked. It's not up to you to make the judgment on your injuries, whether you're swinging the bat well, whether you can hit this guy or that guy. You simply come to the ballpark and put yourself in the hands of the manager.

That's what's really interesting to me about the streak. My first manager was Earl Weaver, and then Joe Altobelli, and then my dad, then Frank Robinson, Johnny Oates, Phil Regan, Davey Johnson, and on and on. I didn't force the streak on any of them. I just showed up to play, and it was a byproduct of that. The streak was created by a group of managers who kept writing my name in the lineup. I had no say in that. I just performed, and that was Dad's influence.

When you play the game of baseball, at any level, you have an obligation to your team and a responsibility to yourself to come ready to play. That's all the streak was. I was never obsessed with it.

Dad was a realist, someone who rolled up his sleeves and showed up to work. It was the only way I knew how to play, because it was the only way I was taught. It's what was expected of me, and I honestly feel it's the approach every athlete should take. I was simply fortunate that I was able to do it for a long time, that I was able to perform at a high level and at the same time establish myself as a regular player. It all flowed from my father, Cal Ripken Sr.

taking grounders
ALEX RODRIGUEZ
PROFESSIONAL BASEBALL PLAYER

Eddie Rodriguez was my baseball coach at the Boys & Girls Club in Miami, from the time I was 8 years old until I was about 16. Everyone kind of feared him, but it was a good kind of fear. You felt safe with Eddie, like being with him was the place to be. He played in the Chicago Cubs organization for a while, but ultimately he landed in Miami, in Coconut Grove, working with kids, and in more than 30 years he's coached about 35 future Major League players. That's an incredible track record.

I grew up a New York Mets fan and an Atlanta Braves fan, but really, down in Miami, my idea of big league baseball was playing for the University of Miami. That was the big time. As a kid it was kind of an unclear dream to play college baseball. But as I grew older, my dream became more clear and I thought I could make it. That was Eddie's influence. That was going to the Williamsport tournament, going out to play in San Francisco, winning all these championships. Even now, a lot of my closest friends are the people I used to play ball with at 9 or 10 years old. We were a tight-knit group, and that was Eddie's doing too. He was so passionate about the game and so dedicated to it that it rubbed off. And it's stayed with us.

> " you felt safe with Eddie, like being with him was the place to be. "

He didn't mess with our mechanics very much. He thought you needed to give kids time and room to grow. And it worked pretty well. With me I was always a shortstop, but back then I was a much better fielder than I was a hitter, probably because I was playing with kids who were so much older than me. It wasn't until I went to high school, playing with kids my own age, that I started to hit. It was a surprise to me but not to Eddie. He said he always knew I would hit.

To this day he still makes it to a lot of my games. He picks up on little things, and we talk about them. I don't make a big decision without talking to Eddie. Baseball, business, life—I trust him completely. It's a nice relationship to have after all these years. It's very pure.

When I made the move to the Yankees, I had to switch from shortstop to third base. It was Eddie I called to talk it over. It was Eddie who met me at the field immediately after the deal was made and started hitting me grounders at third, getting me ready, just like he used to do when I was 8 years old.

long may you run
JOAN BENOIT SAMUELSON
OLYMPIC MARATHON RUNNER

Running is a selfish pursuit. When I first started out I was a selfish runner. I didn't mean to be a runner though. I played other sports too, and I made the varsity field hockey team as a freshman in high school. I warmed the bench in basketball. I played tennis in a recreational league. When I was younger, I swam for the Portland [Maine] Seals, a local swim team.

But my true passion back then was skiing. My whole family skied. We used to go to Pleasant Mountain—it's now called Shawnee Peak—almost every weekend. My father was in the Army's 10th Mountain Division, so skiing was a big deal. It's amazing how many athletes I come across, particularly skiers, whose parents or grandparents were in the 10th Mountain Division. It was a ski troop that trained at Camp Hale in Colorado, then went over to Europe during World War II. Ironically the winter they won the war there was a drought and there wasn't any snow in the Alps, but my father still skis. He's 85 years old and he still teaches in the ski program for people with disabilities at Sunday River in Maine, and he skis with us on the weekends at Sugarloaf. So of course we all have skied since we could walk.

I started skiing competitively when I was in junior high. I broke my leg when I was a sophomore in high school, and that really turned the tide for me in terms of athletics. I started running as a form of rehabilitation, and by the next winter I didn't have the nerve anymore to compete on skis. No guts, no glory—that kind of thing. I was very hesitant in the gate.

So I turned to running as something I could do year-round, something I was good at, something that could replace the competition I was used to getting on the mountain. I had to work at it, but I had two older brothers who ran and I always enjoyed watching them run, so that's what I did. I was always looking for places I could run where people wouldn't see me, because I was trying to shed this tomboy image I had in high school.

When I was growing up, there weren't a lot of athletic opportunities for young women in Cape Elizabeth, Maine. The gender bias prohibition of Title IX was passed in 1972 and I graduated from high school in 1975, so the doors were just starting to open. We weren't at any kind of level playing field just yet, but more opportunities opened up every year. The boys' track coach, Keith Weatherbie, also happened to be my biology teacher my sophomore year and my physics teacher my senior year. I started running with the boys my junior year because I didn't think the girls were working hard enough.

> " you did well here today, but it doesn't mean anything if you can't match it tomorrow in your exam. "

I skipped study hall and went running—I'd run four and a half or five miles and get back in time for my next class. Coach Weatherbie pushed us as hard in practice as he did in the classroom. I can remember him picking me up off the track after one of our practice sessions. "You did well here today," he said, "but it doesn't mean anything if you can't match it tomorrow in your exam."

Like I said, running is a selfish sport, and looking back I realize how selfish I was to go off and train with the guys and leave the girls behind. I still competed with the girls, but I trained with the boys.

I won the state mile during my senior year, although I didn't have a very good race. I went out and watched the boys run in the morning, and then when my race came I went out way too fast but it was enough to win. At our school awards ceremony that year I didn't win the Most Valuable Player award. I was the only one on the girls' team to even go to the state meet that year, but I didn't get the award. I mumbled something under my breath during the awards ceremony when my name wasn't called. But the girls' coach was right in not awarding me the MVP because I didn't deserve it after leaving my team and training with the boys. She taught me a huge, huge lesson, because in truth I didn't deserve the award. I had been selfish, running with the boys like that.

The marathon was the next logical challenge for me. In 1979, when I was still a student at Bowdoin, I decided to run the Boston Marathon. It was meant to be my first marathon, but I actually ran a marathon in Bermuda that January. I'd only planned on running half the distance with some friends as a kind of tune-up, but when we made it to the halfway mark the race marshals told us we wouldn't be able to get a ride to the finish line until the last runner passed, so we decided we would get there faster if we ran. So the 1979 Boston Marathon wasn't my first marathon, but it was the first one I meant to win. And I did, in just over 2 hours and 35 minutes, setting an American record for women.

I'm always nervous before a race, and naturally I was nervous this first time on such a big stage. But it's a good thing to be nervous. If you're not nervous before a competition, something's not right. I remember not really knowing what I was doing or where I was going. The only thing I knew about the Boston Marathon was that there was supposedly this killer hill—Heartbreak Hill—somewhere along the way. I kept waiting for it and waiting for it. I even passed a guy on the hill and asked him how much longer it was until Heartbreak Hill. He looked at me like I was crazy.

I never look at marathon courses before I run them. What I don't know can't hurt me; that's the attitude I take. I tend to run faster wanting to know what's around the next bend in the road.

the right decision
RON SARGENT
CHAIRMAN AND CEO, STAPLES

I used to work for a lady who taught at my school. Her name was Mary
Dunlap, and I was mowing her grass one day and had stopped to take a
break, and she came out to inspect how I was doing.

We talked a little bit and she asked me a question that was kind of
profound, although at the time of course I didn't realize it. She said, "Do
you plan on going to college?" It was 1967, I was 12 years old, and I was
growing up in Covington, Kentucky. Nobody I knew had ever gone to
college, except for Miss Dunlap, and at the time it didn't seem like an
important conversation, but it got me thinking.

I said, "I've never really thought much about it."

And she said, "Well, you've got a good head on your shoulders. You
should think about it."

And so I did. From that moment on, I began to consider things a little differently, and to think that maybe education was the way.

I went to a high school where probably 10 percent of the kids went to college; I did well. All along my only model for making my way in the world had been my father, George Sargent, and he of course had never gone to college. He was a mechanic. He worked on heavy equipment: bulldozers, tractors, cranes, you name it. He worked long days, and every day he'd come home from work covered with grease from head to toe.

He worked for the same company for nearly 40 years, and I think he enjoyed the work. He liked fixing things, he liked solving problems. He took a lot of pride in the fact that a job site might have been shut down because the crane had broken down and he could go in and in a day or two get the crane back up and operational again. He was very good with people and was a very solid citizen. He didn't want to rule the world, but I think he was very important in my life and in instilling the values I hold today. Not a week goes by when I don't think about something he said or something he did, and I have a tendency to pattern my life after him. Even at 12, I guess, I was inclined to pattern my life after him, which I suppose is why college had no place in my thinking before this exchange with Miss Dunlap, but that one conversation changed everything.

> " from that moment on, I began to consider things a little differently, and to think that maybe education was the way. "

I ended up applying to two colleges. One was the University of Kentucky, near where I lived. All of my friends, the 10 percent of students who were going off to college, most of them were going there. I also applied to Harvard. I was accepted at both schools, so I had a dilemma. I could go to Harvard, which was a thousand miles away, but I wouldn't know anybody there and my family probably wouldn't be able to afford to send me there anyway, or I could go to the University of Kentucky, which would have put a lot less stress on my family.

Over the summer, between me and my dad and the Harvard admissions people and the federal government for the loans, we figured out a way I could go to Harvard for a year. My father was thinking college was a big deal. But the University of Kentucky was so much more affordable than Harvard and it made sense to him on so many different levels that it was where he wanted me to go.

He wanted the best for me, but I think he thought college was college was college. He didn't see that there was any difference, except for the cost and the distance. But I thought I should try something different and try to grow up a bit, and that's why I went to Cambridge. Once I was there, that one year became two, and two became three, and I wound up spending six years there. My father supported my decision to go there, but he was not excited about it. He was even less excited when I wanted to get my MBA four years later. He thought it was time to go to work. But it made sense to me to try something different and to push myself a little bit. I was 17 years old, getting set to go a thousand miles away from home, where I didn't know a single person.

My first plane ride, in fact, was flying from northern Kentucky to Boston. My father drove me to the airport with all my freshman possessions. I remember the fear and uncertainty I felt getting off in Boston's Logan Airport and trying to find my way to campus. It took maybe a half hour to figure out you had to catch a bus to get to the T, the Boston transit system, and then when you got to the T there was a map showing all the different train lines, and I was terribly confused.

I finally sought out a guy at one of the turnstiles and said, "I'm trying to get to Harvard." He took one look at me, with all my possessions, and somehow I failed to strike a sympathetic chord. He shot back that I needed to take the Blue Line for six stops, and then the Green Line for two stops, and then the Red Line to the end of the line, except I hadn't gotten acclimated to the Boston accent or attitude and I didn't quite get it the first time. So I had to ask him a second time. He offered up the directions again, and this time he was a little more annoyed.

Finally, after a couple hours, I was able to get to Harvard Square. I distinctly remember walking up the steps from the subway and reaching the top and seeing a whole group of Hare Krishna men. This was 1973, and there were probably 20 men dressed in saffron robes, with the hair and the finger cymbals, and I remember how shocked I was. I thought, "So this is what I've gotten into." And then I thought, "Dad was right. This is a long way from Kentucky. Maybe I made a mistake." It took me several months before I realized I could make it there.

On the other side of things, I think it took my father a while longer to realize I'd made the right decision. We talked about it all the time during my visits home. I remember one specific conversation while I was in business school when I said, "Dad, I think I can come out of business school and make x dollars." Now you have to realize that x dollars, whatever that figure was at the time, was probably more money than my father could expect to earn in several years. And he said, "I don't think you're *ever* going to make x dollars."

Sure enough, a year later I came out of business school and my starting salary was x-plus, maybe a couple thousand dollars more than we'd talked about. And my dad took me aside one day and said, "I think I understand all of this a little better now. I think you made the right decision."

And to think that it all flowed from that one conversation with that teacher. I'm certain I would have been drawn to the idea of college sooner or later, but it was Miss Dunlap who first planted it. It was Miss Dunlap who first got me thinking I had something to offer, and I was always grateful for her interest. In fact she continued to teach until her mid-80s, and I stayed in touch with her even after she went into a nursing home. She died in 1995, at the age of 103, and every chance I had I tried to thank her. If she thought about it at all, she probably chalked it up as just one of the many things she was involved in over her long life and that I was just one of the many people she had a chance to help.

Ron Surgent

prescriptions for success
JOHN SCHUERHOLZ
GENERAL MANAGER, ATLANTA BRAVES

A couple of people had a real impact on my decision making, my leadership compass, and my sense of dealing with people. The first was my dad. One of the very first memorable exchanges we had was when I was 10 or 11 years old. My father had been a professional athlete. He took me to a game at Memorial Stadium in Baltimore, my hometown, and he began to introduce me to people who were his friends. I was awestruck. These were people who had played with him, people who respected him. And he would introduce me, a young, skinny kid, and I'd reach out and shake their hands.

After a while my father pulled me aside. He must have observed that I wasn't shaking hands with the gusto he thought was appropriate. He said, "Look, I want you to shake the man's hand like you really care about meeting him, like you enjoyed meeting him. And I want you to look him in the eye."

It was a wonderful lesson, not so much about how you present yourself, but how the person you're meeting feels about your interest in them.

When I began my career in baseball with the Baltimore Orioles, I was interviewed by Lou Gorman, director of player development. I walked into his office with nothing but a dream of getting into baseball. I was teaching eighth-grade English and world geography, but I was fortunate enough to be offered a job, and with that job came the great opportunity to work for Lou Gorman. He taught me the most important thing, and it was sort of a continuation of what my dad taught me. Every day, sincerely and without phoniness, Lou demonstrated by his actions how very vital it is—more than anything else—to understand and appreciate the people who work with you. Yes, read about the work responsibilities you have, learn the history of the game, study the work documents that guide us in what we do. Do your job well, learn your job well, but always remember that the people you work with are your most valuable asset. Embrace them. Honor them. Respect them.

Lou did more than that. He showed joy, appreciation, and kindness daily. And this wasn't a Boy Scout troop, it was a baseball team. Yet Lou always put people on a pedestal and always by example—never in sermon, never in lecture, just by his actions.

Eventually I left my beloved hometown of Baltimore when Lou was hired by the expansion Kansas City Royals and Ewing Kauffman—an owner who was one of the most dynamic, brilliant, and heartfelt leaders of people that the industrialized business community had ever encountered. Ewing Kauffman started his own pharmaceutical company, Marion Laboratories. He wrote a book called *Prescription for Success* that's one of the best books on leadership you'll ever read.

What struck me right away about Mr. Kauffman was his vision and his clarity and his dynamic and positive personality. His positive energy was so strong that I never picked up a negative vibe or aura or feel or look or view. Never. He approached his life and work with the attitude that anything can happen, anything can be done—with good work, good people, a good plan, and high-energy commitment.

Lou Gorman taught me the value of people. Now I got to work for a man who sent that message in neon lights and capital letters daily. Mr. Kauffman wasn't just talking the talk. He made all of the workers at Marion Laboratories shareholders in the company. It was part of their compensation plan, and he told them the stock would be far more valuable than any extra money he might pay them in salary or bonuses. That was his message: Trust me, believe in me, believe in this company. And they did. I can't tell you how many people retired from Marion Laboratories as millionaires: support workers. janitors, truck drivers, line workers. They believed in Ewing Kauffman and they retired as millionaires because of it—and because Ewing Kauffman believed in them as well. He recognized the strength in motivating and engaging and partnering with people at all levels. That's how he operated the Royals too. He would talk to the receptionists and the line workers in our office like he did to his workers at the pharmaceutical company, and they felt loved and appreciated by him, and they would work their fingernails off for Mr. K.

> " he approached his life and work with the attitude that anything can happen, anything can be done—with good work, good people, a good plan, and high-energy commitment. "

I put that positive attitude to the test right away. I was named general manager of the Royals in October 1981, and in 1982 I made a deal with the San Francisco Giants to acquire who everyone in baseball believed was the most dominant starting pitcher in the game at that time, Vida Blue. We gave up a pitcher named Atlee Hammaker and several minor leaguers. Vida Blue and an outfielder named Jerry Martin came back to us in the trade, but what also came back was a pox upon our clubhouse in the form of drugs. After FBI investigation upon FBI investigation, the whole case became public. Here I am, a young general manager. I'd just made what I'd thought was a wonderful trade, and instead not only did we not play as well, but we had players we loved and cared about going to jail.

I'm not here to condemn Vida Blue or any of the other players involved. That's been done, and the investigative and police records speak for themselves. I just felt so bad that I had allowed such a thing to happen on my watch. I had made this deal, and now every day I had to stand in front of the media defending it, explaining it, talking about how it was affecting our organization, how it was affecting the players, how it was affecting me. It was a big, big story, and it went on for weeks and weeks and weeks, and it was a very, very difficult time. As the spokesperson for the team, I had to explain the situation and at the same time provide strength and comfort to our fans that we were going to confront it and be honest about it.

In a matter of weeks, I was summoned to Mr. Kauffman's office. This was the first time I'd heard from Mr. Kauffman since the news broke, so I didn't know what to expect, but I was prepared for the worst.

It was just the two of us in his office, behind closed doors, and he sat in his chair smoking his pipe. He always smoked a pipe. After a moment he took it from his mouth and put it down and swiveled his chair around and looked me directly in the eyes with his clear, bright, electric-blue eyes. And he said, "John, the reason we made you general manager of this team is because we have confidence in your knowledge, your ability, and your aggressiveness. I do not want the results of this trade to cause you to lose your aggressiveness, to pull in your horns. We have all the confidence in the world in you. You can deal with this. You can get through this. Our organization, under your leadership, can get through this. And I expect you to come out the other side a better man."

That was Mr. K at his finest. The great lesson to me then—and now—is that when you have confidence in someone, when you believe in their honor and their work ethic and their capabilities, and when that person has proven his or her commitment to your organization, then you have to be there with support when that person fails or falters on occasion. That's when it's appropriate for you as a leader to reach down and help him back up and dust him off and get him going back in the fashion he was before. That's leadership.

John Schuerholz

effort is everything
BUD SELIG
COMMISSIONER OF
MAJOR LEAGUE BASEBALL

It was my mother, Marie, who got me interested in baseball. She loved the game. I remember her taking me to the ballpark when I was 3 or 4 years old. I was born and raised in Milwaukee, but she took me to games in Chicago and New York as well. She really knew and understood the game, which was unusual for a woman in the '30s and '40s. In fact, she used to play baseball when she was a young girl and on into college, so her interest was genuine. She listened to ball games on the radio, and by the time I was 6 or 7 I was a real baseball fan. Of course I played, and I was a pretty decent center fielder too, but there was only one problem. One year they started throwing curveballs, and that was the end of my career. If I wanted a career in baseball I'd have to find a different way.

My father, Ben, liked baseball well enough, but only so he could spend a lot of time with me. So he and I would go to Chicago together. My mother was the real fan. She took me to New York for my 15th birthday to see the Yankees because I was a big Yankee fan in those days. Growing up I had it in my head that I was the heir apparent to Joe DiMaggio, my all-time hero, and then of course along came Mickey Mantle. By that time I'd realized I would have to move on. By that time, I'd realized I couldn't hit a curveball.

> " whatever abilities you have, you have to use them. Do the very best you can and that's all anyone can ever expect. "

My parents both came to the United States from Europe when they were very young. My mother came from Russia, and she went on to become a schoolteacher. My father was a self-made man. He came from Romania when he was 4 or 5, went to high school, graduated, and worked for the local paper. He became a Ford dealer at a very young age, one of very few Jewish Ford dealers in America at that time. There are a lot of things I quote my dad on—one line in particular. "Buddy," he used to say, "there's nothing good or bad, except by comparison." It's a great line, and it's true.

Education was important to my parents, and it was always understood that we would go to college. What was unclear was what we would do after college. I was a history major and I wanted to be a history professor. The only career advice my father ever gave to me when I got out of the service was to try my hand in business first. I never liked to say no to my parents so I gave business a try. I'll always wonder what it would have been like to have been a history professor.

My mother was especially tickled when we got the team. It was 1970, I was 35 years old, and I had spent five years trying to bring a major league team back to Milwaukee. My parents were both very proud, but my mother was ecstatic. She never missed a home game until 1988. She was a Brewers fan through and through.

The economic side of the sport always was interesting to my father. I remember when we signed our first $100,000 player, George Scott, the big first baseman. My father was stunned. It was just such an astonishing figure to him, and I wonder what he'd think of the salaries of today's players.

Mom was such a die-hard fan that I used to call her to get the scores when I was on the road. This was back before ESPN and the Internet, and I could tell by the way she answered the phone whether we'd won or lost. She really lived and died with her Brewers.

During the 1982 World Series, she missed a step on her way into the ballpark and fell and broke her hip. I was out on the field, and here comes the team doctor running at me, saying, "Marie fell down." They took her to Jewish Hospital in St. Louis, and I called her in the fourth inning to check up on her. The Brewers were winning big that day—but I was worried about my mother. And I said, "So how are you doing?" Her answer was, "Well, I'm not doing so well, but I'll tell you, the Brewers are doing great."

My parents were wonderful role models in every way, and I had another role model once I got into baseball. John Fetzer, the longtime owner of the Detroit Tigers, took me under his wing almost from the very first owners' meeting I attended in 1970. Outside of my father he really had more influence on my career than anybody. He was a lot like my father, come to think of it: kind, generous, smart. He taught me all about baseball and life. After every meeting, I'd fly through Detroit, which was kind of a pain in the neck, only because I wanted to spend the extra time with him.

By the time I got into the game he was the real patriarch of the American League and one of the great visionary leaders of our sport. And he had no children, so I guess he wanted to pass on some of what he knew to the next generation. But he was also a competitor. His Tigers were out to beat my Brewers, but he never let that get in the way of our friendship. He taught how the game of baseball transcended in importance over an individual franchise. I'd say to him sometimes, "Well, why did you vote for that?" And he'd say, "If it's good for baseball, it's good for the Detroit baseball club."

I've also admired a great many people I've never even met. JFK, FDR, Harry Truman. Vince Lombardi, with whom I shared a secretary. He really put into words what my mother and father believed and what John Fetzer tried to pass on to me.

Whatever abilities you have, you have to use them. Do the very best you can and that's all anyone can ever expect. So it's the effort, really, when it comes down to it. Vince Lombardi was quoted as saying, "Winning isn't everything, it's the only thing." Based on what he stood for, what he meant to say, I think, is that it's the *effort* that's everything. It's the *effort* that's the only thing. And that was the great lesson I took in from John Fetzer and from my parents. Do the best you can. Take the time to make a difference.

My parents took pride in what I was able to accomplish in baseball. I know they did because of a story Bowie Kuhn told me the night my father died.

It was 1975, and the All-Star game was played in Milwaukee that year. While my dad was at the stadium, he got to talking to Bowie, who was commissioner of baseball at the time. All kinds of people were there, baseball dignitaries and other dignitaries too. Henry Kissinger was there, and of course back then the All-Star game was nothing like what it's become today, but it was a very exciting thing for the team and for the city.

At one point my dad turned to Bowie and said, "How many people are going to watch this on television?" And Bowie said, "Oh, about 75 million." And when he heard this my father's eyes moistened up a little bit and he smiled and said, "If I die tomorrow, I'll be the proudest and happiest man on Earth." Then he turned and walked away.

My dad died the following January. I was on my way to a Major League Baseball meeting in Chicago when I got the call. I'll never forget it. It was a miserable snowy night, and I remember driving back and feeling lonely and sad. When I got home it was about one o'clock in the morning, and I was looking for a letter my dad had left me when the phone rang. It was Bowie Kuhn calling to tell me that story. He'd never said anything about it to me before, and my father had never shared it with me either. But Bowie thought it was important for me to hear it the night my father died. I'll always be grateful for that.

Bud Selig

see it now
BERNARD SHAW
RETIRED TELEVISION JOURNALIST

Two people played an important role in shaping my career. One has become a dear friend and one I never met. The one I never met was the inspiration for me in broadcast journalism: Edward R. Murrow.

When I was 10 or 11 years old growing up on the South Side of Chicago, we got our first television—an old, 12-inch black-and-white set. *Howdy Doody* had just come on the year before, so we didn't miss much.

I used to watch CBS News and Murrow all the time. When I was about 13, I declared to my family and friends that I wanted to be just like that man. I got looks of puzzlement, but I used to stand up my dates just to watch Murrow, and later Walter Cronkite. Murrow was my inspiration and Cronkite was my idol.

I grew up in a neighborhood called Washington Park adjacent to Jackson Park, which bordered the University of Chicago campus. Every Sunday

I'd leave our basement apartment and walk the 12 blocks from my house
to get a copy of *The New York Times,* and then I'd sit there on the campus
of the University of Chicago and read. My family couldn't afford to send
me to the University of Chicago, but I always wanted to go to that school
and Northwestern, in that order. The atmosphere of that place is hard to
describe. There were people like Saul Bellow walking the streets. Clifton
Utley and his wife did news and commentary on the local NBC television
station, and I would see him from time to time and we would stop and talk
on the street about current events. It was an incredibly exciting place and an
incredibly exciting time.

My father worked for the railroad and my mother scrubbed floors, but
reading and learning were intense currency in our house. My father read
four newspapers a day and our apartment reeked of newsprint, much the
way Bernard Kalb's office used to at the Washington bureau. My mother
used to complain about the smell of newsprint in the house. I learned to read
when I was 4 and I still remember the 1945 headline in the *Chicago Times*:
FDR DIES. That's where I got my first taste of news and reading, so it was
cultivated for a long, long time.

I grew up at a time when Chicago had four dailies: The *Tribune* and
the *Sun-Times* in the morning, and a great newspaper—the *Chicago Daily
News*—and a Hearst newspaper—the *Herald-American*—in the afternoon.
Plus we read the two black weeklies, the *Chicago Defender* and the *Pittsburgh
Courier*. On top of that we read the Sunday *New York Times*, which I got
to first on the University of Chicago campus. So my interest in the printed
word and in news was sacrosanct.

As it turned out Walter Cronkite and I met when I was in the Marine
Corps stationed in Hawaii. I was tracking everything he did. One day I was
sitting in my cubicle in the barracks reading the *Honolulu Advertiser*, the
morning paper there, and I turned the page and there was this big black-
and-white PR photo of Walter and Betsy Cronkite with the tail section of a
United Airlines jet behind them. It said CBS correspondent Walter Cronkite
was in the islands shooting scenes for his *Twentieth Century* TV program,
and that he and his wife were staying at the Reef Hotel. That's all I needed.

I called the Reef Hotel and left 34 messages over a period of three days.
I explained briefly in the messages to Mr. Cronkite that he was my idol and
I needed very much to talk to him. I received no response and I thought he

had stiffed me, but on the fourth day I came back from work and I found a message. It said, "Mr. Cronkite returned your call. Please call."

I called. He invited me down to his hotel and said he could speak to me for 20 minutes. My squadron gave me the day off, and I dressed up in my Marine tropical uniform and went down to Waikiki. I was waiting in the lobby, waiting and waiting and waiting, and I started to think the meeting was going to fall through, but just then I heard this voice say, "Gee, sergeant, I hope I haven't been keeping you waiting too long."

I was a lance corporal. He had just promoted me two ranks.

He was with his wife, Betsy. He said, "Well, come on upstairs." And then he looked at Betsy and she gave him a stern *don't even try this* look. So he said, "Well, we've got a black-tie dinner we've got to go to very shortly, so why don't we just go over here and sit down?"

> " I said, "what is the most important thing I need to do to prepare myself?" He looked me in the eye and said, "read, read, read." "

We sat and talked, and 20 minutes expanded into 30 minutes, and then after 40 minutes I said, "You have a banquet to go to. I've already had mine." Meaning, of course, what he shared with me in our conversation.

During my 40 minutes, I asked him what I should be thinking about when I got out of the Corps and went back to school. I didn't want to major in journalism—I'm old-fashioned that way—and I wanted to get his thoughts on it. We talked about everything: racial problems, world events. I said, "What is the most important thing I need to do to prepare myself?"

He looked me in the eye and said, "Read, read, read."

And I share that with every young person I can.

He explained: "When you get started in this business, you'll be a general assignment reporter and you will have to know something about everything—politics, music, art, sports, medicine, science. And you can only acquire a sense of these subjects by reading, reading, reading."

That was the most seminal piece of advice I ever received. I was out of the Marine Corps two years later and back to school at the University of Illinois at Chicago. My first real job was at the first all-news radio station in Chicago,

WNUS. I was working there in the evening into late night and going to school in the day. My only goal in life was to be a CBS news correspondent.

For whatever reason, the CBS news ethic was in my pores. I was drawn to it. I said I wanted to become a correspondent by age 30. I missed it by a year, but in 1971, 10 years after meeting Walter Cronkite in Hawaii, CBS News hired me in its Washington bureau. About six weeks after I was hired my first piece made it to the evening news. The announcer came on and said, "Direct from our newsroom in New York, this is the *CBS Evening News* with Walter Cronkite." And then he did that part where he said, "With Roger Mudd in Washington, Bernard Shaw in Washington," and so on. And as he read my name I could see that Walter Cronkite actually had a slight smile on his face. It was just the slightest smile, but there it was.

And it all came full circle.

A few years ago I received the Cronkite Journalism Award from the School of Journalism at the University of Arizona, which of course is named after Walter Cronkite. And Walter himself presented it to me. This was just a couple years after I'd received the Edward R. Murrow Award from Murrow's alma mater, Washington State. And Walter told that story of our meeting in Hawaii. He said, "I've never seen a more determined person in my life."

That was 1961, of course, and we've been friends now for more than 45 years.

Bernard
Shaw

oh man, i've become my father
JOHN SINGLETON
MOTION PICTURE DIRECTOR/
SCREENWRITER

My father was 17 when I was born, and we grew up together. He was learning how to be a man and a father and passing on what he learned as he was finding out about the world. It couldn't have been easy, but he taught himself to be tough and compassionate. Today he's one of the most compassionate men I know. The strongest, toughest men all have compassion. They're not heartless and cold. You have to be man enough to have compassion—to care about people and about your children. It's easier for me than it was for him, raising a son in South Central Los Angeles, but that's what he taught me. That's what we figured out together.

It was just the two of us and for a long time he struggled. Now he's working in real estate and he's doing OK, but it wasn't always like that. When he was in his early 20s, he worked at a Thrifty's drugstore as a manager and he was very proud of that, even though he did not like working for someone else. In fact he hated working for someone else. He used to talk all the time about wanting his own business and the frustration he felt at not having his own business.

When I was little we used to read self-help books because we were living in a really bad neighborhood and we were desperate for any help we could get, any edge. At night there'd be gunshots up and down our street. A couple times my father would have to shoot at people to keep them from breaking into the house. It was all chronicled in my first movie *Boyz N The Hood*. They tell you at film school to write what you know, right? Well, this was what I knew.

For as long as I can remember, my father tried to build himself mentally. It was like a workout. He'd work out physically, he'd go out in the yard and lift weights, but he was always working on his internal self so he'd have the strength to run his own show. If he had to, he used to say, he'd sell pencils just to be the master of his own destiny. And so we'd read these books. Napoleon Hill, *Think and Grow Rich*. George Clason, *The Richest Man in Babylon*. He exposed me to all these books when I was a teenager. He told me to do mantras, to think positively, to prepare myself to be the master of my own destiny. And I bought into it, because it let us build ourselves mentally to where we felt we were able to accomplish everything we wanted to do.

> " my father always told me, "you can do anything you want in life, and don't let nobody tell you different." "

When I was interested in getting into film, there weren't a whole lot of black people I could look at who were doing what I wanted to do. We certainly didn't know anybody who had a career working in film, so to say I wanted to be a filmmaker at 9 years old, that was kind of different. Where we lived, every kid wanted to be a football player or a basketball player. That was it. Those were your options. But my father always told me, "You can do anything you want in life, and don't let nobody tell you different." So that was my attitude.

Every week, we went to the movies together. The first movie I remember seeing with my dad was probably *Snoopy Come Home*, and I think it made me cry at the end. The first real movies I remember were *The Chinese Connection* and *Superfly*. During some of these movies, he'd cover my face whenever there was a naked breast on the screen or something else he didn't want me to see, but it got to a certain point where he went to cover my eyes and said, "Aw, you're gonna see it anyway." Or maybe he just realized I'd already seen everything there was to see.

The most significant movie he took me to, of course, was *Star Wars*. It was 1977 and I was nine years old. We saw it at the Chinese Theater on Hollywood Boulevard, back when it was still Sid Grauman's Chinese Theater. We sat there in that big movie palace and I really got the message that I could be anything I wanted to be. It was a very powerful thing. That's when I decided I wanted to make movies. My father encouraged me in that in whatever ways he could. He told me to follow my dreams. You know? A lot of fathers would have looked at me like I was crazy, but he was very positive about it.

One time my father took me to see a movie, and we were laughing out loud. You know how black people are in the movie theater, right? So we were laughing, and a guy sitting right in front of us turned around and said, "Can you keep it down?" And my father kicked the back of his chair and said, "Don't you ever think you can tell me to do anything! Just shut up and enjoy the movie."

Flash forward 15 years. I'm at USC film school when *Colors* comes out. *Colors* was a Dennis Hopper movie about two white cops in South Central L.A. They were billing it as the next big thing, and it was supposed to show us what gang life was like in my neighborhood. I was a USC film student, just trying to find my way, trying to find out what I wanted to do with what I was learning, and I was incensed because there were hardly any black people in the theater for the screening. There was this producer on stage, pontificating about where I grew up from a kind of voyeuristic perspective, and I was angry about it. I thought, "What does he know?"

And here I am, one of the only black people in the theater, fuming and muttering under my breath and talking, and this guy in front of me turns and says, "Can you keep it down?" So I kicked his chair and said, "You shut up! Don't you ever think you can tell me to do anything!" And then I calmed down a little and thought, "Oh man, I've become my father." So I think I can say my father gave me the guts to be able to say, "You know what, I'm gonna forge a career in a field where very few people like me have ever made it, and to try to do it in my own way, the best way I can, and to find my own way and make myself unique."

There's a person in every family who can spin a yarn and tell a good story. I always point to my father as being that person in our family—someone who's long-winded, who likes to hear the sound of their own voice, but when they talk they're so entertaining, so engaging. Growing up with my father, I learned to be able to tell stories verbally before I even put them to paper. Then after I put them to paper, I put them on the screen.

You have to be able to express yourself, and my father could always express himself. He used to tell me that the best way to sell people on things is to get them to sell themselves on the idea that they really want to do something and they need whatever it is you're selling. It doesn't matter if it's pencils or a story you're trying to tell on screen, you have to be able to do that. I think that's why I was able to direct my first film at the age of 22 and have the career that I have today.

first responders
DENNIS SMITH
RETIRED FDNY FIREFIGHTER, AUTHOR

One day I saw a man direct a thousand first responders, and I came to an utter realization of just how important leadership is in our lives. The day was September 11, 2001, and the man, named Pete, was a deputy fire chief assigned to the first division in the New York City Fire Department.

At 8:46 on that Tuesday morning, as the first plane flew by his office window on Lafayette Street, Pete saw the shadow and heard the roar of the jet's engines. Low, he thought, too low. Experienced in the city's busiest fire stations, Pete knew that the sound of the airplane crashing through the World Trade Center's Tower 2 announced the biggest and the worst job of his life. He was in his car, and then in control of operations in the North Tower, within minutes.

A 30-year veteran of the fire department, Pete has the determined bearing of a gladiator and the keen blue eyes of a professor who has read everything in the library. He is an inquiring person and little escapes his interest. Most of all he is learned in the skills and technology of emergency command. On that day fire company after company filed past him and he delivered orders to each. He saw an old friend, Captain Jay Jonas of Ladder 6, and said, "Jay, just go up and do the best you can." Jonas knew that there is just one mission: Help those who need help to get out.

After little more than an hour the South Tower collapsed and a huge cloud of rubble covered Pete and the others working in the lobby of the North Tower. Pete dug himself loose and quickly found another firefighter near him, this one mortally wounded. It was Father Mychal Judge, the department's beloved and longtime chaplain, dead from a massive coronary. Pete and a few others carried Father Mychal out of the building and gave him to a group of rescuers. Then Pete went back to his job.

Emergencies start with chaos. The experienced incident commander chips away at the disorder and frenzy until, little by little, calm and order are established. But Pete immediately realized that there would be no order and no calm for many weeks, maybe months. The towers of the World Trade Center were awesome in scale and profoundly tragic in the consequence of their attack, fires, and collapse.

A fire chief usually gets only one chance to save a life, and so the early decisions in an emergency are vital. But on September 11 the sorrow of the world fell to the ground as those buildings fell, and Pete knew it. The death toll would be horrendous: 2,749 at the World Trade Center were killed by political and religious hatred.

Pete was buried in debris again as the second tower fell. As he found his way to an open area, he saw a fire truck that had not been completely buried. He climbed to the top of the truck and stood on its cab. Surveying the immense destruction before him, he began giving orders to the other chiefs and captains around him: "Take five men and start climbing." He began sectoring the area in his mind, realizing that a search effort had to be mathematical. There was no time to waste in searching an area twice. Soon company after company of firefighters and contingents of police officers were directed this way and that, as Pete integrated in his mind the areas being covered. If there were trapped victims to be found, they would find them.

When word came that 14 people were trapped in the debris of the north tower—Jay Jonas among them—Pete directed his officers to where he believed they were. "We are coming to get you," he called into his radio. Several hours later, the men and one woman were led to safety, and Jonas reported to Pete.

> " the sound of the airplane crashing through the tower announced the biggest and the worst job of his life. "

Jonas recorded that he saw a tear in Pete's eye as the chief said, "Good to see you, Jay."

Pete stayed on top of that fire truck for the next 10 hours, watching, directing, and internalizing the greatest loss in the history of any fire department. He worked 14- and 16-hour days for the next six months, directing the rescue and then the recovery efforts. He felt the sorrow and the despair of the loss at least as keenly as anyone. But he also knew that someone had to lead, stand in front, and let all of those working at Ground Zero know that there was a strong and dedicated professional person directing the combined energy of thousands.

I will never forget this man. His training as a fire officer and his clear, direct speech inspired all at the World Trade Center site to work harder and longer than anyone might expect. His determination to serve and the aura of his character were reassuring to all first responders and to all New Yorkers.

Dennis Smith

each one, teach one
STAN SMITH
RETIRED PROFESSIONAL TENNIS PLAYER

I grew up in Pasadena and I had the great benefit of playing tennis under a patrons association started by Lou and Linda Crosby. Lou did car commercials so he was pretty well-known in the community. Linda did some commercials too. They had three daughters and the whole family played tennis.

We got together at Pasadena High School every Saturday morning, about a dozen of us in the beginning, and we would play for about five hours. It eventually grew to about 300 kids, but this was back when there were just a few of us. I think I was 15 years old when we started. They still had wire nets on most of the public courts and we played with white balls. At some point early on they hired Pancho Segura to do the coaching, so it really was a great opportunity for me to play tennis at a pretty high level.

Lou was a little bit of a father figure to a lot of us. He took me to some tournaments and really pushed me in my tennis. He said he saw something in me. Fortunately I didn't have to live with him. If he were my father, it would have been tough.

> " look, you're going to be meeting
>   with all kinds of people and you're
> going to need to learn some table manners. "

He really took an interest in me. One time I was over at his house and he said, "Look, you're going to be meeting with all kinds of people and you're going to need to learn some table manners." He had a little card table all set up for me with a formal table setting. He showed me how to hold the fork, the spoon, and the knife, how to wait for everyone else at the table to be served—it was kind of embarrassing. But it was his way of encouraging me. I still think about how concerned he was to see that I got off to a good start. Meanwhile, I played basketball all through high school. I was tall. And we had a good basketball team my senior year. One guy went to UCLA and played with Lew Alcindor. One guy started at USC and another guy played at a smaller school, so we had a good team. I played tennis two days a week and on weekends during basketball season. After the basketball season ended, tennis was my focus. But I had to catch up with the other players who were way ahead of me, because the tennis season in California is pretty much year-round and the other players were playing all the time.

At some point, I started driving to a tennis club in L.A. every day. But I also kept coming back to the program that Lou and Linda started. We'd play from 8 in the morning until about noon every Saturday—and that included lessons from Pancho Segura—and then we'd drill. From noon until about one o'clock we'd give lessons to the younger players. "Each one, teach one"—that was the motto, and we really took it to heart. Teaching those kids really helped my game. It forced me to analyze what I was trying to do. When you articulate how to play the game, it makes it clear in your mind. That was Lou's thing: Take what you know and what you love and pass it on; keep it going.

Stan Smith

don't be ordinary
ROXANNE SPILLETT
PRESIDENT, BOYS & GIRLS CLUBS
OF AMERICA

We didn't think of ourselves as poor. We sure didn't think of ourselves as rich. We just had enough to get by. There were three kids in my family. My father was a baker.

My mother was an incredibly talented artist and had enormous expectations. She was forever finding little ways to let me know she was counting on me. I'm not artistic in the least, so it wasn't about that. It was about meeting expectations and pushing myself above and beyond. She was very, very clear on this. She was also amazingly generous.

I look at some of the families we serve in our clubs across the country, and I recognize that a great many of our children who are doing well come from households where a great deal is expected of them. The push I always felt as a young girl was my mother. I kept hearing from her, "Whatever you do, don't be ordinary." Whether she actually ever used those words, I don't know, but it was implicit in everything she said.

I don't think my mother ever felt she was ordinary. She was talented and she knew it. And yet she was living a relatively ordinary life, at least by outward appearances. She lived in the suburbs. Her husband was a baker. But she was truly extraordinary and she knew it. She had this uncanny ability to create in any medium.

She did most of her work at night. I remember one night we were sitting at the kitchen table talking about something and she ripped something out of the newspaper that caught her eye. I went to bed and when I woke up the next morning she had done this incredible woodcut of an image from the newspaper. She could whittle; she worked in ceramics. Oils were her big thing. "Mom was up all night," we used to say, because if she was up all night it meant something had been created.

She was very hard of hearing. Later in life she was almost completely deaf, but when I was in middle school and high school we could still communicate. She could read lips. The older she got, the harder our conversations became, but we would pass notes. We would find ways to talk to each other.

Ironically my father didn't talk much when I was young. He never articulated his feelings about what he expected of me. For most of my younger life I don't think he even knew what grade I was in. All he knew was that I was a good kid and I was going to be fine. His job was to go and bake and earn the money; that was his idea of being a father. So my father wouldn't talk and my mother couldn't hear, yet between them I got the message that I had a job to do.

> " she was forever finding little ways
> to let me know she was counting on me. "

I have so many of my mother's pieces. My favorites were the flat oval ceramic pendants she used to make. They're small, like a brooch. There'd be a hole in them, and on them she would paint beautiful faces. Each one was different, and each was just gorgeous. She did loads and loads of these faces, and people would tell her all the time that she should sell them because she could get a lot of money for them, but she'd just say, "No, I'd rather give them away." And she did. She gave them away with a piece of ribbon threaded through the hole, but most people would put them on a gold chain or a piece of leather. She used to put the backs of pins on the ones she gave me because I liked to wear them as pins.

When she died a few years ago, my family decided to wear them to her funeral as a kind of tribute, and we each picked out our favorite ones. But it turned out that we weren't the only ones to remember her in this way. When I went up to give a little talk at the service, I stood up and looked out over a sea of beautiful ceramic faces. It took me completely by surprise. The place was packed, and almost every woman who had come to the funeral was wearing one of my mother's pieces.

Some were my mother's oldest and dearest friends, but many others I didn't know at all. And what struck me was how many people my mother had touched. It was more than how many people she had known well enough to give one of her pieces, but how many people felt so connected to her generosity and her extraordinary gifts that they all thought to remember her in this same way.

Roxanne Jillette

pride of a yankee
GEORGE M. STEINBRENNER III
PRINCIPAL OWNER, NEW YORK YANKEES

I have truly been blessed, but not for the reasons you might think. It's not because I am the principal owner of the New York Yankees or had a horse run in the Kentucky Derby or even because I almost shared the television screen with Jerry Seinfeld. No, it's because of Rita O'Haley and Henry George Steinbrenner II, my parents. They gave to me the ultimate gift that a parent can give a child—a sense of value and worth—that today is referred to as self-esteem, although back then I don't think we gave it a name.

My parents shared a great many similarities and differences, strengths and weaknesses, and it made a wonderful environment for my sisters and me to grow up in. They maintained their individuality, and yet they were more than just husband and wife. They were partners in life, in marriage, and in raising their children. And we kids never knew quite what to expect, except that we would be treated fairly and lovingly and with tremendous patience and respect. My father was German, physically tall and strong, a brilliant student and an outstanding athlete and competitor. He was highly disciplined and extremely determined. He stressed discipline and distinction, relentlessness, and he always encouraged his children to be the very best we could be. He taught us to always learn from and concentrate on our mistakes, to surround ourselves with people who were a lot smarter than we were, and to never, ever give up.

> " they gave to me the ultimate gift that a parent can give a child— a sense of value and worth. "

My mother was Irish, no bigger than a minute, a good student, and the kindest and most generous woman you could ever hope to meet—a genuine sweetheart. She might not agree with you, but she always understood. She constantly reinforced my inherent potential in life, as she taught me to relate to others and share with those who might have less. It's because of her influence that I was able to find my personal purpose and place in the world.

Together, my parents loved my sisters and me unconditionally. They gave us opportunity and taught us that there wasn't anything we couldn't achieve, and that all we had to do was try. I am what I am today because of them. It's that simple. The rest is irrelevant and history.

in spirit
GLORIA STEINEM
COFOUNDER, *MS.* MAGAZINE

It's harder for women to think of role models and mentors than it is for men. There were just fewer out there when I was growing up. My main mentor and role model was Louisa May Alcott, a dead woman, because I read her adult novels as well as her novels written for young readers. They were very aspiring, political, feminist, personal novels.

Louisa May Alcott was a lifeline because there were no living role models out there for a young woman—at least not if you wanted to be something other than a wife and mother with a job "to fall back on." True, there was Eleanor Roosevelt, but that only said to me that you had to marry a president, which seemed unlikely. There was Mary McCleod Bethune, a great leader who started the National Council of Negro Women, but she seemed beyond my world. There was Sonja Henie, but I couldn't skate, and there was Doris Day, but I couldn't sing. The poverty of role models wasn't even something we talked about, we just assumed we had to marry and support someone else's dreams.

Of course, later in life, after the women's movement had begun, I discovered many inspirations closer to my age. Bella Abzug had a great sense of history, a great sense of humor, and a great ability to deal with conflict. I campaigned for her from the beginning, when she first ran for Congress. She was a great leader of the peace movement and the feminist movement.

There is also Alice Walker, a world-class writer who can empathize her way into all living things and helps us to do the same; Wilma Mankiller, who became chief of the Cherokee nation and should have been president of the United States; Dorothy Pitman Hughes, a community activist in New York who started the first multiracial, nonsexist child care center and was my lecture partner; and Flo Kennedy, a smart, courageous civil rights lawyer whom I also learned a lot from when we traveled and lectured together. These women would become my friends and my inspiration, but they all came later.

" the poverty of role models wasn't even something we talked about, we just assumed we had to marry and support someone else's dreams. "

In those early years, a political life was out of reach. The only way a woman could get into high office was to marry a man who held the office and wait for him to die. As Margaret Mead often said, in a patriarchy only widows are honored with authority. In business, a husband might die, but usually the son—or even the son-in-law—took over.

I only realized later that my mother had been a newspaper reporter years before I was born. She was a pioneer who had to write under a man's name at first in order to get published at all. She eventually became the woman's page editor and then the Sunday editor of the *Toledo Blade*, and that was rare. But by the time I was born, she had given up her work because my father moved us all to rural Michigan where he was trying to start a summer resort. My mother gave up her friends, the work she loved, everything, and became a kind of isolated, broken-spirited person. She was an example of the price you pay when you give up your dreams.

In private and more internal ways, though, she was very much a role model. She loved poetry. She could recite much of Edna St. Vincent Millay by heart. She taught me how to open new books carefully and run your thumb along the spine with each page so that you didn't damage the binding. She also had a wry sense of humor and made me feel connected to politics by telling me how poor we'd been during the Depression and how Roosevelt saved us. But in terms of self-sufficiency and career, she was kind of an emblem of worry and powerlessness.

I suppose that's why I turned to Louisa May Alcott. I think I probably discovered her books on my own. In the wintertime when the summer resort was closed, my father made an insecure living by buying antiques at auctions and selling them to dealers. He used to buy whole libraries in order to get one first edition, and then he'd dump the rest of the books in our garage. So I'd go out there and read whatever looked interesting.

I must have read *Little Women* first. I remember it was a book populated by females talking about the Civil War and coping with poverty and the other big problems of their lives all on their own. And because their father was off fighting in the war, their mother was the figure of wisdom and authority and kindness in their lives. The fact that there could be a society of women who cared about the whole wide world was a revelation.

Having fallen in love with Louisa May Alcott, I searched out her other books. There was a wonderful novel called *Work* that was set in a time of abolitionist and suffragist struggle. The more I read about her real life, the more I admired her. She took part in the utopian living experiments of her era, and she worked so hard to make a living that her hand became crippled from writing. I used to fantasize that she would come back to life, and I would try to figure out what things in my world I would show her first, from cars and planes to white bread.

It speaks to the power of the written word that someone who is not present—but whose spirit is in a book—can really be a mentor.

Gloria Steinem

God's gift
RUBEN STUDDARD
RECORDING ARTIST

The biggest influence in my life has been my mother. She's the one who taught me how to read and focused so much on my education. Basically, she taught me how to be who I am. My mother and father were both educators, and they taught year-round. My mother kept telling me how important it was to stay in school and go to college and get my degree.

My musical influences mostly came from church. I remember going to a summer camp called Camp Jimmy Goodwin, and that was where I first remember performing outside of church. During the week we would always have contests—you'd get points for having the cleanest cabin, points for winning all kinds of things, and the biggest event was the talent show. Songs, plays—we'd do it all, and the cabin that won would get this big watermelon feast. We usually won. We'd have the best songs.

I sang in my first school talent show when I was about 11 years old. I sang some New Edition song, a capella, and there were all these girls out in the audience screaming really loud. I was on the stage thinking, "Man, this is something I have to do for the rest of my life."

My mother didn't care about the screaming girls. She wasn't so sure about me making a career in music. Her big thing was always making sure I got my education, making sure I finished school, making sure I had something to fall back on. The foundation—that's what she was all about.

The hardest thing I ever did was tell her I was dropping out of school. I was at Alabama A&M, three and a half years into my degree in music education, and I quit to pursue a career in gospel music. I was in a group called God's Gift, and I wasn't the only person in the group who was close to finishing school. It was hard for all of us, but I don't think any of us wanted to be 50 years old, wondering whether we could have pursued our dreams.

I came home to talk to her about it, and she said, "Can't you wait?" She thought we could have done everything we needed to do and kept on in school. We could have, but we wanted to keep our focus and give it our all.

" basically, she taught me how to be who I am. "

It was really rough at home for a couple days, but after my mother saw I was serious she cooled off. She knew the group and she knew we were all serious, so she cooled off. But she made me promise that if I didn't make it in five years I'd go back to school and finish and become a music teacher.

We worked hard. We practiced nearly every day. We did some gigs. We had a couple record contracts that didn't go anywhere, and after awhile the group broke up and I started singing with this jazz band called Just a Few Cats. The whole time, my mother kept reminding me of our deal. Five years, if it wasn't happening, I'd go back to school. I'd promised, and I would have kept that promise, but three years in *American Idol* happened, and that changed everything.

Ruben Studdard

speaking into our lives
COURTNEY B. VANCE
ACTOR

My high school history teacher was a big influence. His name was George Browne. My mother still speaks to him. He really played an important role in my life.

He was my track coach too, and I wouldn't have run track at all if it weren't for him. I went out for track because I wanted to be with Mr. Browne. All the athletes at school adored him. He was one of those hard-as-nails, military types, but that was just a gruff exterior. He really cared about his students and most of all his student athletes. If you worked hard for him, he'd go to the wall for you.

One summer when I was about to start high school, he invited me back to be a counselor, working with him, and it was at that time he talked to my parents about Detroit Country Day School, a private school where he taught. We didn't know anything about it. I'd gone to public and Catholic schools.

We couldn't afford a private school like Country Day, but Mr. Browne thought I might be eligible for some kind of scholarship.

Education was important in my family. My father was a manager for a local supermarket. My mother was a librarian. We grew up around books and my parents instilled in us that we would get good grades and go to college. They spent a lot of time with us, taking us to museums, to libraries, to plays and concerts and movies. During the week we weren't allowed to watch television, unless it was Jacques Cousteau or Mutual of Omaha's *Wild Kingdom*. On Saturdays we could watch cartoons in the morning and we could watch the *Wonderful World of Disney* on Sunday nights, but that was it. Whatever we were watching, at 8:30 p.m. we were on our way up to bed. During the summer, whenever the streetlights came on, our feet had to hit the steps to our house. Whenever those streetlights came on, if my parents came out of the house and I wasn't sitting on the porch, I was in trouble.

Mr. Browne must have seen something in me that left him thinking I belonged at a place like Country Day. He knew I could handle the discipline and the structure—or maybe he knew my parents well enough after those first few summers that he knew what a private school education could mean. He arranged for us to visit the school, and after just one visit I knew I wanted to go there. But I also knew it was too expensive for us. I just said, "Oh well, I'm not going here." But my father took me aside and said he'd talk to Mr. Browne and see if there was anything we could do. He said, "If that's what you want, we'll try to work it out."

It changed the direction of my life. There were so many things to do there, so many different activities, positive activities. For a young black kid, or any child, you want to keep him busy with as many positive activities as possible. My parents knew that once I was there I'd be in a good environment. They could stop worrying about me.

I did everything. I played football and basketball, and that first spring I went out for track. I didn't know how I'd do, but I wanted to be with Mr. Browne. Country Day's motto was "mind, body, spirit." The school really celebrated the student athlete, and everybody talked about what a great coach Mr. Browne was and how he looked out for his athletes.

He worked us hard, on the field and in the classroom. Academics at Country Day were rigorous. Between all the sports and my classes and all these other activities, there wasn't time for anything else. I'd come home at

7 or 7:30 after a game or a practice, put in two hours of homework and go to sleep. By the time I graduated, I was exhausted. I got to Harvard and ran track my freshman year, but after that I just started doing theater because I had done all these things in high school. I was burnt out.

" Courtney, do you realize you're going to be a senior next year and the whole school is looking to you for leadership? "

All those teams I was on helped me to realize there's a gracious way to lose. That's what sports can teach you. Sometimes you're going to miss that layup in front of everybody and be completely embarrassed and have to go back to school and run the announcements the next day. And you'd have to just say, "Hey, I had a bad day. We'll get 'em next time." You've got to learn how to lose. Sometimes that's more important than winning or being the star of the team. Being gracious in defeat—I got that from Mr. Browne.

I also got his love of history. That ended up being my major in college. I love to look at where we've been and project where we're headed, and I got that from him too. And a great work ethic. He wouldn't tolerate low grades in his class or in anyone else's. You couldn't run for him if you couldn't keep your grades up. He spoke into my life in a meaningful way.

George Browne wasn't the only one. There was an English teacher who pulled me aside one day. I'd become a real happy-go-lucky kid, trying to make everybody laugh in class, and I guess she thought I wasn't serious enough. She said, "Courtney, do you realize you're going to be a senior next year and the whole school is looking to you for leadership?"

That's all she said, and she walked away. I don't know if that was true or not, but all I could think was, "Wow!" I came back my senior year and I was on point. And I kept thinking about this English teacher's charge. That's what put me back in line and sent me on my way. She just spoke into my life in this one little exchange. It wasn't even a conversation. And I think back on it and wonder what happens to kids who don't have anyone to speak into their lives the way Mr. Browne and this English teacher spoke into mine.

the best I could
with what I had
MICHAEL VICK
PROFESSIONAL FOOTBALL PLAYER

Poo Johnson was the executive director of the Boys & Girls Clubs in Newport News, Virginia, where I grew up. I was there all the time, and so was he. He kind of took me under his wing. I guess he took every kid under his wing. That was how he was. He took an interest in everyone and was always making sure everybody was on the right track, doing the right things.

I still hear from folks who grew up in that club. Most of them tell how Poo helped them walk the right path and helped them to become a man. He was tough too. He kicked me out of the club four or five times, but after a couple days he'd always let me back. That was his discipline. It's not like I did anything terrible, but he was very demanding. I never got in trouble with my parents for getting kicked out—Poo's punishment was enough.

It wasn't like getting kicked out of school. It was something extra, something I wanted to do for me. If I couldn't be there, if I couldn't play football or basketball or anything else, I was only hurting myself. Really, it was the only place I could go, the only outlet outside of school. Other than that, I'd be running the streets, so after a while I figured it out and made sure I stayed on Poo's good side. My mother said she didn't know what would have happened to me if it weren't for Poo Johnson.

> " everywhere I looked, there he was.
> It's like there were six or seven of him,
> and each one was watching out for me. "

But it wasn't just Poo. A lot of folks made a difference. My high school coach, Tommy Reamon, helped me progress and grow as a man and take my game to another level.

It wasn't until high school, I guess, that I thought football might be my ticket. I was hoping and praying and dreaming, but I knew I was a long shot. There weren't too many African-American quarterbacks when I was growing up, but I was just doing the best I could with what I had. Poo would come by wherever I was, whatever I was doing, and he'd give me some encouragement. He was everywhere. Now, of course, I realize he must have had an office and other responsibilities and that I probably only saw him when he was making his rounds. Still, everywhere I looked, there he was. It's like there were six or seven of him, and each one was watching out for me.

in a heartbeat
MANNY VILLAFANA
CODEVELOPER, ST. JUDE HEART VALVE,
SERIAL ENTREPRENEUR

My siblings were mostly out of the house when I was growing up. I was born 10 years after my youngest brother. My mother was 48 years old when I was born. My father was 59. When I was 10, he died from a heart attack.

Everyone in my family died of a heart attack, including my brothers, and that's a very important part of why I do what I do. I knew that I had this genetic predisposition to heart disease. I had somehow landed a job with a company that handled medical devices, and before I knew it, I had figured out a way to develop a better pacemaker than what was currently on the market. I didn't set out to do it, but it happened.

Pacemakers back then were about the size of a hockey puck, and they'd last somewhere between 12 and 18 months before they had to be replaced.

I came up with the first long-life pacemaker. We used microchip electronics and lithium batteries. Plus, we sealed it so the blood and fluids from the body would not get into the pacemaker and keep it from operating perfectly.

I went to college for a little bit, but it didn't make sense for me to keep going. I was a kid from the South Bronx, and we had nothing. I mean, nothing. I remember one year getting a Christmas present and it was a single shiny dime. And that was it. After my father died it was just me and my mom, and we struggled.

The truth is I almost didn't make it out of high school. I went to Cardinal Hayes High School in the Bronx and I was in and out of trouble. The Boys & Girls Clubs used to run an ad on television where they showed a kid jumping over a fence and running down a street and all over the city until he finally slows to a walk at the club. The line was that he was running away from drugs and gangs and all that sort of thing.

> " nothing was more important to Archie at that moment than setting me straight. "

I used to do that. I used to see that ad and think, "Hey, that was me." There was a gang looking for me, and I knew they'd kick the crap out of me if they ever caught up to me, so for about a year I had to run through the back alleys in the Bronx, run to the subway, run to the Kips Bay Boys Club where I was a member. I couldn't even walk down my own street, so I don't know what would have happened to me if it hadn't been for the club.

My mother didn't have it easy, I'll tell you that. It was hard enough to raise a child on your own in the South Bronx in the 1950s, but she was an old woman by the time my father died. She worked as a seamstress and she didn't have the time or the energy to chase after me, so it was a blessing that I found the club when I did.

My big memory of the club was the time I got caught pinching some coins from the pool table collection. I was about 13 years old and they put me in charge of the pool table, which meant I had to collect the money from the kids who wanted to play. It was something like 5 or 10 cents for a half hour, and unfortunately—or maybe it was fortunate—I stole some of that money. I pocketed it. One of the staff saw that I had taken a couple nickels, whatever it was. I'd never done anything like that before, but when I was faced with the temptation of having some money in my hands, that's what I did.

The next day I was called into the office of Archie Mangini. He kind of ran the place. He was a fixture there for most of my life and a real icon in the Boys & Girls Club movement. He was the physical education director of the Kips Bay Club. Everybody knew him and he knew everybody. There might have been a thousand kids in the club at the time, but he made everyone feel like he was there just for them.

So he called me into his office and I was in there for about an hour. It seemed like an eternity. He didn't yell; he talked in a very fatherly manner. He told me that what I had done was wrong and what it meant. I got a ton of advice for those few nickels, and it was something I needed.

Archie was the father figure in my life at that point. I was a kid and I could have been lost on the street, and here was this man, crouching down to speak to me at my level, eye-to-eye. And it was wonderful. There was no punishment, just a talking-to, and of course I had to give back the money.

I don't think he even told my mom. It was just between me and Archie. And the thing that was most amazing was the crime wasn't big but the attention was. He gave me every minute he thought I needed. There were all those other kids running around also needing his attention, but nothing was more important to Archie at that moment than setting me straight.

"Manny, do you know what you're doing?" he said. He was very patient. Like I said, he didn't yell. He didn't threaten. In fact he ended up giving me even more responsibility when we were through, things to do around the club. Of course I rose to those challenges now that I had Archie's attention.

The memory of that hour in his office and the relationship that grew out of it was so great that when Archie finally died not too long ago, I went to pay my respects, and for some reason I wound up alone with him lying in his casket. Just me and him, saying goodbye. I stayed with him for two or three hours. There was no one else around, and we talked. Well, I talked. I remembered all the times we shared at the club. I remembered that time in his office. I remembered how he saved my butt, not just that one time but a bunch of times. And once again, we took all the time we needed.

"I believe in you"
ANTONIO R. VILLARAIGOSA
MAYOR OF THE CITY OF LOS ANGELES, CALIFORNIA

My mother was a single mom with four kids, and she worked all her life. Sometimes she worked two jobs. She was a secretary for some time, but she had many talents. She was a high school graduate, a Latina in the 1940s with a straight-A average. She spoke five languages and read Shakespeare and Dickens to her kids. She was a great, great lady—very erudite, very positive. A woman of indomitable spirit and unconditional love for her children. And she never complained. It was a pretty tough household when I was a little kid before my father left—domestic violence, alcoholism, all that sort of stuff. But she never complained. She had an unbreakable faith in God, family, and community.

We were latchkey kids from time to time, but my mother made an effort to get me involved in all these great programs. She had me in the Boy

Scouts. She had me going down to the Boys Club. She had me signed up at the Y. She was always trying to put me in situations where there were male role models and authority figures because I didn't have one at home. I was definitely an at-risk kid. I wasn't a gang kid or anything like that, but I was definitely a kid who got into trouble. I was very angry. She saw me fighting all the time and she always was working hard to shelter me and protect me from that.

One morning—I must have been about 15—I'd come home with a tattoo, which I've since taken off. I'd gotten into a fight the night before and I was pretty battered. I'd just been kicked out of school and anyone could see I was on a downward track. My mother came into the kitchen that morning at breakfast and saw my tattoo. She broke down and cried, and after she was through crying she looked at me and said, "You don't believe in you, but I believe in you." I never forgot that. I don't know that I heard it then, but I've never forgotten it, so I must have heard it on some level.

When people ask me if I ever dreamed I'd be speaker of California's State Assembly or mayor of Los Angeles, I say I never dreamed about it, I never thought about it, it never entered my mind. But it entered my mother's mind. From when I was a young boy, she saw me as destined for greatness. That's the kind of woman she was. She believed in her children, and not just me. All four of us did well, we all went onto college, and we all grew up in the same really tough neighborhood in East Los Angeles. She lifted us up.

College was a given in our household. My mother always spoke about it as a given, even though I went through a real rebellious, angry period when I didn't think I'd make it out of high school. I was kicked out of one high school, Cathedral High School, and I dropped out of another, Roosevelt High School. But I went back to Roosevelt and managed to graduate. I actually remember my high school graduation much more than I remember my college graduation. It meant more. I was proud of myself, because I had dropped out for about a half a year, but then I went to night school four nights a week in addition to regular classes and I was able to graduate with the rest of my class. I was proud of that. I felt like I redeemed myself.

I had a little help from a teacher named Herman Katz. He turned out to be one of those adult male role models my mother was always seeking. He had me in a basic reading class and he realized I was much sharper than that, so he made me take a test. After that he put me in a power reading class.

He got me to study for the SATs. He even offered to pay for me to take the SATs, and he really helped me focus on college and pushed me to apply. I ended up going to UCLA in large part because of him. He was a wonderful man—a real mentor, a real inspiration—and I talk about him everywhere I go. And my mother encouraged that relationship because she knew how much I needed someone like that in my life. And I did; I truly did.

> " she knew good things were coming
>   even when I was on the wrong path. "

Of course my mother was brokenhearted when I was kicked out of high school and after that when I dropped out, because I was always a smart kid, but she never wavered in her support of me. Her love was unconditional. She always believed in me, even when I gave her every excuse to write me off. Think about it. In the 1960s she was a single mom raising four kids, not in abject poverty, but we were relatively poor, and in that era, all four of us doing well, all four of us going to college, with no father, it was really incredible. It's a tribute to my mother really.

She died before I made it to the California State Assembly, became speaker of the Assembly and then mayor of Los Angeles, but she got to see me have some success. Thank God for that. I had a good job, a beautiful family, a beautiful house. And she knew good things were coming. Are you kidding me? She knew good things were coming even when I was on the wrong path. She was prescient. She was definitely someone who believed in self-actualization. She believed that if you dreamed it and if you worked toward it, it would come. And I've come to believe in that myself; I truly have. Without question it's the motor that drives me, the catalyst for my growth as a person over the years.

the most important day
DICK VITALE
BASKETBALL ANALYST

Wow. I've been living a dream, man. It's been unbelievable. Making a living
doing something I love, talking about the game of basketball. I mean, I'd
do this for nothing. Are you kidding me? Sit at courtside and get paid? To
watch the greatest games in the country? Duke/North Carolina? Kentucky/
Florida? All these big-time games? And I owe it all to my mom and dad.

Man, I've been so lucky. Even though they didn't have a great education,
they had a doctorate of love, and they taught me that if you have drive,
desire, discipline, and determination, beautiful things are going to happen.
That's what I call the four Ds of life, and I learned that from them. And then
there are the three Es of life: energy, enthusiasm, and excitement. All you
have to do is listen to me do a game and you can tell I learned that lesson,
too. But that's not all I learned. I learned about a work ethic. I learned about
pride. I learned about giving your best.

My dad worked in a factory and then as a security guard. My mom used to sew coats. Both of them taught me to never believe in the word *can't*.

I'll never forget coming home as a young coach, a high school coach chasing the dream to be a college coach, and all my buddies would tell me, "There's no way, man." And my mother used to say to me, "Don't believe those people, Richie." In her Italian way, she would encourage and inspire me. She'd say to me, "You're gonna make it, because you have spirit."

What a family! My aunts and uncles would gather with us every Sunday, and we'd have our bagels and our coffee, go to church, and come back and argue about our favorite players. My dad would throw in how much he loved Joe DiMaggio or Mickey Mantle, and I'd throw in how much I loved Willie Mays, and we'd go at it all day.

" they had a doctorate of love. "

Those days were special, and underneath all the noise and arguing we all really cared for one another. To me that's what life is all about. You know life is very simple. It's about decisions. You make good decisions and a lot of good things happen. You make bad decisions and a lot of bad things happen. I learned that from my parents too.

Yes, they were my greatest inspiration. I miss them so much. I only wish they were living so they could share in the beautiful things that have happened in my life—the places I go, the speaking engagements, the commercials. I've actually written seven books! Seven! That's more than I ever read as a kid— are you kidding me? But I'm really blessed, and it's all because of the guidance and direction and love I received from my mom and dad.

They taught me that winning is simply the ability of an individual in pursuit of a goal or a dream to do your best. If you can look in the mirror and say, "I gave it my best," then you've won.

You know, there's an old saying: So many of us worry about yesterday, and it's gone; so many of us worry about tomorrow and it may not even come. We forget about the most important day of our lives, and that's today. Take care of today, man.

head and *heart*
KERRY WASHINGTON
ACTRESS

I grew up in the Bronx where my grandmother used to call me Sarah Bernhardt, because I was such a dramatic child. I was blessed with very supportive, creative parents who also both worked full time, so rather than just have me sitting at home in front of a television, I was into everything.

On Mondays, it was gymnastics. Tuesdays was ballet. Wednesdays was the children's theater company. Every day there was something else, and I guess acting was the thing that stuck. It got to the point in ballet and gymnastics where they wanted me to study or practice five or six days a week, and I didn't want to give anything up. Theater was the one place where I could do it all: I could sing *and* dance *and* act.

It wasn't until I got to college at George Washington University that I put it all together. I'd always felt there was this disconnect between being intellectual and creative—that you had to be one or the other. But at school

I met this wonderful professor named Stacy Wolf. She was the first person I knew who represented the amalgamation of both. She was a professor in the theater and dance department, but she taught performance studies and theater history. She put the thing that I had loved the most into an intellectual framework.

I had an incredible experience in 10th grade playing Ophelia at the same time we were studying *Hamlet* in English class. It was serendipitous and the first time I was able to apply what I was learning in the classroom to what I was doing on stage. It was brief but exhilarating, and I wondered if it would ever happen for me again. And then I met Stacy, whose whole life was all about theater as more than just imagination.

Imagination is fundamental to what I do, but one of the things I love most about acting is placing it in the context of the history and sociology and psychology and politics of a certain time or place. I really learned how to do that with Stacy. I did a play with her called *Why We Have a Body*. Until then acting hadn't been a craft for me. I understood it as being emotional and energetic, and I worked a lot off my charm and my emotional availability. Theater was the place where I brought my heart and my very full, rich emotional life; class was where I brought my intellect.

In the production I was playing a lesbian. A couple of lesbians came to see the show about five nights before we were opening, and afterward they came up and said they just didn't buy it. I had a talk with Stacy, and she and I realized we had been trying to present this character as someone without all of the stereotypical lesbian mannerisms—I hadn't wanted it to be cliché. But what I hadn't realized was that I had also avoided giving this character any kind of physical reality. I learned that there's a way heterosexual women behave with their bodies that's about not challenging the strength of men. But that's not the way this woman was going to walk in the world, and so it took letting go of that heterosexual woman neurosis. You know, "You can't be too big, or you can't be too powerful. You have to be a lady." So I just let go of all of that and let her be a woman. It was just a subtle thing, but it made a huge difference in how I held my body while I was on stage, how I thought about space, how I sat, how I stood, how I walked. I brought more of a sense of presence and entitlement to the role, and I got that from Stacy.

I brought the best of myself to her classes and productions. She was creative, artistic, and courageous, and she lived her life the way she thought it should be lived. She had what I wanted—a successful career and successful relationships—so she was a role model for me. She took care of her body, took care of her work, took care of her relationships.

" she was creative, artistic, and courageous, and she lived her life the way she thought it should be lived. "

During my junior year I was going through a difficult time in my personal life and I was taking two classes from Stacy. She could have let me off the hook with some of my work, but she didn't. She gave me the extensions that were appropriate, but other than that she pushed me to show up for myself. That was an important lesson. I always had been a perfectionist who would shut down if things weren't exactly right. Stacy pushed me to show up and take a risk. Give what you can give today—that was her big thing. And that's what matters.

one clear call for me

DAVID WOLPER
MOTION PICTURE AND
TELEVISION PRODUCER

My father was a big man, about 6 foot 4, 280 pounds, and during the Depression he worked as a collector at a jewelry store that used to sell jewelry on time. He was the muscle. My mother sold bonds at Bloomingdale's. The store had a stand where they sold savings bonds and later war bonds, and she would go there every day.

My father was lucky to have a job. That in itself was a victory. One time he had to go into this house and he told me to wait for him in the car. He came out of the house, and people were throwing things at him and screaming, and he got in the car and took off. I cried. I went home and told my mother, "Nobody likes my daddy." I thought, "He's such a nice guy and nobody likes him." I was very upset. I didn't realize what he was doing.

I was an only child and I needed a place to go after school. We lived in the South Bronx, and there was a Boys Club not far from where we lived, so I used to go there every day. They brought me up, basically. It was like a storefront operation. It wasn't a big place. This was New York, so there were buildings all around. There was a candy store just up the block. There was a fenced-in yard outside, but there wasn't room for a full baseball diamond or anything like that. Inside there was only room for a half-basketball court.

There was a study area where you could study if you wanted, but mostly we played games. We played a lot of checkers, as I recall, and dodgeball. You stand up against the wall while the other team throws balls at you. For three years it was a big, big part of my life. There wasn't a lot of money around for the club, so for a while the Police Athletic League threw in with the Boys Club because it was a way to save on costs.

There was no trouble on the streets in those days, but if I didn't have the structure of the club, I would have been out playing stickball every afternoon, and my parents didn't want that. They wanted me to be where there was someone looking out for me. They wanted to make sure I'd get my studies done before I started playing ball.

We were a pretty rough bunch of guys in school. By rough I mean we used to give the teachers a hard time, throwing stuff in class, all that sort of thing. We were not a particularly easy bunch. And then one year this English teacher came, Mr. Field. He was a strong, skinny guy. He taught poetry and went straight ahead with it. We would talk and throw things and create all this ruckus, but he just kept on going, and by God, if that guy didn't get to us—every one of us, sooner or later. By the end of the year, he had us all loving poetry and loving his class. I write poetry today because of that teacher. To look at him, you'd have thought nobody would ever listen to him, and to look at us you'd have thought none of us would ever take an interest in something like poetry. But that's what a good teacher can do. He had us reciting poetry like we'd done it all our lives.

Sunset and evening star
And one clear call for me
And may there be no moaning of the bar
When I put out to sea
But such a tide as moving seems asleep
Too full for sound and foam

When that which drew from out the boundless deep
Turns again home.

That's Tennyson, and that was one of the first poems he taught us. I still remember it, all these years later. If somebody would have told me I'd get caught up in this poetry, I'd have thought they were mad, but a great teacher can do that.

When I got older we started playing baseball at Van Cortland Park in the Bronx. It was all organized, with put-together teams. I was a pitcher, and a good one, too, I thought at the time. I ended up playing for USC, but only for about one season before Rod Dedeaux threw me off the team.

> " that's what a good teacher can do. He had us reciting poetry like we'd done it all our lives. "

Rod Dedeaux was a great, great baseball coach. He coached at USC until the mid-1980s. He coached pitching greats like Tom Seaver and Randy Johnson. He took me aside one day and said, "Wolper, one year with you is enough." Dedeaux, too, was a great teacher—just look at his record—but he didn't do much for me. I was a mop-up guy at USC.

I left USC before I graduated because there was a new thing called television and I thought I'd better get into that. It was the beginning of a new business and there was opportunity. My friend's father had a bunch of old films, and he came to us one day and said, "Do you guys want to sell them?" So I agreed, left school a little early, and started selling these films to stations all across the country. The baseball team didn't miss me at all. And that's how I got my start.

Along the way I became the teacher. I was never a teacher of the rank of Mr. Fields or a fellow like Rod Dedeaux. There were a lot of people who helped me, people like Grant Tinker who became president of NBC and Lee Rich who was one of the big buyers on the advertising side. But there was nobody to show me the way or how things were done, because nobody had ever done this sort of thing before. I was making it up as I went along.

Along the way I decided to make my own documentaries. I bought some exclusive Soviet space footage. The United States was in that great race with the Soviet Union at the time, so we put together a documentary called *The Race for Space*. No one was doing independent documentaries at the time.

The networks would air their own documentaries, but they wouldn't take them from independent producers, and yet somehow we got it on the air. And then in 1960 we did *The Making of the President* for ABC, and that was awarded the Emmy for the best program of the year—after all the other networks had turned me down. That felt pretty good.

We had some tremendous people working for us. Jim Brooks was an editor. William Friedkin was one of our filmmakers. David Geffen was an assistant editor. They called it The Wolper School, rather than a company, and that's really what it was.

We all were learning. My style was just to throw my people to the wolves. I had all these young people coming in, and I was very gutsy. A guy would come in who'd never done a documentary, and I'd say, "Go out and shoot this. Let's see what you can do." A lot of them came back with great stuff. You learned on the job—that's how I learned—and from documentaries we moved into miniseries, which no one else was doing at the time. *Roots* was the first one, followed by *The Thorn Birds*, and then a 26-hour epic called *North and South*. It was all new and exciting, and like nothing else on television.

I'll finish up with Rod Dedeaux, because it ties it all together.

One game, he brought me in, bases loaded, two outs, and I gave up five runs. So Dedeaux came out to the mound and said, "Wolper, I hope you're not planning to take this up as a profession because you're gonna starve." So I left the team, and soon after that I left USC, and for years afterwards Dedeaux would take credit for me becoming a success in show business.

I wouldn't say the credit was actually deserved, but it makes a good story, don't you think?

David J. Wolper

the game of work
MARTIN WONG
NECKWEAR DESIGNER

I played a lot of games as a kid: chess, checkers, board games. I remember playing carom, which was a lot like pool and played with sticks. You had to knock the ball into the corner. There was some skill to it, but there was also a lot of strategy.

I was always very self-motivated, and when I think back on the important influences in my life, I keep coming back to games and playing to win. Most of the games I played, I taught myself. I watched the older kids playing and I figured it out. Or maybe some counselor or teacher actually sat down and taught me and I took it from there. I played all the traditional sports too: baseball, tennis, chess. I still play games. I still play chess. I fish. I play tennis. I play poker. And I've started to see that the way I approach games is a lot like the way I approach my business.

My parents were not competitive people. My dad was a communications chief for Napa County in California where we lived; my mom was a legal secretary. They both worked traditional 9-to-5 jobs. Even as a kid I knew I wanted to do something different.

For a while I thought I'd be a stock broker. I was a finance major in college, and one afternoon this guy from Dean Witter came to talk to us and I thought, "That's what I want to be," and I continued all the way through school with that idea in mind. But then I graduated and I got my resume together, and I ran into a chain letter that changed the course of my life.

It was April 1980, back when pyramid letters were popular. I guess I liked the game aspects of it, because I decided to go for it. I was always looking for some kind of edge, so I sent in $1,000, and seven days later I had $16,000. It actually worked, and that money kept me from having to look for a traditional job. It was a windfall.

> " it was just like a game, really.
> I watched how other people went
> about it, and then I figured it out. "

I started looking for opportunities. A girl I knew was able to sew, so we started making ties in my parents' garage. It was just a project at first, a challenge to see if we could take this idea and make some money with it, but it could have been anything. It didn't have to be neckwear. It turned out to be a combination of good business acumen, good timing, and good taste. We were making a fashion statement. We made a skinny leather necktie that was popular with a small group of people at the time, but it was the beginning of what we now consider the young men's neckwear market, and we were there from the start.

Our first order was for a consignment shop in Napa Valley. We made the ties for about 6 bucks, sold them to the consignment shop for $12, and the store put them on sale for $25. We put a dozen ties in the store, and we had a reorder within three weeks. That was very exciting.

We went from store to store selling our ties. It was a struggle at first, but we figured it out. It was just like a game, really. I watched how other people went about it, and then I figured it out. Within six months, we got into Macy's, which was a target account in my area, and I remember thinking,

"OK, this is going to work." Whatever it was, however I'd gotten into it, it was going to work.

When I was a kid, I wasn't preparing myself for a career in business. But looking back, that's really what I was doing. Being successful and trying hard to improve my skills, working with a group of people as a team, pushing myself as an individual—it all goes hand-in-hand.

Success is really like winning, after all—and games can be important teachers, much like mentors. A game like chess forces you to develop your tactical abilities and to think ahead. It's all about survival and outthinking your opponent. You have to be patient. You have to plan your approaches. There are rules and guidelines you have to work within, and all of those elements are still a part of me.

Lately, I've been playing a lot of poker—No-limit Hold 'Em. I look at poker like I look at work. I see people come in aggressive, and when I know them personally I know that's how they handle their business. For me, I bring the same approach to my game of poker as I do to my game of work. I'm cautious. I'm steady. It's an interesting correlation, and at bottom it's a game, just like everything else. You play to win, you play the angles, and you hope for the best.

into a great tomorrow
JOHN WOODEN
RETIRED COLLEGE BASKETBALL COACH

I was raised on a small farm in southern Indiana, in a little town called Centerton. There wasn't much going on in Centerton, just a post office, two country stores, a grain elevator, a dozen or so houses, a grade school, and a church. That's about all. We raised corn, wheat, and tomatoes for a canning factory during the season, and hay, timothy or alfalfa, and corn for the livestock. We had cows. Just a small, simple family farm is all it was, and we worked it until we lost it, my sophomore year in high school.

I had three brothers, and what I remember best about Dad was how he always used to say there'd be some time for play, but only after our chores and our studies were done. He read to us every night, poetry and Scripture, and I think that's probably the reason I've always had an interest in poetry. He was a kind man. I never heard him speak an ill word of anybody. I never heard him make excuses for anything. I never heard him use profanity.

My favorite American was always Abraham Lincoln. He had so many wonderful statements, and I'm reminded here that he once said, "There's nothing stronger than gentleness," and when I hear those words I think of my father. He was not a heavily muscled man, but he was very wiry and he was very gentle. He could take fractious forces and calm them down and pull them together, whereas someone else would just rip them apart and they'd never see eye-to-eye. And through his influence, even though there were no athletic scholarships in those days, all four of his sons got through college on their own, and I know Dad was very proud of that. Certainly it was his influence in starting us out, along with Mother of course.

He was always teaching. He gave us two sets of threes, and we all tried to live up to them. One was "Don't lie, don't cheat, and don't steal." I remember him telling us that if you never tell a lie you'll never have to remember what you said. Another set of three he gave us was "Don't whine, don't complain, don't make excuses. Just do the best you can."

When I graduated from our small country grade school, he gave me a card. I still keep a copy of it in my wallet. He said, "Son, try to live up to what you'll find on this card." On one side was a verse from the Reverend Henry Van Dyke. It said,

Four things a man must learn to do / If he would make his life more true
To think without confusion, clearly / To love his fellow man, sincerely
To act from honest motives, purely / To trust in God and Heaven, securely.

On the other side was a seven-point creed. I may not have these in exact order, but it went like this:

Be true to yourself; help others, that's where you get your greatest joy
Make each day your masterpiece
Drink deeply from good books, especially the Bible
Make friendship a fine art/build a shelter against a rainy day
And, pray for guidance and give thanks for your blessings, every day.

Words to live by, wouldn't you agree? Anyway, I've tried to.

He always went by the name of Hugh, my father. I never knew of a man with more common sense. He'd gone to high school, but he was mostly self-educated. Through his influence—making us study in grade school, no play until the chores were done—his four sons were outstanding students. We all became teachers.

Being from Indiana we were all expected to play basketball, so of course that's what we did. I played at Purdue all four years, although baseball has always been my favorite sport. I hurt my throwing shoulder, but it didn't seem to bother me too much on the basketball court. I was named Player of the Year in 1932, the year I graduated, and Dad was naturally proud—but then he was proud of all his sons. He wasn't a particular basketball fan, but he was a fan of his sons, and I wouldn't say he took more pride in one of our accomplishments over another.

" there's nothing stronger than gentleness. "

He's responsible for a lot of what I've accomplished. His influence in writing verse, especially in my first years of teaching, was considerable. He gave me a verse that I quickly committed to memory:

No written word / No spoken plea / Can teach our youth / What they should be
Nor all the books / On all the shelves / It's what the teachers are themselves.

That sort of reflected what Dad was trying to teach us. You're as good as anybody, but you're no better than anybody. It's a philosophy I embraced in my coaching, when I used to tell my players to be more concerned with their character than their reputation, because character is what you really are while reputation is merely what others think you are. That all came from my dad in one way or another and I passed it on.

There's another verse I've always kept close. It was from a prominent teacher named Glennice L. Harmon, and she offered it upon her retirement in response to a question all teachers must answer at some time or other. I share it here in its entirety, because it had such a profound impact on me:

They ask me why I teach / And I reply
Where could I find such splendid company?
There sits a statesman / Strong, unbiased, wise,
Another later Webster / Silver-tongued,
And there a doctor / Whose quick, steady hand
Can mend a bone / Or stem the lifeblood's flow.
A builder sits beside him / Upward rise
The arches of a church he builds, wherein
That minister will speak the word of God,
And lead a stumbling soul to touch the Christ.

And all about / A lesser gathering

Of farmers, merchants, teachers / Laborers, men

Who work and vote and build / And plan and pry

Into a great tomorrow. / And I say / "I may not see the church,

Or hear the word / Or eat the food their hands will grow,"

And yet—I may. / And later I may say / "I knew the lad,

And he was strong / Or weak, or kind, or proud,

Or bold, or gay. / I knew him once / But then he was a boy."

They ask me why I teach, and I reply,

"Where could I find more splendid company?"

I think about all the players I have coached over the years, all the students I have taught—lawyers, teachers, doctors, dentists, ministers—all professions. And I think back to that poem, because truly I've been in splendid company all these years.

Recently I was invited back to Indiana to honor the McDonald's High School All-Americans. I've been involved with the McDonald's High School All-American program since 1976, ever since I retired. Each year I speak to the players, and when I do I speak mostly about education and very little about basketball—except about how it will open doors for them. After that they have to do the job.

This particular year the game was played in South Bend, where I used to teach high school so many years ago. There was a luncheon in my honor, and there were more than 20 men in attendance who had played for me in the 1930s when I first started coaching, either on my basketball or baseball teams. Twenty! The oldest was 88 years old, and I think the youngest was probably 80 years old. That was really something, to have touched so many young lives and to live to see those lives grow and flourish to where they have, in turn, touched so many more.

I stood there on that day, on that proud, proud day, and I thought once again of my father, because whatever I've been able to accomplish, whatever positive influence I've had over all these lives, all started with him. Joshua Hugh Wooden, my father. And I thought, "No, there is nothing stronger than gentleness after all."

John Wooden

the bottom of things
BOB WOODWARD
JOURNALIST

I went to work for the *Washington Post* in September 1971. I was 28 years old.
I had worked at a weekly paper in Maryland and had served five years in the
Navy as a communications officer. I loved working at the *Post* on the night
police beat, and it was nine months after I started that the Watergate burglary
occurred. Carl Bernstein and I worked on that and wrote stories about the
involvement of the White House and Nixon's reelection committee.

What was interesting was the owner and publisher of the *Post*, Katharine
Graham, and her reaction to our stories. I'd only met her in passing, and
here we had written these stories that were being challenged by lots of people
who didn't really believe them, including people in the *Washington Post*
newsroom. The Washington Post Company stock had just gone public and
had tanked because we learned later that part of the Nixon administration
strategy was to challenge the television licenses that the *Post* had. So the

credibility of the newspaper was in jeopardy, the stock was in the toilet, and the business was in peril, to put it frankly.

One day, Mrs. Graham invited me up for lunch. It was January 1973. Carl was not there, because he had to go to a funeral that day, as I recall, but of course I went. She served eggs Benedict—I had never had eggs Benedict for lunch—and as we sat at the table I saw what kind of manager she was. I later described it as "hands-off, mind-on." She was intellectually engaged in what we were doing and what the newspaper was writing about, but she wasn't trying to do other people's jobs.

She had a staggering understanding of Nixon and Watergate at that point and of everything we'd written. She had a series of great questions. She read all the papers, not just her own. She knew Henry Kissinger, who was the national security adviser for Nixon, and she had some comments about what Kissinger had said about some of Nixon's people that tended to validate some of the things we had written about them. But we were out on a limb. She kept asking questions: "What about this?" "Where are you going with that?"

At the end of the lunch she asked a killer question—which is what a good CEO or publisher always does. She said, "When are we going to find out the truth about Watergate?" Carl and I felt it was a criminal conspiracy, as we had written. Because the Nixon campaign and the White House frightened people so much, and because they had compartmentalized information, there was this wall—which was later labeled stonewall and turned into a verb—my answer to her was "Never."

She looked across the lunch table with this pained, almost stricken look on her face, and she said precisely the following. I'll never forget it: "Never? Don't tell me *never*!"

" beware the demon pomposity. "

I left that lunch a motivated employee. It wasn't a threat; it was a statement of purpose. Our job, Mrs. Graham said, was to get to the bottom of things. To not let the *never* defeat us. To use our resources as reporters, the resources of the paper, to get to the bottom of things.

This was important, she said. There was a lot on the line for the newspaper and a lot on the line for the country. And so what she meant by "Don't tell me never" was "Go do it." Go find out the truth. Don't put limits on yourself. Don't ever accept that you can't talk to so-and-so or that you can't find the answer to a particular question. To Mrs. Graham, "Don't tell me never" meant to fully engage, and I took it as a statement of purpose because it was exactly that.

It was stunning, really, and it was a wonderful lesson. And so we kept at it, and Mrs. Graham provided a kind of protective cocoon for us—as did Ben Bradlee, the editor. He would edit, she would take care of the business side, and our job was to go out into the night and find out what really happened.

Since that lunch meeting, I've done many projects for the *Post*. I've written 13 books, and they're all an outgrowth of that statement of purpose. Don't just pass things by. You're not going to understand everything in a week or a month, so just keep digging.

Less than two years after that lunch, right after Nixon resigned, Mrs. Graham sent Carl and me a letter. She wrote, "Keep loving, keep laughing, keep digging." And then she passed on this very good piece of advice: "Beware the demon pomposity."

We would go on to become friends and neighbors, and we worked together for a long time, but I always think back to that first lunch we had together. It had everything. The themes of engagement. How you manage people. How you try to inspire them. How you try not to do their jobs but let them know you're watching. You can't do better than that.

Bob Woodward

beyond the rim
JAMES WORTHY
RETIRED PROFESSIONAL
BASKETBALL PLAYER

My parents set the tone. They sent me and my brothers the message that we were going to college, and they sent it loud and clear. We couldn't miss it. My mother was a nurse because 22 years after she graduated high school she went back and earned her nursing degree, so education clearly was important. We could all see what it meant. My father only had an eighth-grade education, but he had a good job in shipping and receiving, and he also stressed how important it was for us to do well in school.

I had no interest in sports when I was little. My brothers Danny and Ervin were the athletes. I was pretty much a mama's boy. I grew up in Gastonia, North Carolina, and the Boys Club in town was just an old wooden house that had been refurbished. My brothers would have to babysit me, and I'd go wherever they went, so I followed them to the Boys Club. There was an old-fashioned drink machine and some wooden board games, and I seem to remember a bumper pool table or a Ping-Pong table. No pool. No gym. It was just a couple blocks from where we lived. We used to call it "The Square." In the black neighborhood, that's where everything was. It wasn't even a town square, just a square block where everyone in the neighborhood would meet and socialize and do their thing. There was a Laundromat, a pharmacy, a barbershop, a pool hall, and pretty much everything we needed right there in that little area. And a Boys Club too.

But like I said, we didn't have a gym. There was a dustboard in a little wooded area in back of the house, just down the hill, with a bicycle rim nailed to the tree over a dirt patch. There was no pavement, just red dirt. My brothers would go down there to play, and I'd be up at the house playing checkers or painting. I had no interest in the game, no interest in sports, but that dustboard, that's where I first learned how to shoot. Underhanded. When there's no backboard, you have to be accurate.

My brother Danny was my first coach. He taught me how to shoot. He gave me my first tennis racket, taught me how to drive a stick car, how to play baseball, everything. He was tough—not mean, but hard on me.

I remember a Punt, Pass & Kick contest I entered in 1969. I was 8 years old and the biggest kid in the competition. Because I was so tall, everyone expected me to win and go on to Atlanta for the next round, to be held during halftime of an Atlanta Falcons game. All week leading up to it, practicing with Danny, I was throwing the ball well and kicking it well; it was looking good. And then when I got to the competition I put the ball on the tee and kicked it—down into the ground, about a yard. That was my distance. Then I threw it and it slipped out of my hand and went straight up in the air. It was the worst performance you can imagine. Somehow I still managed to come in third place, but Danny let me hear about it afterward. He was just trying to toughen me up. Even when I started having some success, he was my toughest and best critic. The more success I had, the harder he was.

As I got bigger, sports became more and more important. I was 5' 11" when I was in the seventh grade, and the next year I grew to almost 6' 7", and at that point basketball pretty much took over my life.

I started to get recognized, and along with that I started to let things slip a little bit in school. I always tell people I was a strong B- student, but in eighth grade I brought home two Ds and a C, and my mom wasn't too happy. She was a high school athlete herself, so she knew what it meant. She played on the state championship team in 1945 and was the Most Valuable Player back when they played with six women on the court: three offensive players on one side of the court and three defensive players on the other side. She didn't like that I wasn't excelling in the classroom like she knew I could.

> " it was good to win, but he maximized your life and made you conscious about it. "

It's no wonder. I was playing for my school team, for the Boys Club team, for my church team, and for the local YMCA team—four teams in all. She thought that was too much, and she was right. Imagine coming home from school, going to practice, going to games, trying to get all this stuff done. And it wasn't just my grades that started slipping. You know, the trash wasn't getting taken out, the leaves weren't getting raked on time, the grass wasn't getting cut. So my mother called my junior high school coach and told him I couldn't play anymore. I'd had a few warnings, but then the report card came and that was the end of my basketball season. It turned out to be a blessing in disguise because I knew to focus on my school work after that, and I knew there'd be plenty of time for basketball.

Of course I have to mention Dean Smith, my college coach. To this day he has a major impact on all his lettermen's lives. He truly enhanced whatever my parents were trying to do at home. To Coach Smith, Michael Jordan was no different from our team manager. No one was any different in his mind. Winning? Yeah, it was good to win, but he maximized your life and made you conscious about it. I had that from my parents, but he took it to a different level. He used to send out Christmas gifts where he'd sponsor a child in Africa or somewhere, and he'd do all the work and all you had to do was write the child a letter. He's just a very conscious, conscious man.

I'll never forget his first recruiting visit to our house. It was 1979, and I'd received a letter from just about every college. I can't even tell you what it feels like as a high school senior to know that all these schools have offered you the world. And when a coach comes to the house, you expect to hear all these things. But when Coach Smith came in, the only thing he did was shake my hand and go straight for my mom and dad.

He talked to them for about two hours. I was sitting there in my tennis shoes and my letter jacket like any blue-chipper, and after about 20 minutes I started getting frustrated. I wanted to hear what my deal was going to be, how much playing time I was going to get, how many pairs of sneakers, whether I was going to start right away. You know, you want to hear how great you are, because all they do is tell you how wonderful you are. When Coach Smith got up, he said, "James, it was nice to meet you. If you decide to come to North Carolina, there are a few things I can guarantee you."

I thought, "OK, here it comes. This is the part about the shoes and the playing time." Instead he said, "I can guarantee that you'll go to class every day. And I can guarantee you'll go to church first semester of your freshman year, unless your parents send me a note saying otherwise." He went on to tell me what a great school North Carolina was and how he was going to do everything he could to make sure I graduated on time.

I was floored. After hearing all this stuff from all these other schools—all these coaches promising me the world—it wasn't at all what I was expecting. But I could see it really impressed my mom. I knew at that moment, regardless of what I was going to say, she had decided where I was going.

I'll tell you what else I remember. We were playing for the title in 1982. We had lost the championship the year before to Indiana, but we were fortunate to get back the next year. We were down one, time running out, and Coach Smith called a time-out.

It looked like Georgetown was getting ready to clamp down on us, and Coach Smith had never won a championship. But he was just the calmest, coolest cat in that time-out. He took some time to look around and take in the moment. He was just looking around our huddle, smiling at everybody—really smiling. And it dropped all the tension. He said, "Hey, we're in control. This is where we want to be. We're in control of winning or losing this game." And then he drew up a beautiful play for Michael Jordan, and he was in such total control. I'll never forget that. Not because Michael would go on to hit the shot and we would go on to win the championship, but because of that moment. That time-out. That confidence we were able to draw from Coach Smith. That feeling that this was our time.

the path to purpose
DENZEL WASHINGTON

So there you have it—a couple dozen stories from a couple dozen leaders in a couple dozen arenas. And the resonant message of each is that we don't go it alone. We don't get from there to here without a gentle push or an outright shove and we shouldn't even try. I repeat myself, I know, but the message is all-important and all-around, and in my own life I look to my faith as the steadying counterweight to everything I've accomplished. It's that belief in someone or something bigger than myself—whether that someone or something is my parents, my teachers, Jack Coleman, Billy Thomas, or God himself—that has driven me to become more than I could have ever hoped to be. It's the fire lit by Bob Stone, the Fordham professor who sang my praises, and Ruth Green, the woman who sat beneath the hair dryer in my mother's beauty shop and prophesied that I would speak to millions, that ignited everything that came after.

At the Boys & Girls Clubs, we have a saying: "If you want to change the world, start by changing the life of a child." That's the great lesson of these success stories as well. Sure, some of the folks you've just met found that push a little later on in life and some might tell you they're still looking for it, but at the end of the day it's all about the positive influences that rain down on us in childhood. That's where we find our shape, and our confidence, and our strength. That's where we take root.

Truth be told, I set out to write a book about my experiences with the Boys & Girls Clubs of America, to shine a light on an organization that continues to touch millions of lives just as it continues to touch mine. But as I put these final thoughts to paper I realize that was merely a good place to begin. The real story, the universal story, is that we all stand upon another set of shoulders. We are, all of us, the sum of our influences. We've all been taken by the hand and led to a better, more purposeful place. It doesn't matter if you're the CEO of a major corporation or an inventor of an artificial heart valve that's helped millions of people or an Olympic medalist. If you've achieved anything in this life, if you've overcome any kind of obstacles, odds are you've had some help, and we'll do well to acknowledge that help and pass it on.

I still look back on my childhood as the time of my life. Don't get me wrong, I love where I'm at right now. I love the work I'm doing. I love my wife and kids. I love where I'm living, how I'm living, *why* I'm living. I wouldn't change any of it for anything. But those childhood years, those childhood influences will always be my core. It's what defines me. And it wasn't easy. It might have been the time of my life, but it was no picnic. Absolutely we had it tough. Like I wrote earlier, I don't want to create the impression that we were poor or struggling to make ends meet, because we had it better than most. We were *striving* more than we were struggling. We were all right. But it sometimes seemed my parents were so busy making a living that they didn't have time for us kids, which is why they made sure our heads were on straight and our hearts in the right place. They took the time to lay a strong foundation. All those good clichés, that was us. Absolutely I got into my share of trouble. Nothing too serious. Nothing I'm ashamed about. But I didn't always make the best choices or put myself in the best situations, and yet at the same time I have to think I made *better* choices because of the extra efforts of my parents and teachers and coaches, and I put myself in *better* situations than I might have if I'd been going about it on my own. I had a *better* chance to find my way because I was open to so many positive outside influences.

And I did find my way—thank God for that. From the very first time I stood onstage, wearing a $2 Beatles wig in a color-blind cover band lip-synching "I Want to Hold Your Hand" for a local talent show to landing my first bit parts in professional productions to winning an Academy Award, I've had all kinds of help. A hand to guide me? You better believe it, and I wonder now if I knew I'd need to do all that reaching all the way back at that childhood talent show. After all, I was singing "I Want to Hold Your Hand," so maybe it all ties in. Maybe that was me asking for the help I knew I'd need to lift myself up and out.

I have some final thoughts on the Boys & Girls Clubs, while I have your attention. It's been the place where I found my energy as a child and the place where I've put my energy as an adult, and I can't think of a more noble or fulfilling calling than to work to make this world a better place for our children—one child at a time, like the club motto suggests, but it all adds up. Today there are more than 3,700 local clubs, in all 50 states, serving more than 4.4 million children. No one has taken the time to figure it out, but I'm guessing the number of living alumni runs into the tens of millions. Think about that! It's an enormous number, a nation unto itself, but it's probably a lowball estimate, given the scope and reach of the clubs. And every year we extend that reach a little bit more, to where there are now clubs in our poorest neighborhoods and our richest, clubs in our most remote regions and in our inner cities, clubs on Native American land and in Puerto Rico. There are 415 clubs on U.S. military bases in the United States, Europe, and Asia. There's even a club at the U.S. Naval Station in Guantanamo Bay, Cuba. That's not bad for an organization that started more than 100 years ago, serving just a handful of communities in and around Boston.

These days our streets are a hundred times more dangerous than they were when I was growing up in Mount Vernon, New York, in the 1960s. And our worries don't end on the street. Today's children are assaulted with such a constant barrage of negative influences it's a wonder anyone amounts to anything. But we do, don't we? We manage. We redouble our efforts and refocus our priorities and find a way to light a positive path for our children. We rise above the world we've inherited, and we aim to go our parents, our teachers, our coaches, our role models one better. And our aim is true because we keep hitting our marks, time and time again.

It's an incredible thing, the human spirit. It's what keeps us reaching, ever upward, and as I flip through these pages one last time I'm reminded of the powerful role we can play in someone else's life. The good people you've heard from here have all benefited from a guiding hand or two or three. They've been on the receiving end of some profound words of wisdom, or they've patterned their lives after men and women of principle. They've seen one good turn and helped it blossom into another. Or they've made a mistake and managed to learn from it and move on. And that's the great lesson we can all take with us as we set this book aside and return to our lives. Keep open—to possibility, to opportunity, to wonder—or remain forever shut off to the encouraging outcomes that await us all. Change happens. The key is to keep reaching for that guiding hand and to keep extending our own.

So go ahead. *Train up a child in the way he should go...* and watch what happens.